Better Homes and Gardens®
Annuals
You Can Grow

©1978 by Meredith Corporation, Des Moines, Iowa. All Rights Reserved.
Printed in the United States of America. First Edition. First Printing.
Library of Congress Catalog Card Number: 77-085873
ISBN: 0-696-00285-X

BETTER HOMES AND GARDENS BOOKS

Editor: Gerald Knox
Art Director:
 Ernest Shelton
Associate Art Director:
 Randall Yontz
Production and
Copy Editors:
 David Kirchner,
 Paul S. Kitzke
Garden and Outdoor
Living Editor:
 Beverly Garrett
Garden Book Editor:
 Steven Coulter
Associate Garden Editor:
 Douglas Jimerson
Senior Graphic Designer:
 Harijs Priekulis
Graphic Designers:
 Faith Berven,
 Sheryl Veenschoten,
 Richard Lewis,
 Neoma Alt West
Contributing Editors:
 Lorraine Burgess,
 Diane Nelson,
 Ann Reilly

CONTENTS

Annuals in the Garden ————————————— 4

Annuals for Show ———————————————— 6

Annuals for Special Uses ————————————— 20

Annuals for Special Situations ———————————— 40

ABCs of Annuals ———————————————— 42

Annual Basics————————————————— 72

Tender Bulbs———————————————————— 82

Index ———————————————————————— 95

Annuals In the Garden

What are they and what can they do for you?

Annuals grow seed-to-flower in a surprisingly short time, producing bold color summer-long. You can grow annuals from seeds on a sunny windowsill in early spring to plant out later, or buy seedling plants in flats at a local outlet.

These quick-growing blooms stand well alone, or as fillers in your newest perennial plots. Plant the sturdy seedlings in good soil, water them well, then stand back and watch while they mature and flower in the boldest colors.

It is difficult to dream up a color, shape, or size that's not available in annual flowers. If you love zinnias and want a small flower in a rosy hue, consider the dwarf Rose Buttons. Or, for the very brightest red, look for the All-America winner, Red Sun. It almost seems to glow from within. In zinnias, you may choose from giants to dwarfs in shaggy, quill, or button forms. For mixed colors, look for the very large State Fair and the medium-sized Cut and Come again. Zenith and Fruit Bowl have shaggy blossoms in super sizes.

If you're hooked on marigolds, get acquainted with Primrose Lady, Showboat, and Yellow Galore. These are recent award winners of fine substance—excellent as container plants or in separate beds. Marigolds also run the gamut from very big to very small; from carnation pompons

to nugget edgers; and then to the single French marigold best known as Naughty Marietta, a golden yellow splashed with maroon at the base of the petals. Further, there is a whole family of petites, such as Red Pygmy in a mahogany hue. "Spectacular," "everblooming," and "easy-to-grow" are frequent words of praise for marigolds. They give a continuing source of golden color right up until frost.

A third popular annual is the petunia. It doesn't offer tall, medium, and short sizes, but it is available in a host of grandiflora, ruffled, single, and double flower forms. And in each of these, there's a wide choice of colors. Candy Apple is a vivid red; Glacier, an icy white; and Ballerina, soft salmon. All are grandifloras and

are superb as bedding plants or in hanging baskets. If you pick off flower heads as they fade, the plants will bloom from early summer until frost. And as an added bonus, most have a spicy fragrance. In full-flower, the giant doubles have a strong color impact. The bi-colors come in sparkling combinations. Some prefer the multiflora (many-flowered) singles in Summer Sun yellow, Comanche red, or Coral satin. All are vigorous, free-blooming plants of great value in expanding a garden's floral impact.

Hybridizers bring to annuals a steady stream of accomplishment. They've taken the celosia to new heights with Red Fox and Fireglow. They've given us the orange Sunset cosmos, the Bravo dianthus, the Carefree and Showgirl geraniums, Majorette and Silver Puffs hollyhocks, the Golden Gleam nasturtium, and the Blaze verbena.

If you buy annuals in flats from a nursery specialist, arrange in the fall to have unusual plants grown to your order. Ask for gazanias, blue salvia, white or yellow marguerites, salpiglossis, and sweet scabiosa. If you're looking for something different, search out the little-known garden treasures generally listed in major seed catalogs.

The best medium for growing annual seeds is milled sphagnum moss available at most seed stores.

Packed in a plastic bag, the moss should be practically sterile. Wet down the moss overnight, drain away the excess water, and then put the moss in pots or flats sufficient to hold your seed crop. To plant, scatter seed thinly over the top and slip the moist concoction into a plastic bag, holding the plastic film away from the seeded surface with three or four short stakes. Tie the bag closed with a rubber band and place in a warm, light place, free from drafts. The moisture will rise each day, condense on the plastic at night, and return to the container. After two months, transplant seedlings to separate pots.

Annuals for Show

Old-Fashioned Mixed Flower Beds

Make a big splash with just a little cash by growing masses of old-fashioned flowers from seed or from seedlings purchased in flats. Choose marigolds, petunias, zinnias, and snapdragons for brilliant, fresh color, great masses of bloom, and heady fragrance. With a little work, you can parlay a few dollars' worth of seeds or a batch of seedlings into a wealth of beauty. Costs vary from place to place and season to season, but no matter how you figure it, annuals are your best bargain.

Plant the taller zinnias, marigolds, and a few cosmos toward the rear as a backdrop, with snapdragons and petunias midway, and pansies and ageratum up front. Mingle the clumps so they look less regimented than a row-on-row fruit market display.

If you buy a package mix, expect to get tall and short plants in a crazy-quilt pattern. To establish some focus, you can add a few shrub roses or dwarf dahlias to the center of the bed.

Enjoy bright, tumbling color through a long summer season with dahlias, sweet williams, violas, pansies, marigolds, and petunias.

Plant a red-gold mix of dahlias, dianthus, asters, and marigolds.

Old-Fashioned Mixed Flower Beds

Old-fashioned? Yes. Charming? Precisely. There is excitement in the random happenstance of mixed beds. You can create this same beauty in any planting pocket that gets at least six hours of sun a day. We've become so accustomed to the prolific bloom of annuals that we expect success well before it is our rightful due. And these near-instant plants can be a real solace while your perennials are getting established.

To keep the flowers coming after the first big burst of color, learn the art of deadheading. Each week, cut off all faded blooms before they can go to seed. Not only does this keep the beds looking neat, it encourages the plants to continue making blooms as they try to set seed before the frosts come. Plants will flower longer if they don't have to spend their energies producing seed.

Combine California poppies with dwarf phlox and forget-me-nots.

Pink and white petunias, pansies, ageratum, and Iceland poppies form a kaleidoscope of flower color on top of a retaining wall.

Bold color comes from zinnias planted with purple-blue statice, yellow dahlias, and two-toned red gaillardias.

 COMBINATIONS TO TRY

Blue Blazer ageratum with white alyssum
Red amaranthus with pink snapdragons
Orange calendula with orange cosmos
White candytuft with purple lobelia
Castor bean plant with orange tithonia
Cornflowers with white field daisies
Rose-purple cleome with white gypsophila
Blue larkspur with Iceland poppies
Dianthus in pink, red, and white
Forget-me-nots with California poppies
Gaillardia with yellow coreopsis
Godetia with rose-colored nicotiana
Hollyhocks in a mix of colors
Petunias in deep blue with red verbena
Iceland poppies in a sea of blue lobelia
Celosia in a mix of red and gold
Gazanias with blue verbena

Nemesia and bachelor buttons
Red Sun zinnias with red celosia
Coleus with Rocket snapdragons
Dwarf yellow marigolds with pansies
Giant marigolds with tall, pink zinnias
Phlox drummondi with *Nigella damascena*
Four o'clocks with white cosmos
Nasturtiums with yellow petunias
Hartwegi lupines with blue flowering flax
White cleome with giant gold marigolds

Annuals range from tender to hardy depending upon the severity of the climate. Check with your local suppliers for varieties that do well in your region. If your season is short, start your tender annuals indoors.

Flashy Flowers Massed Together

There's a wonderful sense of extravagance in the mass planting of one kind of flower or in the subtle blending of near-colors of the same plant. If you prefer the bold statement, then mass planting is definitely for you. It places focus on a robust strain, gives authority to the design, and makes for easy care.

Carry the strong impact theory further by choosing plants that are round and squat for the widest burst of color. Low mounds, close by each, hog the sunlight and leave little room for weed growth. Tall plants make a big show for a short time, but low mounds tend to survive better against heavy rains and wind. Either way, mass plantings assure bright color and beauty without all the bother.

Petunias remain the showplace favorite. The flowers love bright sun and the plants spread wide enough to support 20 to 30 blooms at one time. The choices are many—double, two-toned, and upright or cascading varieties in a whole rainbow of colors. Many are so sweetly fragrant that they're too sticky to touch. Still, it's worthwhile to pick off dead blooms to maintain the pristine quality of the beds and to keep the showy flowers coming.

Calendulas are easy, almost obliging annuals of medium height. They bloom mid- to late-summer in unbelievable shades of orange and gold. You can sow them in a sunny bed or container and have masses of strong color in a short time. They're great, too, as cutting flowers. Take what you want from the bushy plants; you'll never miss them in your garden. Buy new seed each year, and cut away faded flowers to prevent self-seeding. The volunteers revert to lesser strains and are not as vigorous as the parent stock. Sow calendula seeds in early spring.

White and salmon-colored petunias combine with blue ageratum.

Orange Gem calendulas glow with dazzling color in late summer.

Flashy Flowers Massed Together

Tall-growing salvia is useful as a colorful property divider.

Dwarf dahlias mass well as border plants.

GOOD VARIETIES TO MASS

For sunny areas where heat-resistance is essential, try Joseph's Coat amaranth, four o'clocks, sunflowers, gloriosa daisies, and the drought-resistant zinnias, Classic and Mexican. On a long sweeping curve, set out Jetfire celosia; and as an airy backdrop, use cleome (spiderflower). Statice does well in the garden and dries well for winter bouquets. Remember annual vines for a quick wall cover. Use *Cobaea scandens,* a purple climber, and morning glories in Heavenly Blue, Pearly Gates, and Scarlett O'Hara. For a feathery stand, use cosmos in the orange-reds—Diablo and Sunset. Zinnias may be at the end of the alphabet, but they rank first as bedders. Their range in height, size, and color is remarkable. Because of its low branching habit, Magic Charms dianthus makes showy color spring into fall, in pink, crimson, coral, or white. Rocket and Regal snapdragons make long-lasting companions for medium-to-dwarf marigolds. Use double petunias in Red or Blue Bouquet, or the tawny white Champagne. In yellows, consider Sunburst or Summer Sun. For garden fragrance, try Nicki-Pink or White—the heavy-flowering nicotiana. In shade, use impatiens.

The large-flowered pansy varieties are easily combined to make an attractive low bed.

Beautiful Borders

Add annuals for brighter border bloom.

In days past, a fine floral border was designed around perennials alone. But today, less-classical gardeners use annuals and shrub roses for even brighter displays.

The basic aim of a border is a continuing show from plants that bloom in an overlapping sequence. Beds are generally 4 to 6 feet wide, with taller plants at the rear, and medium and low varieties up forward. Start the bed or beds with good, rich garden loam, or add leaf-mold, manure, or compost as amendments and additives. Remember, this is a long-term project, so do it well.

Plant iris, peonies, daylilies, phlox, and chrysanthemums in large groups or drifts. Then select a few secondary varieties—Shastas and Sweet Rockets with iris, and lythrum or veronica as fillers for peonies, poppies, and phlox.

You can also use annuals to fill the temporary gaps in your border plan. As shown here, add geraniums, petunias, and lobelia to fill in the forward spaces; follow with some medium and giant marigolds in a range of warm colors; and in the rear, include a dozen or so very elegant dahlias.

A floral border tends to peak several times through the summer. For example, first comes iris, trollius, and poppies; later, daylilies, peonies, phlox, and achillea; and toward the end of the summer, hardy asters, mums, liatris, and solidago. For each of these peaks, there are annuals that can intensify the display. Pansies, lobelia, and tiny marigolds are valuable early; petunias, snapdragons and zinnias carry through most of the summer; and cosmos, coreopsis, and calendula can intensify the golden colors well into fall.

Perennials seem to follow a natural sequence of color with the seasons. Blues and lavenders dominate in the spring, accented by touches of yellow here and there. In early summer, the emphasis shifts toward pinks and then reds laced with brighter golden hues. As fall approaches, the colors tend to intensify. Orange rudbeckia, deep purple asters, and bronze and maroon chrysanthemums signal the year's final color fling.

How to Plan a Border

A well-planned garden offers breathtaking beauty every season of the year. Crocus, scilla, then daffodils and tulips inaugurate the frost-free season; primroses, violets, and trollius follow soon after. By late May and early June, peonies, iris, and poppies are the prime attraction. All these are perennial plants, but there are many fine annuals that can be added to enhance a border display.

Sweet alyssum and lobelias make fine front edgings, while petunias and salvia enliven the middle ground. You can use a screen of spiky snapdragons or larkspur to hide the ripening leaves of spring-flowering bulbs. And while geraniums, marigolds, and zinnias dance among the early perennials, they can become so vigorous by midsummer as to claim prime attention in the border.

But always your goal should be toward plant harmony in relative size, color, and texture. The annuals and perennials should be compatible—happily married in one glorious union.

There should be a flow of shape as well as color in a floral border. As the season progresses, low mounds are replaced by bigger, taller plants, rising in time to new dominance in the overall pattern. Delphinium, liatris, and solidago reach upward in narrow spires, while cosmos and cleome spread wide, still keeping pace. The aim is to have at least two or three kinds of plants in fine flower at any given moment.

Keeping a border trim is a continuing obligation. Cut back stems and stalks as they dry or wither, and pull out early blooming annuals as they falter to make room for more robust varieties. Continue watering into fall if you want to extend the prime flowering season. Then, as autumn comes, you can cut back and take away all debris, or retain some dry flowers as standing bouquets to decorate the garden until they're weighed down by heavy winter snows.

A few plants may self-seed and reappear in the spring, but you can pull them up with the weeds or give extra-good seedlings to friends.

FOR AN ALL-ANNUAL BORDER

To plant a border 5x15 feet, select a sunny site, preferably with good garden loam. If you have poor soil that is heavy with clay, mix in sharp sand. Or, add clay if your soil drains too quickly. Manure, humus, compost, and/or leaf mold can be added to improve the nutritional properties of the soil.

As a border backdrop, use larkspur in blue, pink, or white, together with rose or white cleome. Then choose Peter Pan zinnias in their vivid mixed colors, mostly pinks to reds, to complement Gold Galore marigolds for the middle area. On the forward third of the bed, use alternate drifts of petunias in bright red, and ageratum in white or blue. Then, to finish off the design, run a row of wax begonias or sweet alyssum across the front edge of the border.

LATE-SUMMER ANNUALS

These johnny-come-lately blooms are important to the waning floral border. The newer dwarf dahlias listed in seed catalogs will flower in their first season of growth. Blooms are waxy bright in golden yellows, pink, orange, and red. Treat them as you would zinnias.

Rely, too, on annual asters, now available in vivid new tall, medium, and dwarf varieties. Plant out seedlings when danger of frost has passed. Also, try an English introduction, brachycome or Swan River daisy, which produces a thick carpet of purple flowers. It's easy to grow, superb for bedding, and nice for cutting. A gypsy mix of orange and gold calendulas can help carry the season to a glorious end. And the new striped, or pygmy four-o'clocks bloom right up to frost.

Today's hollyhocks deserve an equally high place in the fall garden in all their Madcap, Majorette, and Silver Puffs designs.

Consider, too, oxypetalum or southern star. Its wide arching sprays of silver-blue starry blooms give forth from June till the end of October. Sow directly outdoors in April, then save them for use indoors as a winter pot plant. Polygonum, known also as Magic Carpet, is a vigorous, creeping form with deep-crimson leaves and dainty rose-pink flowers. It's useful as a covering for slopes, or as a spiky border edging.

ANNUALS FOR MIXED PLANTINGS

When planning to add annuals to an existing perennial border, consider these varieties. In the dwarf to 1-foot size: baby blue eyes or nemophila, with cup-shaped blooms; annual candytuft with white flower spires; blue browallia for sun or shade; coleus for exciting color and shape in its foliage; and echium, a light purple favorite of butterflies. Use impatiens for compact plants, free-flowering lobelia in dark-blue as striking edging plants, and all the dwarf marigolds in golden yellow. Also remember nasturtium—now available in dwarf, semi-trailing, and climbing strains—and pansies in solid colors. Use pinks, petunias, vinca, sweet alyssum, verbena, wax begonia, and dwarf zinnias.

Annuals of intermediate height include arctotis, balsam, calliopsis, coreopsis, and clarkia, as well as geranium, gaillardia, and nemesia. Further, consider mignonette, nigella, other marigolds, sweet william, and stocks. And any list should include cockscomb, centurea, and zinnia.

For tall back-of-the-border plants, the choices are wide. There's an annual poinsettia (euphorbia), baby's-breath or gypsophila, tall bachelor's-button (*Centaurea cyanus*), and bells-of-Ireland. Others include cosmos, celosia, gloriosa daisies, heliotrope, kochia, larkspur, marigold, summer aster, nicotiana, snapdragon, salpiglossis, snow-on-the-mountain, and zinnia. All these and more are available, so study the plants before choosing.

As the season mellows, calendulas and snapdragons add to the perennial show, and marigolds replace fading poppies.

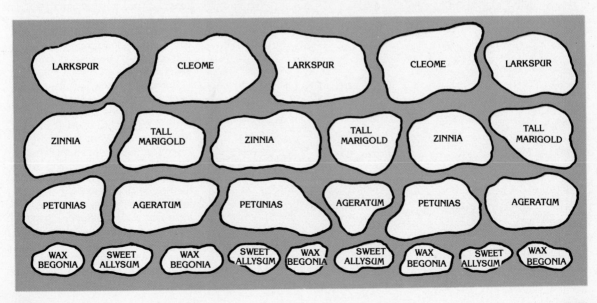

LARKSPUR CLEOME LARKSPUR CLEOME LARKSPUR

ZINNIA TALL MARIGOLD ZINNIA TALL MARIGOLD ZINNIA TALL MARIGOLD

PETUNIAS AGERATUM PETUNIAS AGERATUM PETUNIAS AGERATUM

WAX BEGONIA SWEET ALLYSUM WAX BEGONIA SWEET ALLYSUM WAX BEGONIA SWEET ALLYSUM WAX BEGONIA SWEET ALLYSUM WAX BEGONIA

17

The Versatility of Annuals

The choice of annuals is so vast and versatile, you should be able to find exactly the right variety to brighten any nook or cranny in your garden. Garden annuals are typically a good deal more brilliant than most perennials. They grow in petite, squat, thick, tall, thin, and feathery forms, with near-endless color variety. However, when planting out small spaces, it's best to concentrate on one or, at most, two kinds of plants.

Beside a flight of steps, plant Empress candytuft seeds, and expect flowers in about two months. Try an edging of hybrid dianthus, Snowflake, or Queen of Hearts for fragrance all summer long. And put some zing in life with a mix of Bright Lights cosmos and Sunny Boy calendula.

Gazanias have daisy shapes, but come in wild, exciting colors. Pot them up in the fall to enjoy indoors. For evening pleasure, grow four o'clocks in the striped Jingles and Petticoat strains. Then use zinnias in dwarf to giant varieties, and low-growing Peter Pan in a wonderful mix of luscious colors. Fruit Bowl is taller, with 5- and 6-inch blooms. You can start a prairie garden by adding sunflowers, larkspur, gilia, liatris, and goldenrod to a sunny rise of ground, or give soft color to a tree-shaded corner with *Vinca rosea*.

For a back fence line, plant sweet peas. Revive a few oldies, but test such new hybrids as Galaxy and Jet Set, too. All are sweet-scented. Morning glories Early Call and Heavenly Blue are other favorites. Try the butterfly and wedding bell shapes of snapdragons, along with the Rocket strains. Asters come in new and surprising variations, from Carpet Ball to Super Princess. These and calendulas are good for cutting, too.

If you're weary of lawn mowing, rake up the thatch and try planting a packet of mixed flowers.

Topper snapdragons offer tall flowery spires in vivid colors.

A walk edged with a mix of yellow, gold, and orange marigolds.

Enliven a shady corner with fuchsia and impatiens in many pinks.

Planters for Close-Up Color

Annuals take kindly to pot culture, and because of their brilliant colors, make ideal floral accents in raised beds, hanging baskets, or big containers. What's more, container planting is particularly useful where garden plots are small since it encourages multiple use of terrace space for both plants and people. In addition, you can rearrange containers to change the emphasis, alter the mood, or bring out plants as they come into peak bloom.

With the great development of new colors and strains, there is an extra excitement with annuals. New hybrids extend the color range of the big three—petunias, zinnias, and marigolds—and give us new shapes and sizes. With this accomplished, hybridizers turned their fine talents to snapdragons, dianthus, impatiens, and even cosmos.

Each of these departures is evaluated by the All-America Selections judges, and the best are tagged on seed packets as AAS winners. Each breakthrough can be an adventure for the enterprising gardener, and some winners are so worthy, they remain favorites for years afterward. Container gardening is a good way to study the plants and make your own award judgments. Then, with little effort, you can place your favorites out front where they show to best advantage.

It's easy to garden in pots wherever you live. You can cultivate lush plants on a desert patio, or cacti in a container of gritty sand beside a marshy place. If space is limited, hang baskets from the ceiling or set small pots of tiny plants on a porch railing. And, use window boxes on a ledge or sill for suspended pockets of coleus, geraniums, and trailing ivy.

When choosing material for your low planter arrangements, don't overlook the foliage plants amaranthus, dusty miller, coleus, caladium, and flowering kale. The dusty miller and the kale can be a foil for brilliant zinnias or marigolds. By contrast, the coleus and caladium have enough exceptional coloring to stand alone.

Another great advantage of planter boxes and containers is that they let you tailor the soil to the needs of special plants. More often in the garden, you must grow only what your soil can support.

While we're extolling the virtues of container gardening, we should also be aware of its handicaps. Soil in raised planters or containers tends to dry out faster, and therefore needs more watering. But frequent watering washes away soil nutrients faster and that means more care and replacement. And, because container plants are viewed close-up, there may be a greater inclination to primp and trim. But altogether, these are minor obligations, and relatively painless. Just don't choose containers that are so large and heavy you can't move them about. If you must think big, build yourself a small dolly to roll your plants around. Or use three short lengths of pipe for the same purpose.

Spanish brocade marigolds vie with green-eyed gloriosa daisies.

Low retaining walls of brick, wood, or stone can 'contain' a garden plot to good purpose by directing traffic to other sections of the garden or doubling as casual seats or benches. They permit you to introduce rich garden loam into a limited area, and also make watering chores much easier. Low walls and raised beds strengthen the garden design, and also make weeding and cultivating easier, with less stooping. If you're short of brick or stone, lay up chunks of broken sidewalk concrete as a dry wall, cascading petunias along the top and adding succulents to the outer crevices. If your soil is sandy and drains too quickly, first line the planter with several inches of clay.

Choose your flower colors with the thoughtfulness of an artist. For a rounded sphere of dappling color, mix tiny blue lobelia with dwarf marigolds and white sweet alyssum in a moss-filled basket. Add a few of the seedlings to the sides of the basket as you mound the moss across the top, putting the biggest and stoutest plants in the center. Water at least every other day, except when the rains do it for you, but withhold water when the moss feels soggy. For other surprising combinations, try flowering kale interrupted by little button zinnias in many colors, scarlet carefree geraniums in a bed of English ivy, or Jewel Box celosia in a velvet mix of colors.

Raised beds, close by a terrace, can offer another kind of beauty and one we often overlook—fragrance. There is an ongoing debate about the merits of marigold and nasturtium, but most will concede the nicotiana and scented geraniums are a real delight. Some find petunias too sweet to live with, dianthus just right, and carnations a bit spicy. Annuals you may choose from include the sweet pea, sweet sultan, and sweet alyssum, mignonette, four o'clocks, stocks, verbena, candytuft, and heliotrope. Tansy and chrysanthemums, like marigold, have pungent odors. Add some herbs like basil, thyme, dill, fennel, and mint to the flowers for an unforgettable scent combination.

All-America zinnias Rosy Future and Torch are astoundingly big and brilliant. They make a great color show in a patio corner.

Planters for Close-Up Color

Movable gardening is a practical concept when you have handsome wood planters and patio boxes to work with. The well-designed boxes below can be spread across a window wall, picked up and moved in line as a barrier on the edge of a terrace, or placed on a wide flight of steps. If you start with a good basic design of square or rectangular shapes, you can interlock the boxes in a zigzag fashion, or group them around a central point. You can rearrange them at will.

Timing is another trick to be learned early. In the boxes below, icy-white Glacier petunias were bought as starter plants, set out first, and then nasturtium seed was sown around them. In mild climates, you can plant pansy seed around spring-flowering bulbs in the fall. But in harsher climes, wait until spring and add pansy plants as the tulips or daffodils send up leaf blades to show their location.

Calendulas can be sown in a bed of primroses, to come into flower as the primroses lose their punch. And blue petunia seedlings can be planted in a bed strewn with annual forget-me-not seeds. Both should come to maturity at about the same time and keep good company. If you're looking for an easy-care garden, combine low-growing coreopsis with white Carpet of Snow sweet alyssum. And after planting your favorite petunias, start a casual planting of Iceland poppies and statice between.

If you want to set a style for your garden, you should decide whether you prefer pastel flower shades or a far bolder mix of brilliant and sometimes clashing colors. Fortunately, most annuals are available in gentle and vivid hues so you can have the kind you want.

However, if none of the colors pleases you, try concentrating on neutrals with gray and white. This will take some doing, as an all-white plot needs the drama of various flower forms—the feathery spider flower, the ubiquitous daisy, the white zinnia, and even the white marigold.

Style comes, too, from careful design as well as controlled color. If you want the casual look, show it in random planting and a loosely-woven design. Or if you prefer to be earth-shaking, gather all

This trio of flower-filled boxes can be viewed from either indoors or out. The petunias and nasturtiums flourish in the bright sun.

In a trough made from railroad ties, three kinds of marigolds mingle with petunias and ageratum. Curly parsley adds a crisp note.

the wild colors you can muster, and juxtapose them one against the other in big bold beds.

Although it looks quite permanent, the long planter box shown above is indeed movable, and provides a fine display of color at the edge of a concrete patio. Eight-foot railroad ties are stacked two-high, joined together with 2-foot end pieces, and held in place with heavy spikes. The framed unit has no base and sits directly on the concrete deck. The wood container is filled with good soil, heavy with humus and well-laced

with sand for good drainage. In it, a concentrated planting of robust annuals produces a wide display of maximum brilliance.

If you have a sheltered garden where the winds are gentle, try growing taller annuals in containers. There is dancing beauty in a wiry stand of pink cosmos, giant asters, or the very bright Flaming Fountain amaranthus. And although compact plantings of stout marigolds give intense globes of color, a loosely-branched display of marguerite, celosia, or cleome also can be a delightful surprise. If you

stay with cosmos or cornflowers because they do best, you can still work wonders by putting individual colors and heights in separate pots.

Houseplants that have been moved outdoors for the summer can be embellished with extra bits of annual color, too. Seedling plants of lobelia or sweet alyssum can be added to full-grown geraniums to cascade over the rims. Or a scattering of sedum seeds might be dropped in scuffed soil around the base of a jade tree. If the sedum crowds the jade, dig it out and pot alone.

23

Annuals for Specials Uses

Bright Spots on City Windows

Window boxes are a great way to improve your city view *and* share your flowers with neighbors. Below is one with extras: tubs of geraniums plus strung-up vegetables and indoor plants. It's rigged with six shelf brackets screwed to a balcony wall (with the landlord's OK), but the same setup would work with a conventional window, too.

If your balcony gets little sun, use shade-loving plants—wax begonias or impatiens—to keep the area colorful. It's perfect, too, for starting new plants from stem cuttings that the wind might knock off, or for snippets from shaggy houseplants. Use a ball of twine and a couple window-top appendages to build a morning glory cage by running strings at 3-inch intervals around the rim of the window box and up to a U-shaped rod above. Soak the seeds overnight and plant in groups of three around each string upright. Then plant a flat of giant pansies in the remaining space; you can pick them for indoor use.

Build a saddlebag planter by joining two boxes to fit over your porch or balcony railing. A third box is mounted on the saddle bridge to sit, nail-free, on top of the rail. The three-part unit is secured by wiring the saddle boxes to a couple of railing uprights. Plant the top box with petunias, add morning glories at either end to trail along the rail, then start vining nasturtium or black-eyed susan vine in the remaining space for further screening.

With window boxes and railing units, arrange your plants first for indoor view, and then for outsiders looking in. For added privacy, include a few tall plants, or use scarlet runner beans or climbing tomatoes to cover the entire window opening. Add a few herbs along the inside edge for gourmet clipping.

Containers are also good set on stair treads and planted with cascading varieties to drape through the balustrade. They're handsome, too, stood on rough-hewn pedestals, 6x6 posts, or fruit market crates as an entry display. Any of these spots can make a setting for browallia, impatiens, wax begonias, or coleus. Monitor your displays, watching for signs of too much midday heat, wind damage, or too much shade. Then rearrange the plants to their individual likings until they seem content.

Most window boxes are built with 1x10 boards. Redwood boxes are most durable, and resist rot. But before adding soil, drill ½-inch holes in the box bottom and spread a layer of screening and 2 inches of perlite or vermiculite to assure good drainage. Then you can either fill with good garden loam or set in a row of potted geraniums and ivy, filling the spaces between with vermiculite to keep the unit light in weight. Remember that a 4-foot window box filled with wet soil can be very heavy. If the box hangs over a sidewalk, you must be doubly sure that the weather or the box's own weight cannot dislodge it to fall to the ground or on passersby.

If you have to go to the roof to find a place to garden, choose a protected corner beside a chimney wall and out of the wind. Spread out some old planking around the edges of your new domain to hold your container plants while distributing their weight across a wider span of roof beams. If your roof is tarred and graveled, you can use a square of artificial turf to protect the surface and give the illusion of a lawn. Then, gather together a group of barrel halves, soy tubs, or surplus window boxes, raising them an inch off the turf or planks for better circulation.

In containers near the chimney and parapets, plant climbing annuals, cup-and-saucer vine, thunbergia, or passion flower vine. String them up to the chimney top or across a portable lattice made from an expansion gate or old ladders. Then add a tray or two of potted pansies, weeping lobelia, sweet william, and shirley poppies. And bring your dracena and variegated geraniums up into a shaded corner for the summer. Garden with commercially prepared soil-less compost instead of earth. It's lighter than normal soil, but contains all needed nutrients.

The rest is up to you—from benches to lounge chairs to canopies to night lights. A roof garden can give you a new view of your life in the city.

Grow bright flowers anywhere within reach of a watering can.

The glorious crimson of far-reaching geraniums makes viewing this window box a two-way pleasure.

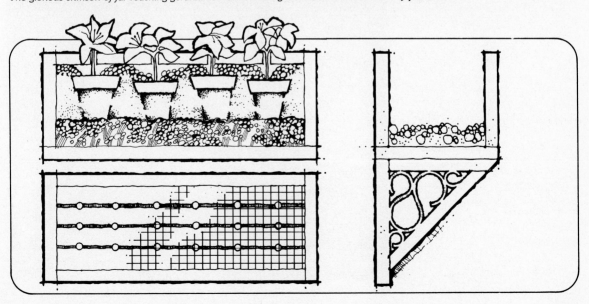

Annuals in Pots

Choose plants with vivid colors to decorate a small porch or balcony, and change them with the season. Use primrose in spring, and mums in the fall.

Maneuverability is your biggest asset in container gardening. You can move plants around at will to put color just where you want it. Try to combine container color with nearby flower borders, or brighten a shady corner with hot-pink wax begonias and sprightly rose impatiens. Think of potted plants as easy accent tools for garden color in any season.

Potted plants are useful, also, to screen out or divert attention from faltering garden flowers. Cascading petunias can hide a multitude of sins and leave the garden visitor none-the-wiser. In fact, you can convert all ground-level space to durable ground covers, then grow flowers exclusively in pots, boxes, and hanging baskets, where care is relatively easy and daily watering is just a simple routine.

A green-gold background of shrubs and new trees or a brick-paved patio surrounded by climbing vines are ideal settings for a container garden. To make your groupings harmonious and cohesive, choose various-sized pots of similar colors in clay, wood, or plastic. And, select plant colors that blend with each other so that a change in pot groupings is never dissonant.

Plan, also, to have an off-to-the-side holding area where you can nurture new plants through the seedling and bud stages and grow replacements. Make it a sunny place, perhaps with a planting bench and—to meet the needs of individual plants—a variety of soil mixes in convenient bins.

Cluster your pots all in one place for maximum show, or divide them between the terrace and a clearing near the rear of the garden. This gives you a near and distant view, and an excuse to wander out for a closer look. Potted plants make good devices for manipulating a party crowd, directing people toward an open lawn area, or keeping them away from a new bed of freshly-seeded wildflowers.

And—another great advantage—whenever your container plants want to reach out or cascade, you can always provide

A lath trellis protects impatiens and other shade-loving plants from strong sunlight.

A low, curved patio wall makes for comfortable seating and a great showplace for tulips, pansies, geraniums, and lilies.

them with the space to grow their merry way.

Give your container plants a well-rounded appearance by grouping four to six plants to a medium-sized pot. Set three to five seedlings on the slopes of a little hill of soil, leaning toward the rim, and one on the top of the mound, reaching straight up. If you want the tall-look, pot up foxglove, lupine, or delphinium seedlings in sturdy containers sheltered from high winds. Or, for both flowers and a crop, try scarlet runner bean seeds set in a big pot with tall stakes for future plant support.

Try some exciting plant combinations, too. Plant up bright pink geraniums in a 12-inch pot edged with sweet alyssum or blue lobelia seedlings to drape over the rim. Consider spring-flowering bulbs for a special spring show. You'll need to pot up the bulbs in the fall and season them in a cold frame outdoors through the winter, but by spring those clusters of crocus, daffodils, and tulips will make it all worthwhile.

Grow one or more hybrid morning glories from seed in a pot fitted with bamboo trellising, or try growing cherry tomatoes within a cylinder of chicken wire set into the pot itself. The opportunities are endless. With pots and planters brimming with colorful flowers, it's possible to turn an otherwise sterile-looking patio into a beautiful, bloom-filled garden in just a few short weeks.

Strawberry Jars

The pocketed strawberry jar still gets occasional use as a container for strawberry plants and their luscious fruit. But each year, more gardeners are using these jars to display many other kinds of plants, including petunias, lobelia, and succulents. In fact, any cascading or semi-trailing plant is a candidate.

Strawberry jar-gardening is simple—mostly a matter of selecting plants that harmonize well with the red clay surface of the jars. Trailers and small bouquet shapes fit best in the tiny compartments, and are generally preferred to larger plants that would overwhelm and hide their interesting containers.

Candytuft or sweet alyssum make a pleasing contrast, and primrose polyanthus pockets well in a cool, moist, and somewhat-shaded place. A mix of pansies and violas, peeking out in all directions, is an amusing sight. And impatiens or fibrous begonias also lend themselves to strawberry jar treatment. Fuchsia and Reiger begonias make a particularly spectacular mild-climate display. And any pocketed jar is ideal for showing a special succulent collection or a gathering of cacti.

If you stay with strawberries, try both the June- and everbearing varieties. Surecrop and Fairfax are outstanding in the first category, and Ogallala and Ozark Beauty in the second. Then there is Fraises des Bois, a tiny French strawberry of exceptional sweetness and flavor.

The plants do best in light-textured soil that is well-drained. The June- and everbearing varieties prefer full sun; the French strawberries, woodland half-shade.

Set plants in the pockets so crowns are level with the surface of the soil. Fan the roots out and down, firming soil over them. Apply 10-10-10 fertilizer about six weeks after planting.

On June-bearers, pick off blooms before they set fruit the first year to channel the plant's efforts into becoming well established and sending out runners.

After the season's growth, move the jar to a sheltered spot and mulch each pocket and the top with straw or snippets of pine branches.

In spring, top-dress with well-rooted cow manure or other fertilizer.

1 To plant a pocket jar, first spread a thick layer of broken crockery or potshards. Cover it with a circle of screening mesh or a layer of nylon hose discards. If the jar is more than 2 feet tall, add a 3-inch cylinder of screening mesh as a central core to assure deep watering. Then, a little at a time, put rich potting soil around the cylinder and in the pockets. Keep the soil lightly textured, and don't hard-pack.

2 After the jar is filled with soil to 1 inch from the top, add the plant seedlings in groups of two or three to each pocket opening. It's a bit easier to plant from bottom to top, turning the jar as each section is completed. On larger jars, some gardeners plant each pocket as the soil is layered in, making it easier to evenly spread out the roots. Be sure to save enough plants to evenly fill out the jar top.

3 Your pocket jar can become a gay ornament almost immediately if you select seedlings that are already in flower or bud. Keep these flowers coming by watering the jar well at the onset and keeping the container lightly moist most of the time. To maintain an equal display on all sides, turn the jar a quarter turn every two or three days (use a turntable or casters under large, heavy strawberry jars).

Trailing lobelia makes an attractive addition to any strawberry jar.

Hanging Baskets

There's a special pleasure in growing plants overhead. They can enclose you in a canopy of flowers, *without* robbing you of vital outdoor living space. If you have a wide roof overhang, an arbor, a pergola, or a pretty gazebo, you have the framework for an overhead garden. So plant your flowers high up, to enclose your yard with color.

All you need is a handful of screw eyes or clothesline hooks screwed into the roof beams, a few wire baskets or clay bowls, and some lightweight chain or rope to use for hanging. Sphagnum moss or lightweight perlite or vermiculite mixed with standard potting mix will make the pot burden lighter.

If your climate is nicely humid most of the time, your plants will grow well in moss-lined baskets. In drier situations, plants do better in clay or plastic pots, saucered to hold moisture. It's true that hanging pots take more attention, frequent primping, and generally almost-daily watering. But this is no great chore if you have the plants concentrated in one place. And it's a small price to pay for showpiece plants that are viewed close-up by visitors.

You also can bring some of your houseplants outdoors for a cool summer under the eaves. Ferns, Swedish ivy, and tradescantia all do well in a sheltered corner with half-light. If you don't want to transplant them to baskets, drill three holes in the rims of their saucers and use chain to hang the saucers and pots together. But be aware of the weight of each pot, and keep the heaviest ones on a rack or table.

In moss-filled baskets grow any of the cascading petunias. Chiffon or Pink Cascade are beauties. Try the cup flower, nierembergia Regal Robe. It retains brilliance in strong sunlight. Start semi-trailing Gleam nasturtiums from seed planted in somewhat-dry soil in a sunny location, and have blooms in six weeks. In filtered sunlight, grow the unusual Amethyst browallia for sheer grace. Plant ivy or scented geraniums by themselves, and the self-branching Carefree with cascading Sapphire lobelia. Combine Button, Lilliput, or Thumbelina zinnias with Linearis, the basket plant zinnia. Or, do a basket with nothing but verbena in a bright color mix—Regalia or the red, white, and blue Spirit of '76.

1 To start a hanging basket, assemble a wire basket frame, a sack of sphagnum moss, a bag of potting mix, and several flats of seedlings—pansies, alyssum, and wax begonias. Then soak the moss in a pail of water (overnight, if you have time), drain off the surplus water, and shape the moss into flat cakes.

2 Line the interior of your wire frame with the moss layers, working the moss around the wires to disguise it. Thicken the moss lining until you have a quart-size cavity in the center. Recheck the lining for thin spots and make the necessary additions, interlocking the moss fibers well throughout.

3 Finish the basket with a cushion of moss around the wire rim. Then carefully fill the cavity with a good planting mix, shaking the mix into all the nooks and crannies as you go. Fill this center soil cavity to the top, then strike the basket on a tabletop until soil settles to 1 inch below the rim.

4 Tilt your basket on its side, then begin planting the seedlings between the wires in dimpled depressions you make with your fingers. Run three ribs of alyssum bottom to top, adding wax begonias between. Round out the arrangement with pansies, planting the remainder on top. Hang the basket with chains and water well.

Hang a basket of sunshine overhead—a dappling of sweet-smelling alyssum and fibrous begonias, with sparks of pansies.

31

Problem Areas

Granted, few of us have perfect garden plots. Some are too hot and dry; others, too wet and shady. Our soils can range from sticky clay to runny sand or coarse gravel. And our sites can vary from windswept hilltops to peaty bogs. We cannot hope to quickly remake the soil into an ideal mix with the right pH. Nor should we expect to grow shade trees overnight or to clear a thickly wooded plot without considerable effort. It's better that we recognize our gardens for what they are and select plants that survive or flourish with the conditions we have to offer.

Too much shade may be the steadiest source of annoyance and concern. We love our trees, but they hide the sun. The plants shown on these pages can come to the rescue. Fancy-leafed caladiums have foliage in reds, pinks, whites, and silver, and prefer moist soil and semi-shade. Wax begonias prosper under shrubs or beside shaded walks, their luminous blooms shining out from the darkest corners. Impatiens also are prime shade plants, covering the ground with gay flower colors, spring to fall.

In very bright sun grow zinnias, big sunflowers, and hollyhocks. And the prerequisites for nasturtiums are a sunny location and dry—even poor—soil.

If you crave privacy, start a tall barrier row of tithonia, the bushy Mexican sunflower with red-orange dahlia-like flowers. Or on wide plains or hilltop sites, grow asters and cosmos for their flexible stems.

Brighten the gloomy pockets of your garden through the summer with caladium—the most brilliant of our shade plants.

Plant pink Carmen and red Indian Maid wax begonias under taller plants and beside a shaded garden walk.

Elfin impatiens—low-growing, self-branching, and shade-loving—offers prolific bloom all summer in a corner that's moist and cool.

33

Problem Areas

Don't let garden problems get you down. Take it easy and approach them one at a time. In solving your first problem, you may well solve a few others, too. If your land slopes away too steeply, modify the angle with intermediate terraces or a graceful flow of steps. To remove abrupt changes in grade, reshape the land with earth fill or a structure framed with railroad ties, redwood timbers, or concrete slabs. Once the angle of repose is established, plant evergreens and flowering shrubs nearby, to mark the way in time. Meanwhile, resort to flowering annuals for instant enhancement of the scene.

A slope planted with spreading juniper is, meanwhile, graced with sweet alyssum.

Heavy timbers serve here to unify steps and retaining walls. While shrubs mature, petunias and marigolds contribute instant color.

An informal planting of petunias, marigolds, caladiums, and sedum fill a curved rock outcropping between a driveway and entry.

Problem areas can well be creative challenges if we learn to think of them as opportunities instead of hindrances. With such devices as retaining walls, fencing, steps, and storage sheds, we can develop stable slopes and privacy.

It's been said that if the task is too easy, we come up with dull solutions. Tough problems, however, lead to exciting solutions. We need to be flexible and willing to make some drastic and irrevocable changes. And the momentum of change can have a valued effect on other problem areas: early success generates new confidence in tackling other garden problems.

There's an excitement in shaping gardens to human needs, in carving terraces into hillsides, in constructing a small deck on a rise of ground, or in pushing back the weeds to make room for a cutting garden. We should look for lively solutions to our problems—an earth berm embankment covered with flowers on a heavily trafficked street corner, or a rooftop haven or balcony retreat where no land is available. Many of us might reconvert the raw, scarred land of a new suburbia to a country landscape awash with flowers.

Don't be afraid to experiment with something radically new or different: sunken gardens filled with bright-flowering annuals and durable perennials, tall hedgings to enclose and enfold, or fast-growing vines to clamber up the walls of a small areaway. And always remember the rumor that the world's best gardens occupy the most difficult sites.

35

Climbing Annuals

A generous planting of annual vines can teach us much about gardening in a single year. These vigorous and quick-growing plants demonstrate the abilities of vines to screen out an unpleasant view, to shade a bald plot, or to enliven a dull corner. They've been labeled the quick-change experts of the garden, and rightly so.

Once you're convinced of the value of vines, you can rely on annuals to continue as temporary foliage while newly-placed perennial vines mature. Sow a fresh packet of seeds, and in a few short weeks, you'll have cover and color just where you wish.

Most packets contain more seed than you'll ever need. This allows you the gamble of an early planting. If these seeds fail, plant again. If you still have a surplus, plant the remainder in a place where you can use a trailing ground cover, preferably in full sun. Annual vines expend most of their energies producing lavish blooms, probably because they don't have to plan for their own survival. Woody perennial vines more often have good leaf-green and less color.

All annual vines climb upward by twining, so it's necessary to give them strings or garden nets to twine upon. Experienced gardeners find it wise to set the strings or nets as they plant the seed, and to sow seeds right where they're to grow. Vines don't like to be moved, especially morning glories. Soak the hard-shelled seeds overnight in warm water to hasten germination, or shake them in a glass jar that has been lined with a piece of sandpaper. The scraping will wear down the tough cover, and is easier than notching the seed one-by-one.

Annual vines are invaluable in small gardens where space is limited. They can clothe harsh walls, or soften unattractive fencing. Used on an arbor, pergola, or trellis, they interrupt a neighbor's overhead view. They're also good as summer cover on a sunny porch or patio, but pull them down in the fall to reopen the space to the warming winter sun. Vines can be useful in many ways—as cover for a dead tree, screening for an ugly storage structure, or to scale an airy cage or a new gazebo. Design a series of pillar plantings, or hang vines over a concrete retaining wall.

The choices are many. Still most favored are the morning glory and the climbing nasturtium. But others deserving your attention are the cup-and-saucer vine (Cobaea scandens), the black-eyed susan vine, the cardinal climber (known also as the scarlet star glory), the moonflower, and the colorful ornamental gourds.

You can grow sweet peas for their flowery cover or for the cutting bouquets they offer. Start these and scarlet runner beans when the weather is cool. The sweet peas grow to 6 feet; the scarlet runners, to 12. Runner beans are also edible.

Grow hops (Humudus japonicus) for good green foliage, or its fancier green-and-white variegated cousin. Look for the tricolor morning glory in purple, white, and yellow.

Reach up to pick nasturtiums from your climbing vine; picking fosters bloom.

Moonflowers offer giant, evening blooms all summer long.

Cobea scandens, known both as the cup-and-saucer vine and cathedral bells, is a delightful oddity. Its flowers change from green to purple-blue as they mature, and it can reach heights of 25 feet under optimum conditions.

Heavenly Blue is a proper name for this outstanding morning glory. Other winners include Pearly Gates (white), Scarlett O'Hara (scarlet-red), and the Early Call (rose or blue). Plant all in full sun and in well-drained soil.

Bouquet Colors to Bring Inside

Enjoy your garden flowers indoors all winter by preserving them. Here are the various techniques, along with recommended flowers for each.

AIR DRYING

Cut flowers when dry and at their best (midday); strip leaves and secure in small bunches with elastic ties. Then, hang them upside down in a dark ventilated attic or room for a period of two to three weeks. Avoid picking flowers after heavy rains or when covered with dew.

Some excellent garden varieties for this method include cockscomb (celosia), larkspur, annual statice, acacia, bells-of-Ireland, blue salvia, Chinese-lanterns, globe amaranth, hydrangea (Pee Gee), delphinium, yarrow, artemisia, heather, honesty (silver dollars), and strawflowers (strawflowers should be picked and wired, if possible, when buds are just starting to open).

Likewise, many of the field flowers such as dock, goldenrod, pampas grass, pearly everlasting, teasel, and tansy dry well using this method.

SILICA GEL

Your favorite garden flowers—including zinnias, marigolds, roses, shasta daisies, dahlias, delphiniums, snapdragons, feverfew, ranunculus, and peonies—are great candidates for desiccant drying. Remember, however, that the finished product is only as good as the original flower specimen you picked to preserve! Try to avoid broken or damaged flowers.

Place a base of 1 or 2 inches of silica gel granules in the bottom of a cookie tin or coffee can and insert the short-cut stem of the flower *face up* in the drying medium. Be careful not to overlap any of the petals between flower specimens. Gently sprinkle more of the granules over the flowers until

they are completely covered with silica gel to a depth of about 1 inch. *Cover tightly* and tape name of flower and date on top of container. Place tin in a dark, dry place for the required drying time (from two to six days, see chart). If in doubt, lift lid and check to see if the petals feel brittle and papery to the touch; if not, replace cover.

When ready to remove, slowly pour off the silica gel and cup your hand under the flower head. Gently shake off drying compound, and if necessary, remove stubborn granules with a soft artist's brush. Store flowers in airtight boxes until ready to use (stem ends may be inserted erect in blocks of dry floral foam). To keep dried material in top condition, especially over prolonged periods or when excessive humidity may be a problem, add 3 to 4 tablespoons of silica gel to the storage container. If a petal should fall off, dab on a small amount of white glue with a toothpick and join it to the flower center.

Though delphiniums and larkspur may be air-dried, they retain form and color perfection in silica gel. Delphiniums, larkspur, rose buds, lilacs, and snapdragons should be dried in a horizontal position. Avoid drying dark red flowers, as they turn black. But don't forget to dry flower buds and leaves for more effect.

Silica gel, available at craft shops, can be reused indefinitely, but must be heated in the oven at 250° F. for one hour when restoration of the blue crystals is necessary.

BORAX

Ordinary household borax also may be used as drying medium. Follow the silica gel directions with two exceptions—place the flower *face down* in the container and leave the *lid off* while drying. Though less expensive than silica gel, it takes twice as long to act as a desiccant, and the color retention is less effective.

PRESSED

For the avid pressed-flower enthusiast, a flower press, complete with blotting paper, is available in craft shops. But for the average pressed-flower lover, a telephone book will suffice. At 1-inch intervals

DRIED FLOWER TIME CHART

Air Drying:
2 to 3 weeks

Silica Gel:
2 to 3 days forget-me-not, viola, coral bells, miniature roses, lantana
3 to 4 days pansy, small zinnia, dwarf dahlia, feverfew, tea rose, larkspur, dwarf marigold
4 to 5 days peony, large zinnia, shasta daisy, delphinium, hydrangea, ranunculus
5 to 6 days large dahlia, marigold, snapdragons, aster, calendula, lilacs

Borax:
double above drying times

Pressed Flowers and Ferns:
3 to 4 weeks

Glycerine Method:
1 to 2 weeks

in the book, spread facial tissue in newspaper. Place flowers flat and avoid overlapping. Cover flowers with tissue, then newspaper, so that newspaper print will not be picked up by the flowers while pressing.

If possible, use an even thickness of materials on each page for even drying. Remember to include buds and curve some stems and leaves for graceful positioning when dried. Weight with books and store for 3 to 4 weeks away from sunlight.

Some garden favorites for pressing include buttercup, daisies, verbena, dusty miller, hydrangea florets, lobelia, delphinium spikes and florets, sweet alyssum, pansies, violas, and almost all types of fern.

When ready to create pressed flower pictures, use eyebrow tweezers and a tiny dot of white glue to anchor the flowers to the background material. Let the finished design dry overnight before

inserting the glass and making the back airtight with tape.

FOLIAGE (GLYCERINIZED)

Leaves such as peony, oak, and beech may be pressed or dried in silica gel, but they will never be as supple and useful as when treated with glycerine. In a jar, mix a solution of one part glycerine to two parts hot water and shake well. After scraping or pounding the cut young branch ends, place them in 2 to 3 inches of the solution. Let stand for one to two weeks, or until leaves have finished absorbing the mixture and feel pliable. Usually they change to dark green or soft shades of brown and rust, depending upon their foliage. The glycerinized material may be used with fresh flowers, too, as water causes no injury.

Additional foliage to treat includes

eucalyptus, holly, laurel, aspidistra, pyracantha, sycamore, yew, and crab apple. Foliage to be treated should be gathered before mid-August while still tender. And the glycerine solution may be used over again if stored in a tightly covered jar.

DRIED ARRANGEMENTS

Combine glycerinized foliage with dried flowers in a foam-filled container, after using floral wire and tape to extend the flower stems. Insert the foliage first, using it as a guide for height and outline (about 1½ times the height of the container). After the filler material, place large and darker flowers in the lower center section of the arrangement for visual interest. Fill in with the rest of the flowers. Place the completed arrangement away from direct sun.

Air drying of tansy, pearly, everlasting, yarrow, lady's-mantle, and three kinds of statice.

39

Annuals for Special Situations

Flowers solve problems—problems either overlooked in the original landscape plan or problems inherited with your remodeling or your site selection. To solve them, rely heavily on annuals for their dependable, long-lasting color. Most will bloom from late spring till frost.

There's an annual for every need, and maintenance isn't at all demanding. For an average of just a few minutes each day, you can hide a strip of foundation, fill bare spots where nothing has grown before, erect living screens for privacy, or blanket a small rocky expanse.

A packet of flower seeds is still the great American bargain. Nowhere else can you get such immeasurable beauty in such a small package to produce such a lasting impression.

For Shady Spots

Annual aster
Calendula
Centaurea
Clarkia
Cleome
Dusty miller (foliage plant)
Feverfew
Larkspur
Lobelia
Nemophila
Phlox drummondi
Snapdragon
Sweet alyssum
Tassel flower
Wax begonia

For Dry Soil

Browallia
California poppy
Celosia
Cleome
Coreopsis
Cornflower
Cosmos
Four-o'clock
Gaillardia
Gypsophila
Portulaca
Rudbeckia
Scarlet sage
Sunflower
Zinnia

For Moist Soil

Annual forget-me-not
Baby-blue-eyes
Blue lace flower
Butterfly flower
Calendula
Mallow
Monkey flower
Nemesia
Nicotiana
Phlox drummondi
Sweet pea
Torenia

For Poor Soil

California poppy
Celosia
Cleome
Coreopsis
Four-o'clock
Gaillardia
Marigold
Morning-glory
Nasturtium
Portulaca
Sweet alyssum
Zinnia

For Tall Borders

Celosia
China aster
Cleome
Cornflower
Marigold (giants)
Tithonia
Sunflower

For Edging

Ageratum
Alyssum
Browallia
Candytuft
Dianthus (dwarf pinks)
Marigold (dwarfs)
Nasturtium
Nemophila
Pansy
Petunia
Portulaca
Sweet alyssum
Torenia
Wax begonia

For Drying

Baby's-breath
Bells-of-Ireland
Celosia
Bachelor's-buttons
Everlasting (helichrysum)
Gaillardia
Globe amaranth (gomphrena)
Statice
Verbena
Zinnia

For Trellises and Screens

Cup-and-saucer vine (cobaea)
Moonflower
Morning-glory
Scarlet runner bean
Sweet peas

For Early Planting

Baby's-breath
Calendula
California poppy
Candytuft
Clarkia
Coreopsis
Cosmos
Gaillardia
Marigold
Petunia
Phlox drummondi
Stock
Sunflower
Sweet alyssum
Sweet pea
Verbena
Zinnia

For Window Boxes

Button zinnias
Creeping sanvitalia
Gazania
Geranium
Impatiens
Lobelia
Marigold
Nasturtium
Petunia
Sweet alyssum
Wax begonia

For Fragrance

Annual carnation
Candytuft
Heliotrope
Moonflower
Nasturtium
Nicotiana
Petunia
Stocks
Swan river daisy
Sweet alyssum
Sweet sultan
Verbena
Wallflower
Woodruff (annual)

For Night Gardens

Candytuft
Canterbury-bells
Cleome (white)
Evening stocks
Feverfew (white)
Four-o'clock
Iceland poppies
Larkspur
Marguerite (white)
Moonflower
Nicotiana
Petunias (white)
Sweet alyssum

For Privacy Hedges and Screens

Amaranth
Balloon vine
Balsam apple
Cardinal climber
Castor bean
Crimson star glory
Cup-and-saucer vine (cobaea)
Cypress vine
Dahlia
Hyacinth bean
Moonflower
Morning-glory
Ornamental gourd
Rainbow corn

For Strawberry Jars

Blue lobelia
Dusty miller
Impatiens
Pansy
Petunia
Sweet alyssum

For Hanging Baskets

Cascading petunia
Ivy geranium
Trailing lantana
Trailing lobelia
Wax begonia

For Cutting Gardens

African daisy
Annual carnation
Bells-of-Ireland
Calendula
Canterbury-bells
China aster
Clarkia
Cleome
Cornflower
Cosmos
Felicia daisy (blue)
Feverfew
Gaillardia
Gazania
Gloriosa daisy
Godetia
Gypsophila
Larkspur
Lupine
Marigold
Pansy
Petunia
Plumed celosia
Statice
Stock
Swan river daisy
Sweet william
Sweet pea
Wallflower
Zinnia

For Wild and Prairie Gardens

Bird's-eyes
Black-eyed susan
Blazing-star
California poppy
Chinese-lanterns
Cornflower
Corn poppy
Lupine
Mountain garland
Painted daisy
Purple coneflower
Queen-Anne's-lace
Tahoka daisy

ABCs of Annuals

Of the top ten flowering plants in the United States, at least half are annuals—and for good reason. Annuals are economical to buy and grow for quick summer color, and bloom all season to frost. They require no winter care or storage, and are heat- and drought-resistant, as well as relatively disease- and insect-free. With their wide range of colors and heights, they permit great freedom in garden design, and adapt to various planting times. And, most important, annuals will bloom for even the most inexperienced gardener. Here, in easy-to-find alphabetical order, are all the annuals, along with details on colors, heights, preferred environments, and culture.

African daisies make fine companions for taller Iceland poppies.

A

ACROCLINIUM
(helipterum)

DESCRIPTION: Double and semi-double blossoms are 2 to 3 inches across on slender 2-foot stems; oval pointed leaves are gray-green. Mixed seed includes shades of pink, white, and beige. Flowers resemble daisies and asters, but are usually slightly smaller and more delicate than strawflowers.

SOIL AND LIGHT: Acroclinium grows best in well-drained, average-to-dry soil that receives full sun.

PLANTING: Sow seed outdoors after all danger of frost. It should germinate in about 15 days and bloom about 6 weeks later. Seedlings may be thinned to 6 to 12 inches apart; they are often difficult to transplant.

SPECIAL HELPS: Flowers may be used in fresh arrangements and are excellent additions to dried bouquets. To dry, cut the whole stem before the flower is fully open; strip foliage. Hang upside down in a cool, airy, shady place so that stems will be straight. The flowers should be dry enough to use in two to three weeks. If desired, spray with hair spray or clear acrylic to help prevent shedding or humidity damage. Keep dried flower arrangements out of direct sunlight to prevent fading.

AFRICAN DAISY
(arctotis)

DESCRIPTION: Daisy-like blooms grow 2 to 3 inches across on stems 1 to 2 feet tall. Arctotis is available in shades of yellow, pink, and brown; but the most common variety has gold-edged blue centers with white petals that are a light purple underneath. Plants have sparse but attractive gray-green foliage. Flowers close at night.

SOIL AND LIGHT: These do best in sandy, light soil with full sun, and adapt to dry conditions. Plants like hot days and cool nights.

PLANTING: Start seeds indoors 6 to 8 weeks before last frost, or sow directly in the ground after all danger of frost. Seedlings may be thinned to 6 to 12 inches apart; prune plants to keep bushy. In mild climates, the seed may be sown in late summer, if desired.

SPECIAL HELPS: Arctotis are effective in mass plantings and in front of borders, especially when planted to receive reflected heat from sidewalks or walls. Attractive flowers and long stems make them desirable for fresh bouquets. Plants are native to South Africa.

AGERATUM
also called flossflower

DESCRIPTION: These 3- to 6-inch dome-shaped plants are almost constantly in bloom. The small fuzzy blooms are most commonly seen in shades of blue-violet, but are also available in white and pink.

SOIL AND LIGHT: Plants are easy to grow and are tolerant of all soil conditions. They prefer full sun, but will adapt to some shade.

PLANTING: Start seeds indoors 6 to 8 weeks before last frost. They germinate in 5 to 10 days and grow slowly. Seedlings are also quite tender, so you may prefer to buy started plants. Plants may be propagated from stem cuttings. Set plants 5 to 9 inches apart; in some areas, they may self-sow.

SPECIAL HELPS: Their mounding, compact shape makes these plants excellent for edgings, borders, and rock gardens, either alone to form a solid mass of color, or in combination with other border plants. Tall varieties make good background plantings. Snip faded flowers to assure constant bloom. Ageratum doesn't tolerate drought conditions, so keep evenly watered. Plants were originally found in Mexico; in 1822, the seed was taken to England where it was first cultivated. Painter's brush and tassel flower are other names sometimes used in referring to this plant.

ALCEA ROSEA
see hollyhock

ALYSSUM

DESCRIPTION: Delicate white, pink, or purple flowers cover these compact plants from spring to frost, scenting the air with honey-like fragrance. Most varieties grow only 3 to 4 inches tall; others may reach up to 9 or 10 inches. Plants tend to spread, making them wider than they are tall. Popular varieties include Rosie O'Day, Carpet of Snow, Royal Carpet, and Violet Queen.

SOIL AND LIGHT: These do best

in full sun, but will adapt to some shade. They're tolerant of all soil conditions.

PLANTING: Sow seed as soon as the ground can be worked, or set out started plants when weather is warm. Space plants 6 to 8 inches apart. Dig up with a clump of dirt around the roots in the fall for a showy houseplant. Plants self-sow in many areas.
SPECIAL HELPS: These fragrant, spreading plants are excellent choices for borders, edgings, rock gardens, bulb gardens, hanging baskets, and window boxes. In warm climates, they will often bloom all year. If flowering decreases toward the end of the summer, trim plants back to encourage new growth. Alyssum is native to the Mediterranean area.

AMARANTH
also called love-lies-bleeding

DESCRIPTION: Tall plants (3 to 6 feet) with vibrantly colored foliage and long, red tassel-like flowers. The drooping flower heads may last up to 8 weeks before fading. Foliage of some varieties changes color in the fall. Often-planted varieties include Illumination, Early Splendor, Aurora, Molten Fire, and Joseph's Coat. Amaranth also is called summer poinsettia.

SOIL AND LIGHT: These plants tend to grow taller in rich soil, and to develop brighter colors in poor soil. Amaranth is drought resistant, and prefers full sun.
PLANTING: Get a head start by planting seed indoors about 6 weeks before the last frost. Space plants about 18 inches apart; they are relatively easy to transplant. Stake the plants, especially in windy locations.

SPECIAL HELPS: Grow amaranth in a spot where you want a temporary hedge, or use them as background plantings or against a wall. The name amaranth is from the Greek, and means "does not wither."

AMMOBIUM
also called winged everlasting

DESCRIPTION: These fairly tall plants (about 3 feet) are characterized by raised ridges on the stems and clusters of yellow-centered white flowers, 1 to 2 inches across. Leaves are soft and silvery.
SOIL AND LIGHT: Plants do best in full sun and light, sandy soil, explaining their Latin name, ammobium, which means "living in sand."
PLANTING: Sow outside as soon as the ground is workable; or start indoors 6 to 8 weeks before the last frost is due. Set out started plants

about 9 inches apart when evening temperatures stay above 50° F. Plants usually survive transplanting at any stage, if it's carefully done.
SPECIAL TIPS: Flowers are traditionally dried for winter bouquets. Cut before flowers are fully opened, and hang upside down in a dry, shady place. Ammobium is native to Australia.

ANCHUSA
also called summer forget-me-not

DESCRIPTION: Similar to true forget-me-nots (see myosotis), this annual features clusters of tiny five-petaled flowers on stiff, hairy stems, 1½ to 2 feet tall. Flowers are usually blue with white centers, but also may be all white. Best-known varieties are Blue Bird and Blue Angel. Another common name for anchusa is cape forget-me-not.
SOIL AND LIGHT: Although they'll tolerate shade, anchusa prefer full sun. They also like rich soil that's more often moist than dry.
PLANTING: Start seeds indoors 6 to 8 weeks before the last frost is due. When it's dependably warm, set plants 10 to 12 inches apart in a prepared bed. Seeds also may be sown directly after all danger of frost has passed. Because of its moderate height, anchusa is good for middle-of-the-bed location in borders.

44

SPECIAL HELPS: Excellent for window boxes and massed beds, anchusa also can be grown as container plants. To stimulate vigorous flowering, cut plants back to about 6 inches after the first bloom fades. Anchusa specimens were first found in South Africa and then taken to England.

ANTIRRHINUM
see snapdragon

ARCTOTIS
see African daisy

ASTER
(callistephus)

DESCRIPTION: Plants range from about 8 inches to nearly 3 feet in height, with blossoms from 1 to 5 inches across. Flowers may be double or single, and shaggy or shaped like a daisy, mum, or pompon in a rainbow of colors. Frequently, centers are yellow. Some varieties of annual asters include Early Bird, American Branching, California Giant, Extra Early, Totem Pole, Perfection, Milady, and Powderpuff. Plants also are called China asters, as a Jesuit missionary found them in China in 1731.

SOIL AND LIGHT: Choose a sunny or lightly shaded location for asters. A rich, well-drained soil is best, but you may need to add a little lime if soil is too acidic. Mulching with peat or grass clippings will help maintain moisture and protect the shallow root system.

PLANTING: Start seeds indoors about 6 weeks before last frost, then space seedlings 12 to 15 inches apart (check seed packages for the correct spacing of specific varieties). Seeds also may be sown outdoors after frost danger. Be careful not to plant asters in the same location 2 years in a row, as they are susceptible to a fungus disease that lingers in the soil. For a continuous show of color, plant some of each of the early, mid-season, and late varieties. Or plant the mid-season and late varieties at 2-week intervals. If flowers fail to develop and foliage turns yellow, the plant may have a virus disease that is commonly spread by leaf hoppers. To reduce this possibility, look for varieties labeled "wilt-resistant."

SPECIAL HELPS: Choose a size, color, and shape to mix with other annuals in any part of the flower bed, but stake tall varieties that may get leggy. Cut flowers are good for fresh bouquets.

B

BABY-BLUE-EYES
see nemophila

BABY'S-BREATH
see gypsophila

BACHELOR'S-BUTTON
see cornflower

BALSAM
see also impatiens

DESCRIPTION: Also known as garden balsam, touch-me-not, and lady slipper, this member of the impatiens family has two varieties. Bush balsams average 8 to 10 inches in height with flowers at the tops of the plants. Other varieties have flowers growing along the stems, which can be as tall as 15 to 24 inches.

The camellia-like blossoms may be double or semi-double in shades of pink, red, salmon, purple, white, or combinations. Flowers are usually 1½ to 2½ inches across.

SOIL AND LIGHT: All kinds of balsams do best in rich, well-drained soil that is kept slightly moist and receives full sun. They will adapt to grow in shade.

PLANTING: Seeds should be soaked in water for 24 hours before planting. Sow outdoors after all danger of frost, or start inside 4 to 6 weeks earlier. For best display of flowers, space plants about 18 inches apart. If you transplant seedlings, dig up a small ball of soil with each plant.

SPECIAL HELPS: This native of Asia is often grown in old-fashioned gardens. Although both types work well in beds and for edging, the varieties with flowers along the stem instead of at the ends make a unique addition to borders.

The common name touch-me-not refers to the plants' seed pods that burst open with the slightest touch, a characteristic they share with other members of the impatiens family.

Cuttings may be taken in the fall for winter houseplants.

BEGONIA
wax begonia or fibrous begonia

DESCRIPTION: Single and double flowers normally cover these rounded plants that average 6 to 9 inches tall. The clusters of flowers are usually white or shades of pink and red. Foliage ranges from glossy green to red to bronze.
SOIL AND LIGHT: Plants will grow under almost any light conditions, and will bloom in shady areas. Soil should be rich and kept moist. Water plants regularly to help them resist hot weather.
PLANTING: Seed is very fine and should be started indoors 4 to 6 weeks before first frost, so it's often easiest to purchase started plants. Space starts 6 to 8 inches apart. Start seed in September for winter houseplants, or dig up plants in the fall. Cuttings root easily.
SPECIAL HELPS: This annual is best in a massed bed of its own or as an edging for a shady perennial border. Begonias do well in pots year round, but may need an occasional trimming to keep bushy.

BELLS-OF-IRELAND
(moluccella)

DESCRIPTION: This old-fashioned plant is named for the green bell-shaped calyxes which grow along the 2- to 3-foot stems. Tiny white flowers are almost hidden inside. Some varieties have a white veining pattern on the 1- to 2-inch-long bells.
SOIL AND LIGHT: Bells-of-Ireland can be grown in average soil, but they'll do even better in rich, well-drained soil. Plant in a sunny location and keep evenly moist.
PLANTING: Although plants occasionally sow their own seed, you'll do better to toss in a few seeds after frost danger is past. Later, space plants about 12 inches apart. In warm climates, sow again in August. Transplanting is not easy, so it's better to sow directly where you want plants.
SPECIAL HELPS: Native to the eastern Mediterranean area rather than to Ireland, these plants make an unusual addition to winter dried bouquets. Cut the whole stalk when flowers are in bloom, then tie stalks together and hang upside down in a cool, dry place. When dried (in 2 to 3 weeks), remove the small flowers from inside bells.

BLANKET FLOWER
see gaillardia

BLUE LACE FLOWER
(trachymene)

DESCRIPTION: Similar to the wild Queen Anne's lace, these plants bear umbrella-shaped clusters of flowers on slender 1½- to 2½-foot stalks; flowers usually are blue. A white-flowering variety is called Lace Veil; trachymenes may also be pink. Each cluster of tiny flowers is 2 to 3 inches across and sweetly scented. Foliage is finely cut and sparse.
SOIL AND LIGHT: Plants grow in well-drained soil and full sun, but they prefer cool regions and do not do as well where summers are hot and dry.

PLANTING: Start seed indoors 6 to 8 weeks before the last frost is due, or sow outdoors as early as the ground can be worked. Space plants about 12 inches apart. Each plant blooms for only about 3 weeks, so sow at intervals for continuous color. When plants are about half grown, you may want to insert brush or stakes in the rows to keep them from toppling in the wind.
SPECIAL HELPS: Use in borders or cut the delicate flowers for a graceful addition to fresh bouquets. Plants originated in Australia.

46

BRACHYCOME
see swan river daisy

BROWALLIA

DESCRIPTION: Compact, sprawling plants may cover a 10- to 15-square-inch area, displaying their small petunia-like flowers till frost. Blossoms have a velvety texture in shades of blue, violet, and white. Size of plants and flowers varies with the variety. Choose from Blue Bells Improved, Silver Bells, or Velvet Blue, among others.

SOIL AND LIGHT: Plants tolerate all soil types, especially if kept moist. They may be grown in full sun or partial shade.

PLANTING: Seeds tend to be slow to germinate; start indoors 6 to 8 weeks before last frost, or buy started plants. For best display, space plants 8 to 10 inches apart. They will usually start to bloom about 12 weeks after sown. May self-sow in warm areas.

SPECIAL HELPS: Pinch plants for bushier growth. Browallia is an excellent choice for hanging baskets, window boxes, or edging plants. It may be cut back in the fall and potted for all-winter bloom on a sunny windowsill.

BURNING BUSH
(kochia)

DESCRIPTION: Also known as fire bush and summer cypress, these plants are known for globe-like, dense foliage. The delicate green,

finely cut leaves turn bright red in fall. Plants average 2 to 3 feet in height. One common variety is Childsi.

SOIL AND LIGHT: Kochia is especially tolerant of hot weather and appreciates full sun. Soil may be of any type as long as it is kept on the dry side.

PLANTING: Sow seed outdoors when weather is warm, or start indoors 4 to 6 weeks earlier. Space plants 18 to 24 inches apart so they can develop into a full, solid shape.

SPECIAL HELPS: Excellent for hot, windy areas, Kochia is sometimes grown in pots on balconies to give privacy; they may be used anywhere as temporary hedges. The plant's origins have been traced from France across Asia to Japan.

BUSH BALSAM
see balsam

BUTTERFLY FLOWER
(schizanthus)

DESCRIPTION: Fragile and lipped flowers with spotted petals resembling butterflies give the plant its name. The bicolored blossoms are predominantly pink, red, yellow, purple, and white. The pale green

foliage is delicate and fernlike. Plants vary from 1½ to 4 feet in height, depending on where they are grown.

SOIL AND LIGHT: This uniquely flowered annual prefers cool regions and does not do well where summers are hot. Give it a garden spot that receives full sun to partial shade. Keep the rich, well-drained soil moist.

PLANTING: Start seed indoors 6 to 8 weeks before last frost. Seed also may be sown directly. Make fall plantings in warmer areas. Each plant blooms profusely, but only for a few weeks; make plantings every 2 weeks for 6 weeks to extend the blooming season. Set plants about 12 inches apart.

SPECIAL HELPS: Show off the gaily colored and deeply cut flowers by letting them tumble over hanging baskets or window boxes. Taller varieties benefit from brush or stakes inserted in the row for support when plants are about half grown. When plants are about 3 inches tall, start pinching to develop more bushy, less straggly plants. These plants also bloom well in a cool-temperature greenhouse. Plants are originally from Chile, and are also called the poor man's orchid. Blooms may be cut for flower arranging.

C

CALIFORNIA POPPY
(eschscholzia)

CALLIOPSIS
see coreopsis

CALLISTEPHUS
see aster

CANDYTUFT
(iberis)

CAPE DAISY
(dimorphotheca)

DESCRIPTION: Silver-green, finely cut foliage provides the background for these silky, cup-shaped flowers on long stems. Single and double varieties are available. The 2- to 3-inch blossoms were originally bright yellow, but now may be found in shades of orange, gold, bronze, red, and white. Petals may be crinkled and edged with a darker shade. Varieties include Ballerina, Mission Bells, Aurantiaca, and Sunset.
SOIL AND LIGHT: Give these a slightly sandy soil in a sunny to partially shady location.
PLANTING: Seed is hardy and usually not hurt by frost, so plant as soon as the ground can be worked. However, germination is slow and the first blooms may not appear for 2 months. Space individual plants 6 to 12 inches apart to allow for spreading. Plants often self-sow.
SPECIAL HELPS: Originally found on the Pacific Coast by Russian explorers, this poppy now is the state flower of California. The brightly colored, open-faced flowers show to advantage in planters and window boxes. Flowers usually don't last when cut.

DESCRIPTION: Choose either the brightly colored, dwarf plants with flat top clusters of tiny flowers, or the taller, sweetly scented type with white blossoms in dense hyacinth-like clusters. Heights range from about 6 inches to nearly 2 feet. Two of the varieties are Umbellata Dwarf Fairy and Giant Hyacinth Flowered Iceberg.
SOIL AND LIGHT: Both types do well in average soil and a sunny location. But if it's hot, they appreciate a little shade.
PLANTING: Plants do best in cooler weather; to give plants a chance to develop before it gets too hot, sow as soon as the ground can be worked. And, to provide continuous flowering, make successive plantings every 2 to 3 weeks. Plants are not easily transplanted, so discard seedlings after you thin plants to about 7 inches apart. Flowers should appear 8 to 10 weeks after seed is sown.
SPECIAL HELPS: The smaller, globe-shaped types add bright colors to rock gardens, borders, and edgings. The taller ones add a dramatic highlight to borders. Trim back both types after the first

flowering to stimulate a second bloom. Both the white and colored varieties are a good choice for fresh bouquets.

DESCRIPTION: Masses of 3- to 4-inch daisy-like flowers characterize these clumping plants which average 12 to 15 inches in height. Petals come in shades of yellow, orange, rose, salmon, and white, usually with a blue- or lavender-shaded underside. Slender stems support the flowers and narrow leaves. Aurantiaca is one popular hybrid variety.
　Cape daisies are often called cape marigolds, but actually they are not related. Cape daisies are tender perennials, native to Africa, which can be easily grown as annuals in colder climates. True marigolds originally were found in America.
SOIL AND LIGHT: Plants must have sun or the flowers won't open. Plant in well-drained soil that is kept dry; they thrive in heat.
PLANTING: Sow outdoors after all danger of frost, or start inside about 5 weeks earlier. Flowers appear 7 to 8 weeks after seeded. In warm areas, seeds may be sown again in the fall for winter and spring bloom.
SPECIAL HELPS: Save cape daisies for a sunny, hot spot in the garden or along a border. Flowers close at night and on cloudy days, so they are not recommended for fresh arrangements.

CARNATION
(dianthus)

DESCRIPTION: These pink, yellow, red, and white flowers rival those from the florist's greenhouse. Blossoms are 1 to 3 inches across with a spicy fragrance on 12- to 24-inch stems. Foliage is blue-gray. Some favorite varieties for home gardens include Chabaud, Dwarf Baby, Giant Enfant de Nice, Giant Marguerite, Juliet, and Pixie Delight.
SOIL AND LIGHT: Give plants full sun and a light soil mixture that's kept moist.
PLANTING: About 10 weeks before the last frost, start seeds indoors. They should germinate in about 10 days, but they'll need about 5 months to produce flowers. In mild areas, the plants may last for many seasons.
SPECIAL HELPS: Snip faded flowers for continuous bloom. Plants are dramatic when massed in the garden or border. Cut them for long-lasting arrangements.

CASTOR BEAN
(ricinus)

DESCRIPTION: Looking like they belong in the tropics, these exotic plants often grow to 10 feet in one season. Each palmlike leaf may be 1 to 3 feet in length. On some varieties, the leaves will change from red to brown or green as they grow older. These are sometimes called castor oil plants or palm christi. Flowers are nearly hidden by the foliage, appearing on the top and side stems of plants as reddish-brown clusters with no petals.
SOIL AND LIGHT: Plants thrive with plenty of heat, moisture, and sun.
PLANTING: Seeds have a hard outer covering; soak in water or nick with a file before planting. Start seed indoors 6 to 8 weeks before the last frost, or wait to sow outdoors after the weather has warmed. Space about 3 feet apart.

SPECIAL HELPS: Castor beans make an excellent choice for a quick-growing, background screen that may last for several years in mild climates. Seed pods are poisonous and should be clipped before they mature, especially if plants are in an area where children may be playing. Be aware, also, that some people are allergic to both the seed pods and foliage. Plants are grown commercially in India for castor oil.

CELOSIA

DESCRIPTION: Cockscomb (or crested) and plumosa (or feathered) are the common names for the two most typically found celosias. Both names describe the shape of the brilliantly colored flowers that appear in red, yellow, orange, and pink; blooms measure 2 to 12 inches across. Dwarf forms average about 8 inches in height, while taller varieties may reach 18 to 24 inches. Favorite plumosa varieties include Lilliput, Crusader, Golden Torch, Red Fox, Forest Fire Improved, and Golden Triumph. Some top cockscomb varieties are Extra Dwarf, Jewel Box, Empress Gladiator, Fireglow, Floradale, and Toreador.

SOIL AND LIGHT: Plants will tolerate nearly all soil types, and even survive drought; but they must have full sun and usually don't grow in partial shade. They do best in well-drained soil.
PLANTING: Start seeds indoors 6 to 8 weeks before the last frost is due; space plants 8 to 12 inches apart. Seed may also be sown directly in the ground after the weather has warmed. Started plants are generally available.
SPECIAL HELPS: These ornamental beauties are impressive in massed plantings, but should be used with discretion in mixed annual beds lest their strong colors steal the show. Dwarf varieties may be used for edging. Flower heads are extremely long-lasting when cut, and also make excellent dried specimens. To dry, cut when mature, before the black bead-like seeds appear. Hang in bunches, head down, in a dry, airy place. Pot individual plants in tubs for movable accents on patios.

CENTAUREA
see cornflower, dusty miller, sweet sultan

49

CHINESE FORGET-ME-NOT

see cynoglossum

CHRYSANTHEMUM

DESCRIPTION: Yellow, purple, scarlet, orange, salmon, or white usually color these daisy-like flowers. Varieties may have a dark eye, or a contrasting ring of color near the center. Both single and double flowers may be 2 to 3 inches across, on 2-foot stems. Dwarf types grow only to about 10 inches with 1-inch flowers. Popular varieties include Rainbowl, Paludosum, and Golden Raindrops. Leaves are generally smaller and more succulent than perennial types.

Annual chrysanthemums often are called painted daisies.

SOIL AND LIGHT: Plants do best in rich, moist soil with full sun, but they will tolerate some shade. Cool summers are preferred.

PLANTING: Sow outdoors as soon as the ground can be worked. They grow rapidly and can later be thinned to 12 to 18 inches apart. Seedlings are easily transplanted. Pinch back young plants to encourage bushiness.

SPECIAL HELPS: Utilize dwarf varieties as a colorful edging, or plant taller varieties as borders. Both provide long-lasting cut flowers.

CIGAR PLANT

see cuphea

CLARKIA

also called Rocky Mountain garland; see also godetia

DESCRIPTION: Originally a wildflower in the western United States, these have been cultivated to produce double-flowered varieties in shades of pink, rose, scarlet, purple, orange, and white. The delicate 1-inch blossoms appear at every joint along the slender stems, forming spikes 1 to 2 feet tall. Flowers have a deep, penetrating fragrance.

SOIL AND LIGHT: Plants do best in light, sandy soil, and seem to bloom most profusely when soil is low in nitrogen. Set them in a semi-shady location, although they will tolerate full sun.

PLANTING: Sow seeds outdoors as early as the ground can be worked. Don't bother with trying to start them inside; they prefer the cooler outdoors. Plants will thrive where summers are cool, often blooming from July until October. Thin seedlings to about 9 inches apart.

SPECIAL HELPS: These make long-lasting cut flowers, but they do not do well in hot climates. Plants were named for Captain William Clark of the Lewis and Clark Expedition ordered by President Jefferson in 1804.

CLEOME

also called spiderplant, spiderflower

DESCRIPTION: Cleome is a tall plant with an unusual appearance and a pungent scent that some people find disagreeable. At the end of each 3- to 6-foot stem is a rounded flower cluster measuring about 8 inches across. Long, thread-like stamens and pistils extend from the pink, rose, orchid, or white flower clusters. As the flower matures, slender seed pods dangle on 4-inch wiry stems, looking very much like spider legs and giving the plant its common name. Flowers appear continuously, usually from June through August. Three of the most commonly found varieties are Ruby Queen, Helen Campbell, and Rose Queen.

SOIL AND LIGHT: Sometimes described as a "rough and tumble garden plant," these thrive in poor, sandy, or average soil; but rich soil is okay if kept on the dry side. Full sun is best, but plants will tolerate some shade.

PLANTING: Sow seeds outdoors after all danger of frost; thin to 18 to 24 inches. Self-sowing is common.

SPECIAL HELPS: Most people prefer to use cleome as background or screen plantings, especially along a fence or wall. Flowers show up well at a distance, and the strong scent is not as noticeable. They also may be used in tubs, in massed plantings on banks, or in front of tall shrubs. Seed pods add a handsome touch to dried arrangements.

COLEUS

DESCRIPTION: Colorful foliage is the trademark of these plants, with multicolor patterns of chartreuse, yellow, pink, white, red, and green covering the often-ruffled leaves. The white or blue flower spikes are usually pinched off. Plants range from 6 to 24 inches in height. Some of the common varieties are Carefree, Rainbow, Color Pride, Pink Sensation, Red Velvet, Salmon Lace, Sunset Glory, Volcano, and Candidum.
SOIL AND LIGHT: Plants do best in average to rich, well-drained soil that is not allowed to dry out. Give them indirect light or partial shade; they'll tolerate full sun if it doesn't last all day.
PLANTING: Seeds will produce a variety of colors and leaf patterns. Start indoors very early; young plants develop slowly. Started plants are commonly available and allow you to choose desired colors; space them 8 to 10 inches apart. Stem cuttings root quickly in water and make attractive houseplants.
SPECIAL HELPS: Plant coleus wherever you want an attractive foliage accent. Keep plants pinched back to encourage bushiness.

CONEFLOWER
see rudbeckia

CONSOLIDA
see larkspur

CONVOLVULUS
also called morning glory

DESCRIPTION: Also known as the dwarf morning glory, these plants do indeed have similar leaves and flowers. But instead of vines, plants are bushy mounds about 12 inches tall and 18 inches wide. The 2-inch trumpet-like flowers show their colors (blue, pink, lilac, and red) all day. Some double-flowering varieties are available. Others are striped or "tricolor" with a white band separating the yellow throat from the colored petals.
SOIL AND LIGHT: For constant bloom, plant in a dry, sunny location. Almost any type of soil is suitable if it is kept dry.

PLANTING: Seeds have a hard outer shell which should be chipped or soaked to speed germination. Sow outdoors after frost danger, or start inside 4 to 6 weeks earlier. Space seedlings about 12 inches apart.
SPECIAL HELPS: Enjoy these all-day bloomers in window boxes, hanging baskets, borders, or edgings.

COREOPSIS
(calliopsis)

DESCRIPTION: These are hardy plants, despite their feathery, light-green foliage and wire-thin stems. Flowers are daisy-like with toothed petals often appearing in double layers. Blooms show rich shades of golden yellow, mahogany, crimson, maroon, and orange, often with small brownish-yellow centers. Dwarf varieties grow to 12 inches, while taller ones may reach 3 feet.

SOIL AND LIGHT: Sun is the only definite requirement for these plants; soil can be of any type. Plants are especially adaptive to smoky city air.
PLANTING: Seed should be sown as soon as the ground can be worked in the spring. Plants should flower in about 40 days. Seeds were once used to dye cloth. Coreopsis are self-sowing in many areas.
SPECIAL HELPS: This easy-to-grow annual also has a perennial form. Staking will help support the flowers. Use both varieties in borders where they are easy to reach for cutting flowers.

CORNFLOWER
(centaurea); also called bachelor's-button

DESCRIPTION: Most commonly found with blue fringe-petaled flowers, these graceful, easy-to-grow plants are an old-fashioned favorite. Flowers also have been developed in shades of pink, white, red, and lavender. Plants average 1 to 3 feet tall with fine, lacy, light-green or gray-green foliage. Popular varieties include Blue Boy, Pinkie, Snowman, Jubilee Gem, and Red Boy.

51

SOIL AND LIGHT: Choose a sunny location for planting. Average soil is fine, if well-drained.

PLANTING: Seeds are hardy and can be sown as soon as the ground is workable. Seed also may be sown in fall for flowers the following year. Plants often are self-sowing, although flowers tend to become gray-white in succeeding years.
SPECIAL HELPS: Keep faded flowers snipped to encourage continuous bloom. Plants show well in massed groupings since individuals are fine-textured and graceful. Use flowers in fresh arrangements, or hang to dry.

COSMOS

DESCRIPTION: Wide, serrated petals in shades of pink, rose, yellow, red, and lavender surround a yellow-gold center to form these delicate 3- to 4-inch flowers. Foliage is lacy and fernlike, adding to the airy quality of the plants—even though they average 4 to 6 feet tall. Common single and double flowering varieties include Dazzler, Radiance, Sensation, Bright Lights, and Diablo.
SOIL AND LIGHT: Flowers will appear earlier if soil is fairly dry and not very fertile. Full sun is best, although plants are somewhat shade-tolerant.
PLANTING: Start seeds indoors 5 to

6 weeks before the last frost is due; or wait and sow when weather has warmed. Space seedlings about 12 inches apart. Plants grow rapidly. If you live in an area of the country that normally receives a killing frost before the first of October, don't bother with the late-blooming cosmos unless you start the seeds early indoors.
SPECIAL HELPS: If set in a windy spot, plants will benefit from staking. When flower buds first appear, fertilize with a little wood ash from the fireplace to help produce an abundance of bloom. Cut flowers, combined with a little foliage, make a delightful bouquet.

CUPFLOWER
see nierembergia

CUPHEA
also called cigar plant

DESCRIPTION: The common name of this plant comes from the ¾-inch tubular flowers which have black and white tips that resemble cigar ash. Flowers are fiery red in the most familiar variety; others are pink, lavender, or rose. Plants are 10 to 12 inches tall, erect, and bushy with lance-shaped leaves. Other common names are cigarflower, firefly, and firecracker plant.
SOIL AND LIGHT: Cuphea do well in average soil that receives full to partial sun.

PLANTING: Plants are usually purchased, but seed may be started in mid-winter. Set plants about 9 inches apart.

SPECIAL HELPS: Although most widely known as an everblooming houseplant, cuphea make a striking addition to rock gardens, sidewalk edgings, window boxes, and hanging baskets. Plants are perennial in their native Mexico. Young plants should be pruned to encourage bushiness. Make cuttings in the fall for winter houseplants.

CYNOGLOSSUM
also called Chinese forget-me-not

DESCRIPTION: Taller than the conventional forget-me-not (myosotis), these have similar tiny flowers on graceful branching stems that are 1½ to 2 feet tall. Flowers are usually blue, although pink and white varieties are available. A common compact variety with blue flowers is Firmament. Blanche Burpee is taller with different colored flowers.
SOIL AND LIGHT: Plants thrive in light, sandy soil where summers are hot and dry. They're adaptable, however, and will tolerate any type of soil in sun or shade.
PLANTING: Plants grow quickly from seed, so there's little advantage to starting them indoors. Sow as soon as the ground can be worked. Make consecutive plantings for

continuous bloom. Plants often self-sow and may become a nuisance. Seeds are described as "stick-tights" because they adhere to clothing and animals. Set about 12 inches apart.

SPECIAL HELPS: Flowering branches add airiness to fresh bouquets and to mixed annual borders. Plants are sometimes called hound's tongue because of the shape of their petals.

D

DAHLBERG DAISY
(dyssodia)

DESCRIPTION: Also known as golden fleece, these attractive, compact plants feature aromatic, feathery foliage that is almost hidden by bright yellow ½-inch flowers. Plants are 8 to 12 inches tall.
SOIL AND LIGHT: Characteristic of their native Mexico and Texas, plants do best in full sun and light, sandy soil. Hot weather doesn't bother them.
PLANTING: Unless you live in a warm climate, it's best to start seeds

indoors 8 to 10 weeks before last frost, since plants often take 4 months to bloom. Seed also may be sown outdoors as early as the ground can be worked. Space plants about 6 inches apart.
SPECIAL HELPS: Cut flowers make attractive small bouquets. Use plants for accent color in rock gardens, edgings, and borders.

DAHLIA

DESCRIPTION: These bushy plants have dark green foliage and 2- to 3-inch flowers in brilliant shades of yellow, orange, red, lavender, purple, and white. The single, double, and semi-double flowers appear on 12- to 24-inch plants. Taller varieties with

larger flowers are usually grown as perennials. For annuals, choose from these: Coltness, Early Bird, Redskin, Sunburst, Cactus-Flowered, Pompon, and Unwins.
SOIL AND LIGHT: Plants need at least a half-day of full sun and prefer well-drained soil that is kept moist during hot, dry weather.
PLANTING: Started plants are generally available in nurseries, or you can start your own. Sow indoors 6 to 8 weeks before the last frost. Seeds should germinate in 5 to 10 days and be of flowering size in 8 to 10 weeks. Set plants 10 to 15 inches apart.
SPECIAL HELPS: If desired, tubers may be dug in the fall and stored over winter for the next season. Use dahlias in borders where you can easily cut the flowers for fresh bouquets. Give taller varieties extra support by staking.

DELPHINIUM
see larkspur

DIANTHUS
see carnation, pinks, sweet william

DIMORPHOTHECA
see cape daisy

DUSTY MILLER
(centaurea)

DESCRIPTION: The principal reason for growing this 12- to 15-inch annual is its silvery white, fernlike foliage. Flowers are insignificant and seldom seen.
SOIL AND LIGHT: Plants need full sun and tolerate dry soil.

PLANTING: Since they're slow-growing, it's usually best to buy started plants. Set them about 8 inches apart.

SPECIAL HELPS: Dusty miller is an excellent choice for combination plantings with brightly colored, flowering annuals, or as an accent against shrubbery. Since they prefer dry soil, plants do well in window boxes and other hard-to-water locations.

DYSSODIA
see dahlberg daisy

E

ESCHSCHOLZIA
see California poppy

EUPHORBIA
also called snow-on-the-mountain

DESCRIPTION: White-edged green foliage, with an occasional all-white leaf, characterizes these 18- to 24-inch plants. Flowers appear on spikes, but are generally insignificant. Another variety has red-edged leaves and is also known as annual poinsettia, Mexican fire plant, and fire-on-the-mountain.

SOIL AND LIGHT: Euphorbia adapt to any soil, including that usually considered "poor." Full sun is best.

PLANTING: Plants grow easily from seed sown in early spring. Self-sowing habits can make the plant

a "noxious weed" in some areas.

SPECIAL HELPS: Euphorbia provide a showy background or border filler, either alone or with other annuals. Cuttings enhance fresh bouquets, but should be seared in flame or dipped in boiling water to keep the sap from coagulating and clogging the stem, causing it to wilt. When cutting, be careful not to get any of the milky sap in your eyes, mouth, or on skin cuts; it is poisonous. Plants are sometimes called ghost weed.

EVERLASTING
see strawflower

F

FAREWELL-TO-SPRING
see godetia

FEVERFEW
(matricaria)

DESCRIPTION: Sprays of button-like gold, white, and yellow flowers appear on branching but compact plants 8 to 30 inches tall. A member of the chrysanthemum family, feverfew resembles some of the perennial mums; flowers can be single or double. Foliage is generally feathery with a tangy fragrance.

False chamomile is another common name. Good varieties include Golden Ball, Lemon Ball, Snowball, and Capensis.

SOIL AND LIGHT: Plants thrive in cool climates with rich, well-drained soil and plenty of sun. In warmer areas, give them partial shade and a light mulch, especially if it's dry.

PLANTING: Scatter seed outdoors as soon as the ground can be worked; or start indoors 4 to 6 weeks earlier. Space plants about 6 inches apart.

SPECIAL HELPS: Flowers are often used by florists, since plants generally bloom all summer. Plants act like perennials in warm areas.

FLAX
(linum)

DESCRIPTION: These 18- to 24-inch plants have grasslike foliage and white, pink, blue, or bright red flowers that last only 1 day, but are replaced with new ones.

SOIL AND LIGHT: Give flax a sunny location with well-drained, light sandy soil. Where strong winds are common, set plants in a protected spot or add trimmed branches for stakes.

PLANTING: Start seeding as soon as the ground can be worked; repeat

54

every 3 to 4 weeks, if continuous flowering is desired. Thin seedlings to 8 inches. Plants do best where summers are cool.

SPECIAL HELPS: Plan flax into your cutting garden for a charming addition to fresh bouquets. They'll give the same airy quality to annual beds and borders.

FLOSSFLOWER
see ageratum

FLOWERING TOBACCO
see nicotiana

FORGET-ME-NOT
see myosotis

FOUR-O'CLOCKS
(mirabilis)

DESCRIPTION: True to their name, these bright, trumpet-shaped flowers appear in late afternoon, usually staying open until the next morning. Colors are lavender, pink, white, salmon, yellow, and violet. Dense foliage gives the 2- to 3-foot plants a shrub-like appearance. Another name is marvel-of-Peru.

SOIL AND LIGHT: Plants thrive best in a sunny location with average, well-drained soil.

PLANTING: Sow when soil is warm, or start indoors about 5 weeks earlier. Space plants about 12 inches apart. Self-sowing is common.

SPECIAL HELPS: One of the more hardy annuals, these are treated like perennials in warm areas. Colorful and quick-growing, they make a good, low hedge. If desired, dig the fleshy tuber-like

---

roots in the fall; store over winter and set out again the following spring. The resulting plants will probably have larger flowers.

G

GAILLARDIA
also called blanket flower

DESCRIPTION: Sunset shades of red, yellow, and cream grace these 2- to 3-inch daisy-like flowers. Both single and double, as well as shaggy, ball-shaped flowers, are available. Plants are 14 to 24 inches tall. Common varieties include Tetra Fiesta, Gaiety, Lollipops, and Primrose.

SOIL AND LIGHT: These tough plants can take dry conditions and almost any type of soil. They thrive in full sun.

PLANTING: Seeds are slow to germinate, but plants grow fast and will usually bloom 9 to 10 weeks after planting. Start indoors 4 to 6 weeks before the last frost, or sow outside as soon as the ground can be worked. Seedlings are hardy and can usually survive a late spring frost. Space plants 8 inches apart.

SPECIAL HELPS: Since these annuals like hot, dry conditions, they're a good choice for planting in window boxes, tubs, and other quick-to-dry places. Flowers work well in fresh arrangements.

GAZANIA

DESCRIPTION: Single 4-inch flowers in shades of cream, red, bronze, gold, orange, bright yellow, and pink—often with dark-rimmed contrasting centers—grow on 6- to 12-inch stems. The thick leaves are usually dark green on top and white underneath, often with a felty texture.

SOIL AND LIGHT: Windy, hot and dry days with summer temperatures in the 80s and 90s are the ideal conditions for the gazania. Sandy, light soil is best, and, of course, full sun.

PLANTING: Sow seed outdoors a couple weeks after the last frost, or start inside 5 to 7 weeks earlier. Space plants 8 to 12 inches apart.

SPECIAL HELPS: Gazania are an excellent choice for hot, dry locations; but flowers close at night and on cloudy days, so they don't make good cut flowers.

GERANIUM
(pelargonium)

DESCRIPTION: This versatile group includes nearly 600 different varieties. The most common colors are shades of red, pink, and white. Flowers vary in size, with some strictly individual and others growing in clusters. Foliage may be green or variegated, large-leaved or small. Plants range from 4-inch miniatures to 5-foot "trees." Most commonly found are the zonals, with their

55

bush-like structure; the trailing ivies, with their smaller flowers; and the scenteds, whose leaves smell like peppermint, apple, lemon, or rose when rubbed. Other fragrances are also available. Familiar names to look for are Sprinter, Carefree, Colorcade, and Martha Washington.

SOIL AND LIGHT: Geraniums will grow almost anywhere with minimal care. They like full sun, but will adapt to partial shade. For best results, pot them in well-drained soil that is only of medium richness. They especially like warm days and cool nights.
PLANTING: Seeds can be slow to germinate, so allow at least 4 months to produce a flowering-size plant. Started plants are readily available and should be set about 12 inches apart. Sprinter varieties reach maturity faster than others.
SPECIAL HELPS: Although popular as container plants, geraniums also do well set in the ground. Pin the stems of ivy geraniums to train them to grow close to the ground. In fall, take stem cuttings for winter windowsill plants. Ivy varieties, particularly, do well in hanging baskets.

GLOBE AMARANTH
(gomphrena)

DESCRIPTION: These mounding plants, 6 to 24 inches tall, are continuously covered with ¾-inch clover-like blossoms in red, pink, yellow, purple, and white. Common varieties include Cissy, Buddy, and Rubra.

SOIL AND LIGHT: Plants will tolerate all soil types, but need full sun. They usually stand up well in wind and rain.

PLANTING: Germination takes 12 to 14 days, so start plants indoors 6 to 8 weeks before the last frost. Or, sow seed outside when warm. Set plants 8 to 12 inches apart.
SPECIAL HELPS: Flowers are an unusual addition to fresh and dried arrangements. To dry, cut flowers just as they're fully opened; hang upside down. Since they don't mind wind or dry conditions, plants are a good choice for window boxes and tubs, as well as beds and borders.

GLORIOSA DAISY
see rudbeckia

GODETIA
also called satinflower, farewell-to-spring, clarkia

DESCRIPTION: Satin-petaled and cup-shaped flowers 3 to 5 inches across grow in shades of pink, rose, lilac, red, salmon, and white on 10- to 30-inch stems. Flowers may be single or double; foliage is gray-green and tends to form mounds. Top varieties are Sybil Sherwood Double, Duke of York, Sutton, and Dwarf Gem.
SOIL AND LIGHT: Plants do best in areas where nights are cool and the air is dry. Give them full or partial sun, and light, sandy loam. Soil that is too rich will produce more foliage than flowers.
PLANTING: Sow seeds as soon as the ground can be worked in spring. Later, thin to 6 to 12 inches apart.

Seed may be fall-sown in mild climate areas.

SPECIAL HELPS: These plants are a showy addition to both indoor flower arrangements and garden borders. They adapt well to cool greenhouses. Give tall varieties brush support or staking.

GOMPHRENA
see globe amaranth

GYPSOPHILA
also called annual baby's-breath

DESCRIPTION: Plants are generally larger than perennial forms, but with similar delicate flowers scattered on many-branched stems that range from 15 to 24 inches tall. The finely cut foliage does not detract from the white, pink, or rose flowers. Covent Garden and King of the Market are two popular varieties.
SOIL AND LIGHT: Typical of their name (gypsophila means "chalklover"), these plants do best in poor soil. Adding lime or wood ash from the fireplace will help them in acid soil. Although plants will grow in richer soils, they will not be as sturdy, making them less resistant to wind and rain. Full sun is best.

56

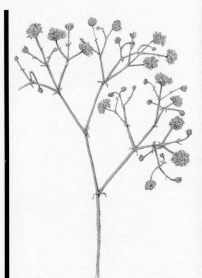

PLANTING: Save your indoor seed beds for other annuals—these plants grow rapidly when sown outdoors as early as the ground can be worked. Blossoms don't last long, so repeat sowings to ensure a continuous supply of flowers. Space plants 8 to 12 inches apart.

SPECIAL HELPS: Plan a few rows of gypsophila in your cutting garden for a light, airy contrast. Sprays of the tiny starlike flowers also add grace to fresh and dried bouquets.

H

HELIANTHUS
see sunflower

HELICHRYSUM
see strawflower

HELIOTROPE

DESCRIPTION: A Victorian favorite, these 12- to 24-inch plants bear clusters of 6- to 12-inch lilac-like flowers in dark violet, white, or heliotrope blue. Depending on the variety, flowers may be scented. Choose from Marine, Regale, Mme. Bruant, Cherry Pie, or Pacific, among others.

SOIL AND LIGHT: Plants do best in rich, well-drained soil. Give them full sun or light shade, and keep evenly moist.

PLANTING: Although it is easiest to buy plants, seed may be sown in mid-winter (in a warm place) for summer flowers. Space plants about 12 inches apart, and try root or stem cuttings to increase your supply.

SPECIAL HELPS: Fragrant as well as colorful, heliotrope can be grown in window boxes, tubs, and borders. Bring the pots indoors, or make cuttings for winter windowsills. Blossoms may be dried for sachets or enjoyed fresh in an old-fashioned bouquet. A native of Peru, heliotrope means "constantly turning face to sun."

HELIPTERUM
see acroclinium

HOLLYHOCK
(alcea rosea)

DESCRIPTION: Two- to six-foot spikes bear single, double, semi-double, and occasionally frilled flowers that are 3 to 4 inches across. Red, rose, pink, and yellow are the most common colors. Some of the variety names are Silver Puff, Majorette, Summer Carnival, Indian Summer, and Triumph Supreme.

SOIL AND LIGHT: Full sun is this annual's only requirement; soil may be of any type.

PLANTING: Start seed indoors 6 to 8 weeks before the last frost, and set outside when night temperatures have warmed. Plants do best when sheltered from the wind and placed 12 to 24 inches apart.

SPECIAL HELPS: Hollyhocks can be annual, biennial, or perennial, depending on their variety and location. They are often suggested as a backdrop for flower beds or as a row of color along fences and walls. But you may want to cut them after the first bloom to encourage another crop of flowers in fall.

I-J

IBERIS
see candytuft

ICE PLANT
(mesembryanthemum)

DESCRIPTION: These creeping 6- to 8-inch plants have dark green, succulent leaves. Foliage sometimes has tiny ice-like flecks, giving the plant its common name. Flowers are daisy-like and usually about ½ inch across in shades of pink, yellow, white, lavender, and red. They close at night and on cloudy days.

57

SOIL AND LIGHT: These will grow nearly anywhere, and even flourish on dry, rocky banks. They do less well in shady, moist locations.

PLANTING: Start plants indoors about 10 weeks before the last frost is due, or sow directly when the weather is dependably warm. Space seedlings about 2 inches apart. Plants started outdoors will bloom later, but tend to last longer.

SPECIAL HELPS: Rock gardens and window boxes are a natural habitat for these dry-loving plants. They also do well in windy locations.

IMPATIENS
see also balsam

DESCRIPTION: These compact plants—usually 6 to 18 inches tall—mound to cover a wider area. The flat blossoms look like violets and appear all over the plant in shades of pink, red, purple, orange, and white, plus some bicolor varieties. Choose from hybrids

such as Zig-Zag, Elfin, and Imp, or standards such as Glitters and Sultani.

SOIL AND LIGHT: Partial shade is the first choice of these flowering beauties. Rich, moist soil is preferred.

PLANTING: Sow seed indoors 6 to 8 weeks before the last frost is due. When weather warms, set plants outside, but be forewarned that they are quite sensitive to cold. Started plants are usually readily available; they may also be propagated by cuttings.

SPECIAL HELPS: Also known as busy lizzie and patient lucy, this plant has a seed pod that easily breaks and scatters seed at the slightest touch. Pot them in hanging baskets or planters for easy transport to a sunny window in the fall. For bushier plants, pinch back the tips of young plants. Before a killing frost, take some cuttings inside to grow in water during the winter.

K

KOCHIA
see burning bush

L

LANTANA

DESCRIPTION: Lantanas are available in both bushy and trailing varieties. As a stiff-branched shrub, the common lantana averages about 3 feet in height; dwarf varieties are 12 to 18 inches tall. Clusters of tiny flowers appear in pink, yellow, white, red, and bronze. Trailing varieties usually have yellow-centered rosy flowers that grow in clusters.

SOIL AND LIGHT: Both varieties prefer rich, well-drained soil and full sun, although they will tolerate partial shade.

PLANTING: Seeds are slow to germinate and develop, so new plants are more easily propagated by cuttings from established plants. Or, buy nursery-started bedding plants. Space plants 12 to 18 inches apart in the garden.

SPECIAL HELPS: With both bushy and trailing varieties available, you can use lantanas nearly anywhere in the garden—from hanging baskets and tubs, to borders, edgings, and rock gardens. In warmer areas, the trailing variety can be used as a ground cover. You can bring plants inside for the winter, too. Cut them back 6 to 8 weeks before the first fall frost is due, and pot. You can leave them outdoors for several weeks to allow them to adapt to their container.

LARKSPUR
(Consolida regalis)

DESCRIPTION: This old-fashioned favorite is often identified as the annual form of the perennial delphinium. Predominantly known for their spikes of purple or blue flowers, larkspur also comes in shades of rose and white; flowers may be single or double. Plants can either be branching with a flower spike on each stalk, or hyacinth-like with only one large flowering stalk. The foliage is bright green and lacy. Common varieties are usually 3 to 5 feet tall, but a dwarf variety that averages 12 inches is also available. Look for Dark Blue Spire, tall, vigorous Supreme Mixed, and White King All-American winner.

SOIL AND LIGHT: Light, well-drained fertile soil is preferred, but plants adapt to other types. Full sun is best, but plants need a little shade in hot climates.

PLANTING: Larkspur seed can be planted in the late fall or very early spring (as soon as the ground can be worked) because seeds need cool temperatures to germinate. For continuous bloom, do a second planting in 3 weeks. Seedlings are not easy to transplant, but thin them to 8 to 15 inches apart.
SPECIAL HELPS: If you have a wall or fence to conceal, larkspur will cover it with a mass of color. Taller varieties may need staking to help support the flower weight. Keep faded flowers trimmed to encourage later bloom.

LINARIA
also called toadflax

DESCRIPTION: This 9- to 12-inch plant presents a mound of dainty ½-inch flowers that resemble snapdragons in shape. Flowers are mostly bicolor, with reds, yellows, and lavenders predominant. A popular variety is the dwarf Fairy Bouquet which blooms in abundance.
SOIL AND LIGHT: Give these an open sunny position, and they will adapt to nearly any soil type. They do, however, prefer cool summers.
PLANTING: Plants are not heat-resistant, so seed should be sown in the fall or very early spring.

Transplanting is not recommended. Thin seedlings to about 6 inches apart.

SPECIAL HELPS: If possible, give linaria a spot where they can be mass planted to show off their colors. They also make attractive edgings and spots of color in rock gardens. Arrange cut flowers in a small vase for indoor enjoyment.

LINUM
see flax

LOBELIA
(Lobelia erinus)

DESCRIPTION: Both compact and trailing varieties of this popular edging plant are available. Plants grow to 6 inches tall and are covered with ½-inch flowers. Blooms are usually blue, although they may be white, pink, or lavender. Trailing varieties vine up to 2 feet. Foliage tends toward a dark metallic green color with toothed edges. Good edging varieties are Bright Eyes, Crystal Palace, Blue Stone, and Cambridge Blue. For trailing, plant Blue Cascade or Sapphire.
SOIL AND LIGHT: For best results, give lobelia full sun and rich, moist soil. They will adapt to other soil types, but will not flower as lavishly. If summers are hot, give this plant some shade.

PLANTING: Seeds are quite small and often slow to germinate, needing 2 months to reach flowering size. Start seed indoors 8 to 10 weeks before the ground is warm, or buy started plants. Set plants about 6 inches apart.

SPECIAL HELPS: Depending on the variety, lobelia may be used in hanging baskets, window boxes, or borders. The trailing variety is sometimes used as a ground cover. Potted plants may be kept through the winter in a sunny window. After the first blossoms have faded, cut the plant back to encourage a second blooming.

LOVE-IN-A-MIST
see nigella

LOVE-LIES-BLEEDING
see amaranth

LUPINES

DESCRIPTION: Also known as the Texas bluebonnet, this annual is smaller and shorter than perennial forms. The 1- to 3-foot plants branch from the base, and feature spikes of clustered flowers in blue, pink, lavender, yellow, and white. Bicolored forms are also available.
SOIL AND LIGHT: Lupines thrive in the cool temperatures of spring and early summer; they are not heat-resistant. Give them a rich, moist, well-drained soil and plenty of sun. In climates where summers are intensely hot, plant lupines

59

varieties. Plants range from 6 to 7 inches (dwarfs) up to 2 to 3 feet. All sizes are erect and bushy in nature, with many flowers per plant. A few of the many dwarf double varieties available are Goldie, Bolero, King Tut, and Gypsy. Naughty Marietta is a reliable dwarf single. Taller varieties include Gay Ladies, Toreador, Golden Climax, Golden Jubilee, Senator Dirksen, and Alaska.

SOIL AND LIGHT: Full sun is the only requirement of these hardy plants. They'll adapt to any soil.

PLANTING: Sow seed outdoors after the last frost, or start inside about 6 weeks earlier. Started plants are readily available and seedlings are easily transplanted. Give them a chance to develop their full bushiness by spacing 12 to 15 inches apart, depending on the type.

SPECIAL HELPS: Plant marigolds in beds, borders, and tubs—either singly or massed—as well as in vegetable gardens.

MATRICARIA
see feverfew

MATTHIOLA
see stocks

MESEMBRYANTHEMUM
see ice plant

MEXICAN SUNFLOWER
see tithonia

where they'll get shade for at least half a day.

PLANTING: Plants do not transplant easily, so start them outdoors in early spring. Later, thin to 8 to 10 inches apart. Seed usually needs to be treated with a legume bacteria culture like that used for sweet peas; follow the package directions.

SPECIAL HELPS: Keep faded flowers trimmed, or cut early to enjoy in bouquets.

M

MARIGOLD
(tagetes)

DESCRIPTION: This easy-to-grow annual is known for its flowers of bright orange, yellow, and recently, white and cream. Depending on the variety, flowers may be shaped like a globe, carnation, or mum, and can be either single or double. Foliage is deep green and finely cut. Most have a pungent scent, although this has been bred out in some newer

MIGNONETTE
(reseda)

DESCRIPTION: Fragrance is the best reason for planting mignonette; the flowers are rather drab, appearing in shades of greenish-yellow to brownish-red on 6- to 12-inch spikes. Plants are 12 to 18 inches tall.

SOIL AND LIGHT: Mignonette prefers fertile soil, but will adapt to other types if kept moist. Partial shade is desirable especially where summers are hot, since these plants flower best when temperatures are on the cool side.

PLANTING: Sow outdoors after the last frost, repeating at 3-week intervals to ensure continuous bloom. Seedlings don't transplant well, so it's risky to replant them when you thin; thin to about 10 inches apart. If they are too crowded, the flowering spikes will not show to their best advantage.

SPECIAL HELPS: Plant mignonette where you can enjoy their strong pleasant fragrance—near the patio or doorstep, underneath an often-opened window, or in pots on the windowsill. And as the blossoms are attractive to bees, they'll help garden pollination.

MIRABILIS
see four-o'clocks

MOLUCCELLA
see bells-of-Ireland

MORNING GLORY
see convolvulus

MOSS ROSE
see portulaca

MYOSOTIS
also called forget-me-not

DESCRIPTION: This favorite spring flower may be an annual, biennial, or perennial, depending on the species and the region of the country. Most bloom only in the spring; others may bloom all summer. The small flowers are usually blue, but also may be white or pink. Plants are generally 8 to 12 inches tall and compact in nature. Blue Bird is a reliable annual variety.
SOIL AND LIGHT: As long as temperatures are cool, myosotis will adapt to nearly any soil and either sun or shade.
PLANTING: Seed should be sown in early spring or late fall. Self-sowing is common.
SPECIAL HELPS: This plant is a graceful contrast to spring-flowering bulbs in beds and borders. Use it for indoor arrangements also. Annual varieties of myosotis will often reseed themselves and quickly naturalize a rock garden or woodland setting. They make an especially striking display mixed with English daisies, sweet williams, pansies, or violas.

N

NASTURTIUM
(tropaeolum)

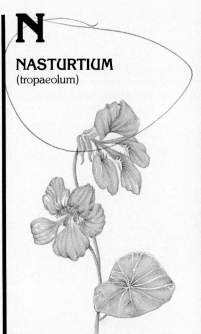

DESCRIPTION: Shiny shield-like leaves and single or double flowers, often with a tart fragrance, identify this annual. It blooms in shades of red, yellow, pink, and white. Bush varieties are usually 8 to 15 inches tall; climbing varieties may reach 6 feet or more. Good double varieties include Cherry Rose and Dwarf Jewel. Dwarf Single is a reliable single form, and Single Climbing is a fine trailer.
SOIL AND LIGHT: A spot with full sun and sandy soil is your best choice for bush-type nasturtiums. Other soils will usually suffice if they are kept dry. Water only if plants become dry enough to droop; too much water will produce all leaves with few flowers. Vining varieties prefer a moist soil and shade from the midday sun.
PLANTING: Seedlings are not easily transplanted, so it's usually simpler to sow seed outdoors after the last frost. Seed should germinate in 8 to 13 days and be of blooming size in 7 to 8 weeks. Thin bush types to about 6 inches and climbers to about 10 inches.
SPECIAL HELPS: If you'd like to have some flowers around the house but don't want to spend much time on their care, nasturtiums may be the answer; they thrive on neglect, including poor soil and little water. Climbers usually want

more water than bush-types; try them on a trellis, fence, or to cover a tree stump. Leaves of both types may be added to salads; they have a taste similar to watercress.

NEMESIA

DESCRIPTION: These compact plants reach about 10 inches in height and bear 3- to 4-inch flower clusters on 2- to 3-foot spikes. The ¾-inch flowers are cuplike and come in shades of yellow, pink, lavender-blue, crimson, and white.
SOIL AND LIGHT: Cool, damp areas of the country are best suited for nemesia, since these plants cannot tolerate heat. They'll thrive in full sun (or partial shade in warm-weather areas) in any kind of soil if it is kept moist. Plants benefit from humus added to the soil.
PLANTING: In early spring, sow seed where plants are to stay, or start them indoors 4 to 6 weeks earlier. Seedlings are delicate, so take extra care if you transplant them. Thin to about 6 inches apart.
SPECIAL HELPS: Nemesia make charming cut flowers. If you don't use them all for bouquets, be sure to cut plants back after the first bloom fades to encourage later flowering. This is also a good time to feed them. Use nemesia as edging plants in the garden.

61

NEMOPHILA
also called baby-blue-eyes

DESCRIPTION: Clusters of white-centered sky-blue flowers on the tips of delicate stems give this plant its common name. Five rounded petals form a cup shape about 1 inch across. Plants mound in 6- to 8-inch heights, about 12 inches across. Foliage is pale green with a hairy texture.
SOIL AND LIGHT: Sun or partial shade and light, well-drained soil are recommended for nemophila. They'll thrive where soil is kept moist and summer nights are cool. Hot, dry days discourage flowers.
PLANTING: Nemophila is hard to transplant, so it's best to sow seed as early as the ground can be worked, even if it's still 1 or 2 weeks before the last frost is due.
SPECIAL HELPS: Try nemophila as a ground cover or edging around flowering bulbs. They'll also make a good showing in a moist area of a rock garden or display bed. Flowers look nice in cut flower arrangements, but they don't last long.

NICOTIANA
also called flowering or ornamental tobacco

DESCRIPTION: Delicate flowers with a pleasant, though heavy, fragrance characterize this plant. Most varieties bloom only in the evening; newer day-bloomers often are much less fragrant. Clusters of trumpet-shaped blooms appear at

the ends of branches; take your pick of red, lavender, pink, rose, chartreuse, or white flowers. Plants are generally 1 to 3 feet tall, although some varieties may reach 5 feet. Leaves are very large with a soft texture and grow mainly at the base of the plant. Try richly-colored Crimson Bedder, Compact Dwarf, White Bedder, day-blooming Daylight, Sensation, or extremely

fragrant Lime Green.
SOIL AND LIGHT: Heat does not hurt these plants, although they prefer partial shade in very warm areas. Full sun is desired elsewhere. Nicotiana tolerate almost all soils.
PLANTING: Seed is very fine and slow to germinate, so you may find it easier to buy started plants. In warm areas, seed may be sown directly into the garden. Space plants about 9 inches apart.
SPECIAL HELPS: Plant nicotiana where you can enjoy the evening fragrance. They look especially attractive when set in front of tall shrubs or perennials.

NIEREMBERGIA
also called cupflower

DESCRIPTION: Dense and spreading in character, these 6-inch mound plants are covered almost continuously with bright violet, cup-shaped flowers. Blooms have a yellow center and measure about an inch across. Purple Robe, a compact, densely blooming variety, is the most widely grown.

SOIL AND LIGHT: For best results, plant in a location that's sunny but not too hot, and where the well-drained, rich soil can be kept moist. In hot areas, give plants some shade and plenty of water.
PLANTING: Start plants indoors 8 to 10 weeks before the last frost; seeds develop slowly so you may wish to buy started plants. Set them about 8 inches apart where they can be sheltered from strong winds.
SPECIAL HELPS: Found wild in Argentina, these plants can be used in rock gardens, window boxes, or edgings. When cut, the flowers make delightful miniature bouquets.

NIGELLA
also called love-in-a-mist

DESCRIPTION: Also called fennel flower and devil-in-a-bush, this 12- to 24-inch plant features very fine pale green foliage and 1½-inch cornflower-like blossoms in blue, rose, pink, purple, or white. The popular variety Persian Jewels has light, feathery foliage.
SOIL AND LIGHT: As long as they get plenty of sun, these plants will tolerate any type of soil.
PLANTING: Seed can be planted in the fall in mild climates, or very early in the spring elsewhere. Seedlings are hard to transplant but should be thinned to about 8 inches apart. Make 2 or 3 plantings about a month apart to increase the blooming period.
SPECIAL HELPS: Flowers are attractive in fresh arrangements, but don't cut them all or you'll miss the large balloon-shaped pods that

follow. The pods, pale green with reddish-brown markings, add a unique touch to dried-flower arrangements. To dry, cut stems when pods mature and hang upside down in a dry, shady place.

O

ORNAMENTAL TOBACCO
see nicotiana

P

PAINTED TONGUE
see salpiglossis

PANSY
(*Viola* sp.)

DESCRIPTION: Face-like markings on large, open flowers characterize this old-fashioned favorite. The five overlapping petals of each flower combine variations of stripes and blotches in shades of purple, blue, yellow, dark rose, and white. Plants average about 8 inches in height and tend to spread out. A host of interesting varieties are available; some of the best known are cardinal-red Alpenglow, large-blossomed white Moon Moth, vigorous Paramount, clear yellow

Coronation Gold, and heat-resistant Imperial Blue.
SOIL AND LIGHT: Plants do best in cool spring weather. Give them full sun and a rich, well-drained, moist soil.
PLANTING: For late spring blossoms, start seed indoors about 10 weeks before planting, or buy started plants. In most areas, seed can be sown in mid- to late summer and the plants kept in a cold frame over the winter for early spring bloom. Space them about 6 to 8 inches apart in the garden.

SPECIAL HELPS: A favorite for edging beds, pansies also make a good show in rock gardens and around spring-flowering bulbs. They adapt well to containers and window boxes. Flowers should be cut to stimulate further blooming; use fresh for charming bouquets. Pinch back young plants to encourage branching. But even with continuous pinching, the plants may look quite leggy and straggly by summer. When this happens, cut back to within 1 or 2 inches of the base and fertilize; or dig out and replace with another low annual. If extra large flowers are desired, allow only four or five flower stalks to develop on each plant.

PELARGONIUM
see geranium

PERIWINKLE
see vinca

PETUNIAS

DESCRIPTION: A number of colors, shapes, and sizes are offered by this popular annual. One main type is classified as multiflora, indicating that it blooms freely. It produces 2- to 3-inch single and double flowers on branching plants 12 to 15 inches high. Many gardeners find that this is the easier type to grow. A second type is classified as grandiflora. These plants are generally about the same height, but bear flowers that measure up to 5 inches across, often ruffled and fringed, and either single or double. Petunias are available in both bush and cascading varieties.
SOIL AND LIGHT: Petunias like at least a half-day of full sun and rich, well-drained soil that is kept on the moist side. For the best display, feed regularly during the summer.
PLANTING: Seeds are small and sometimes hard to start, so most people find it easier to buy started plants. Set plants 8 to 16 inches apart, depending on the variety.
SPECIAL HELPS: Pack petunias into sunny spots in borders, window boxes, hanging baskets, tubs, and planters. To encourage branching, pinch plants back after the first blossoms fade. When the weather turns cold, bring some of the potted plants inside and set them in a sunny window. Good varieties to try are the trailing grandiflora Red Cascade; the hybrid grandifloras Malibu (blue), Happiness (pink), and Sunburst (yellow); and the multiflora hybrids Comanche (red) and Sugar Plum (lilac).

PHLOX

DESCRIPTION: Clusters of flowers show well above the foliage on these 15- to 18-inch plants. Dwarf varieties are available in 6- to 8-inch heights. Flowers may be lavender, red, pink, blue, or white; bicolors are sometimes available. Some favorites include vigorous salmon Glamour, dwarf Blue Beauty, and Twinkle.
SOIL AND LIGHT: Almost any well-drained soil is suitable for phlox. Full sun is desirable, although they'll adapt to light shade. Water during dry periods.
PLANTING: Seed should germinate in 8 to 17 days, depending on conditions. Blossoms generally appear about 65 days later. Plant outside after the last frost, or start inside about 5 weeks earlier. Set plants about 6 inches apart.
SPECIAL HELPS: Keep old flowers clipped to encourage further growth. If plants get too straggly, cut back to about 2 inches above ground. In a few weeks, the plants will be covered with vigorous new branches. Use plants in rock gardens, beds, and flower borders.

PINCUSHION FLOWER
see scabiosa

PINKS
(dianthus)

DESCRIPTION: The common name of this annual refers not to the color, but to the fringed (pinked) edges of the flower petals. Many popular varieites do produce pink flowers, but reds, whites, and bicolors also find favor with gardeners. Plants are usually 8 to 12 inches tall. Try scarlet red hybrid Queen of Hearts, white-edged China Doll, or early-flowering Magic Charms for starters.

SOIL AND LIGHT: Full sun and a light, well-drained soil should give you good results. Lime or wood ash is often added to keep the soil alkaline. In dry weather, be sure to water plants regularly—perhaps even daily.
PLANTING: Sow outside after the last frost, or start seed indoors about 7 weeks earlier. Seed should germinate in 6 to 10 days, producing blooming plants in about 3 months. Space seedlings about 8 inches apart. Mature plants tend to be frost-resistant, and may overwinter in moderate-climate areas.
SPECIAL HELPS: Use the shorter varieties for attractive edging plants or in rock gardens. Save the taller

ones for borders, flower beds, and massed plantings. Seed forms quickly after flowering, so keep plants trimmed; this also encourages new flower formation. Some pinks are very fragrant, but these are usually the perennial forms.

POPPY
(papaver)

DESCRIPTION: The four most popular varieties feature bright, crinkled flowers on wiry stems above clumps of foliage. Flowers may be single or double, and are often fragrant. Alpine is the shortest, averaging 6 to 10 inches. The others usually range between 1½ and 3 feet. The two perennial types are Iceland and Oriental; Iceland has a wide range of colors, while Oriental poppies have the showiest blooms. Shirley, an annual, is the tamed offspring of the black-centered red poppies common in the fields around Flanders. California poppies are the easiest to grow. A popular Iceland poppy is the vigorous Champagne Bubbles; you'll also have good luck with the Oriental poppies Brilliant Red and Queen Alexandria. Try deep pink Sweet Briar or bicolor Double Donna Shirley poppies. Mission Bells, a double and semi-double poppy, and orange Aurantiaca are popular California poppies.
SOIL AND LIGHT: Poppies require full sun, but will adapt to most soil conditions. Cool, moist weather is

best, and wind protection helps preserve the fragile blossoms.

PLANTING: For easier planting, mix the fine seed with sand first. Sow in late fall or very early spring. In areas where summers do not get too hot, make consecutive plantings about 6 weeks apart. Space seedlings 6 to 12 inches apart, but don't try to transplant. Some varieties will self-sow each year.

SPECIAL HELPS: Massed plantings are the most effective way to show off these colorful annuals. To use in bouquets, cut just when the buds start to split open; sear stem ends immediately to conserve their moisture. Keep faded flowers trimmed back.

PORTULACA
also called moss rose or rock moss

DESCRIPTION: This creeping succulent will spread a carpet of brightly colored single and double blossoms over the poorest, driest soil. Foliage is needle-like and usually dark green. Plants are usually only 3 to 6 inches tall. Some of the available types include vigorous, long-blooming Sungalo, colorful Claudia, and double Day Dream.

SOIL AND LIGHT: Full sun and well-drained soil are the only requirements.

PLANTING: Seed is very fine and may be mixed with sand to give better coverage. It needs warm weather to germinate, so sow outdoors after the ground has

warmed. If you want to start earlier, sow indoors in a warm place; they transplant easily and may be thinned, if desired. In most areas plants will self-sow. The flower size and color quality will be diminished the second year, so it's best to start over annually.

SPECIAL HELPS: Rock gardens, planters, and problem areas will support these neglect- and drought-loving plants.

R

RICINUS
see castor bean

ROCK MOSS
see portulaca

ROCKY MOUNTAIN GARLAND
see clarkia

RUDBECKIA
also called gloriosa daisy or coneflower

DESCRIPTION: Hybridized from the wild black-eyed susans, these plants have similar large, daisy-like flowers on stems 18 to 36 inches tall. Petals are usually shades of yellow, orange, or bronze with brown centers, although one variety has a green center. Some of the common

varieties are bright yellow Golden Daisy, green-centered Irish Eyes, and bicolor Pinwheel.

SOIL AND LIGHT: Rudbeckia are quite undemanding as to soil type. Plant them in full to partial sun and they'll thrive.

PLANTING: Plants are very hardy and can be sown in late fall or very early spring. They are also easy to transplant and will usually self-sow, although the colors of resulting plants may not be as strong. Allow 12 to 18 inches between plants.

SPECIAL HELPS: For the best display, plant in clumps along a fence row or in the back of the flower bed or garden. Flowers are long-lasting in cut arrangements and should be kept trimmed to encourage continuous flowering.

S

SALPIGLOSSIS
also called painted-tongue

DESCRIPTION: Salpiglossis is also known as velvet flower because of the texture of its petunia-like flowers. They appear in muted shades of pink, purple, yellow, orange, and red covered with an intricate pattern of veining in a contrasting color. Foliage is sparse on the slender-stemmed 2- to 3-foot plants. Bolero is a vigorous variety that bears large quantities of huge blooms. Also try the dwarf-like, bushy Splash and Colorful Emperor.

SOIL AND LIGHT: Plant in a rich, well-drained soil that is kept moist until the plants are mature, after which it can be allowed to dry between waterings. Full sun is preferred, and protection from the wind with added brush supports is advisable.

PLANTING: Plants develop slowly, so it's a good idea to start them indoors 6 to 8 weeks before the last frost. If you don't mind late-blooming plants, wait and sow seed outdoors after the last frost. Space 10 to 12 inches apart.

SPECIAL HELPS: These richly colored and marked flowers make interesting fresh arrangements and good border or background specimens. Pinch back young plants to encourage branching.

SALVIA

DESCRIPTION: Spikes of intense red flowers characterize scarlet sage, a traditional foundation planting. Plants are usually 12 to 30 inches in height, although dwarf varieties may grow from 6 to 10 inches. Foliage is deep green. Among scarlet sage varieties, try scarlet Blaze of Fire; long-blooming Red Blazer; dwarf, early Scarlet Midget; and early-blooming St. John's Fire. Besides red, you now have a choice of pink, white, and blue varieties that are quite adaptable to lightly shaded sites. Also grow Lavender Love, White Fire, or coral Rose Flame.

SOIL AND LIGHT: Salvia needs full sun for at least a half-day. A rich, well-drained soil is best.

PLANTING: Since the seed needs heat to germinate and grows best under controlled temperature conditions, most people find it easiest to buy started plants. Space bedding plants about 12 inches apart in the garden.

SPECIAL HELPS: Salvias usually bloom from July till frost, making them a good choice for nearly every yard spot as well as balcony and patio tubs. Choose plants in a specific height range for the desired location. But be careful in mixing them with other flowers; some colors—especially bright red—can be overpowering. Flower spikes may be cut for drying; cut them at their peak and hang upside down.

SATINFLOWER
see godetia

SCABIOSA
also called pincushion flower

DESCRIPTION: Flowers are sweetly scented, large, and showy, in white or shades of blue, rose, lavender, red, and coral. Long silvery stamens cover the blossoms. Plants are usually 2- to 3-feet tall, with dwarf varieties to 14 inches. Compact Dwarf Double and double Giant Imperial are two top varieties.

SOIL AND LIGHT: Plants will do best when soil is well-prepared and enriched with humus. Water regularly during dry weather. Full sun is preferred.

PLANTING: Seed germinates in 15 to 20 days and should be of blooming size in 3 months. Sow outdoors after all danger of frost, or start inside about 6 weeks earlier. Space plants 8 to 12 inches apart, depending on the variety.

SPECIAL HELPS: Plan these into a mixed bed, or give them a massed spot of their own. Flowers are especially good for fresh bouquets; keep faded ones snipped.

SCHIZANTHUS
see butterfly flower

SEA LAVENDER
see statice

SNAPDRAGON
(antirrhinum)

DESCRIPTION: Plants range from 6-inch miniatures to 3-foot giants. Each features spikes covered with clusters of tubular flowers in an assortment of colors. Some of the hybrids are the popular heat-tolerant Rocket and Topper varieties, and the semi-dwarf Little Darling. Also try the bedding Coronette Mix and Sweetheart. Giant Ruffled Tetra snapdragons produce stocky plants that bloom later than other types, but with larger flowers.

SOIL AND LIGHT: For best results, plant in rich, well-drained soil that receives full to partial sun.

PLANTING: Plant early enough so plants are well established before hot weather. Buy started plants, or start seed indoors 6 to 8 weeks before the last frost. Transplant outdoors as soon as the ground is workable, setting 6 to 12 inches apart (depending on the variety). Growth is not as good if seeds are sown directly in the garden.

SPECIAL HELPS: Rust can be a problem in older varieties, but most of the newly developed ones are rust-resistant. Early pinching will help promote bushier plants. Dwarf varieties are especially good in rock gardens and borders. Larger ones make attractive backgrounds; staking is recommended.

SNOW-ON-THE-MOUNTAIN
see euphorbia

SPIDERPLANT
see cleome

STATICE
(limonium); also called sea lavender and thrift

DESCRIPTION: This 1- to 3-foot plant features a rosette of scalloped leaves that lies flat on the ground.

Stems holding tiny, papery-textured flowers in shades of blue, lavender, rose, white, and yellow rise from this base.

SOIL AND LIGHT: Statice is found naturally in salt meadows, so it does especially well in seaside gardens. Give it full sun. Plants will adapt to most well-drained soils, but they prefer cool weather.

PLANTING: If the seed you have is enclosed in a husk cluster, break it up before planting. Sow outdoors after all danger of frost, or start inside about 7 weeks earlier. Space plants about 10 inches apart.

SPECIAL HELPS: Flowers work well in both fresh and dried arrangements. To dry, cut when flower is fully opened; hang upside down in a shady place. When dried, flowers will last several months.

STOCK
(matthiola)

DESCRIPTION: Plants are 1 to 3 feet tall with attractive foliage and spikes of tiny, delicately scented flowers. Blooms usually are deep blue, but lilac, white, and pink varieties are available. Try the vigorous, large-flowered Giant Imperial, the early-blooming Early Cascade Blend, or the extremely early-blooming Trysomic Seven Weeks.

SOIL AND LIGHT: Cool temperatures and moist, moderately rich soil will satisfy these plants. Give them full sun unless summers are excessively hot—then give them partial shade.

PLANTING: Start early for best results. Sow outdoors as soon as the ground can be worked, or start indoors about 6 weeks earlier. In warm areas, sow seed in the fall.

SPECIAL HELPS: Remember this fragrant flower when planning the beds and borders around your porch, patio, or near the front entry. Cut for indoor enjoyment.

STRAWFLOWER
(helichrysum); also called everlasting

DESCRIPTION: The daisy-like double "flowers" are actually stiff, modified leaves surrounding the true flower in the center. The colorful petals show shades of red, purple, yellow, or white.

SOIL AND LIGHT: Full sun is preferred, and nearly any soil is tolerated if it is kept on the dry side.

PLANTING: Sow outside after the last frost, or start indoors about 6 weeks before. Set plants about 8 inches apart.

SPECIAL HELPS: Flowers hold their color especially well when dried, but may also be used in fresh arrangements. To dry, cut when half open, strip the foliage, and hang upside down in a dry, shady place.

SUMMER FORGET-ME-NOT
see anchusa

SUNFLOWER
(helianthus)

DESCRIPTION: Most commonly thought of as the 10-foot giant with single flowers that grow 8 to 14 inches across, sunflowers also come in a 2- to 4-foot variety with 3- to 4-inch single and double flowers. Yellow, orange, and mahogany, and bicolored flowers are available. Popular varieties include Teddy Bear (2 feet), Sungold (5 feet), Dwarf Sungold (2 feet), and Mammoth (10 feet).

SOIL AND LIGHT: Sunflowers will tolerate all soil conditions, although the shorter ones need more moisture. Full sun is required.

PLANTING: Plants develop quickly, so there's no advantage to early indoor starting. Sow outdoors after the last frost. Seedlings may be transplanted, but they'll grow taller and bloom earlier if left alone.

SPECIAL HELPS: Tall varieties often are used for temporary hedges; smaller ones may be planted into borders. Flowers may be cut for indoor arrangements, but be sure to leave some in the garden, as they attract birds. Squirrels like the seeds, and you may even want to save some for yourself.

SWAN RIVER DAISY
(brachycome)

DESCRIPTION: Many fragrant ½- to 1½-inch flowers cover this compact 12-inch plant. Bloom colors include blue, rose, violet, pink, and white.

SOIL AND LIGHT: Full sun and rich, well-drained soil is best, and wind protection is recommended.

PLANTING: Seeds should produce flowering plants in about 6 weeks, but the blooming season is short so plant at weekly intervals starting after the last frost. Space about 6 inches apart.

SPECIAL HELPS: Plants do best where summers are cool. Use them in borders, rock gardens, or movable pots. Flowers are short-stemmed, but make attractive arrangements in small containers. Keep the faded blossoms snipped.

SWEET PEA
(lathyrus)

DESCRIPTION: This old-fashioned favorite has enjoyed increasing popularity with the development of hardier varieties. Most are climbers, stretching as high as 8 feet. Bush types, growing 15 to 30 inches, are also available. The fragrant, bonnet-shaped flowers have ruffled or plain petals in nearly every color. Varieties to try include 12-inch bush Bijou, 30-inch climbing Knee-Hi, heat-resistant Cuthbertson Floribunda, and vigorous Summer Flowering Spencer.

SOIL AND LIGHT: Sweet peas do best in cool temperatures, although breeding has given new varieties more heat resistance. Give them full to partial sun and rich, well-drained soil that is kept moist. A light mulch will help protect roots from heat and dryness.

PLANTING: Soak seed before planting, and check the seed packet to see if they need to be treated with a nitrogen-fixing bacteria. Sow as soon as the ground can be worked. Seed should germinate in 2 to 4 weeks and bloom in 2 months.

SPECIAL HELPS: Although new varieties are more hardy, they also may be less fragrant. Vining types make attractive screens and backdrops, while bush types are good in beds or borders. For continuous bloom, pick all faded flowers.

SWEET-SULTAN
(Centaurea moschata)

DESCRIPTION: Pleasantly fragrant, these tassel-like flowers are fluffy and soft, and bloom in shades of

68

yellow, pink, lavender, and white. Plants grow 2 to 3 feet tall with deep green, finely cut foliage. Seeds are usually in mixed color assortments.
SOIL AND LIGHT: Sweet-sultans do well in any soil that receives full sun.
PLANTING: Plants do best in cool weather, so make two sowings about three weeks apart beginning in very early spring.
SPECIAL HELPS: Use flowers in fresh arrangements, or plant in mixed borders. Keep faded flowers snipped to encourage bloom.

SWEET WILLIAM
(dianthus)

DESCRIPTION: Often grown as a biennial, this compact plant may be as short as 4 inches or as tall as 2 feet. Flowers are in flat clusters in shades of red, purple, pink, and white. Reliable varieties include scarlet-red Queen of Hearts, 4-inch Wee Willie, quick-blooming Red Monarch, and richly colored Pink Beauty.
SOIL AND LIGHT: Full sun and moist, light soil are recommended.
PLANTING: Buy started plants, or sow seed indoors about 7 weeks before the last frost. Space 8 to 10 inches apart. In milder climates, sow seed in late summer and cover the seedlings with a layer of mulch during the winter. Plants started in this manner will bloom much earlier than spring-sown plants. Plants usually bloom a second summer where winters aren't severe.
SPECIAL HELPS: Flowers usually aren't fragrant, but they add much color to borders and rock gardens.

T

TAHOKA DAISY
(Machaeranthera tanacetifolia)

DESCRIPTION: These bushy 1- to 2-foot plants have wispy, fernlike foliage and long-lasting, yellow-centered, blue-violet flowers.
SOIL AND LIGHT: Plants resist drought and will tolerate all soil types. Give them full to partial sun.
PLANTING: Seeds need 4 months to produce flowering plants, so they do best in warm climates. Sow in very early spring, or start indoors 6 to 8 weeks earlier. Space plants about 6 inches apart.
SPECIAL HELPS: Blooming continuously from midsummer till frost, these plants are a good choice for borders and beds in areas where the warm season is extended. Flowers also keep well in fresh arrangements.

THRIFT
see statice

TITHONIA
also called Mexican sunflower

DESCRIPTION: Also called the "golden flower of the Incas," this bushy 4- to 6-foot plant features red-orange flowers that are gold on the underside. Foliage is gray-green and velvety in texture. Orange-red Torch is a common variety.

SOIL AND LIGHT: Resisting both drought and heat, plants need full sun and will adapt to any soil.

PLANTING: Plants grow rapidly but often need 4 months to flower. Sow after the last frost or start indoors about 5 weeks earlier. Set about 24 inches apart.
SPECIAL HELPS: Since they're bushy in habit, they make an excellent temporary hedge, especially in hot, dry areas. Flowers last well if they're cut in the bud, seared, and placed in warm water.

TOADFLAX
see linaria

TORENIA
also called wishbone flower

DESCRIPTION: This 1-foot plant displays trumpetlike flowers with flattened enlarged lips and blotches of blues, purples, yellows, and whites. The common name comes from the appearance of the crossed stamens. Foliage is dark green.
SOIL AND LIGHT: Torenia thrive in partial shade, and warm, moist soil.
PLANTING: Seed is very fine and germinates slowly, but plants grow quickly. Sow in the garden after the last frost, or start inside about 10 weeks earlier. Set plants about 8 inches apart. In warm areas, torenia are often self-sowing.

SPECIAL HELPS: Torenia are best suited to tropical and subtropical areas. Cuttings make unusual houseplants on a sunny windowsill in any climate.

TRACHYMENE
see blue lace flower

V

VERBENA

DESCRIPTION: Both a creeping type and an upright mounding type are available. Each bears flat clusters of tiny, fragrant flowers in many colors, usually with white centers. Heights range from 6 to 15 inches. Look for 8-inch Dwarf Sparkle, bush-type Spirit of '76, early-blooming Ideal Florist, and scarlet-flowered Blaze.

SOIL AND LIGHT: Verbenas like full sun and rich, well-drained soil. Most are heat-resistant.
PLANTING: Seeds need two weeks to germinate, so sow outdoors after the last frost, or start inside three months earlier. Started plants are generally available. Space 6 to 12 inches apart.
SPECIAL HELPS: Creeping varieties are especially good ground covers as well as potted specimens in window boxes and hanging baskets. Use others in rock gardens. Keep faded flowers snipped.

VINCA
also called periwinkle

DESCRIPTION: Shiny green leaves and five-petaled open flowers in shades of blue, pink, and white characterize this bushy, 1- to 2-foot plant. Foliage also may be a variegated green and white. Bush types are usually about 1½ feet tall. Annual varieties include dwarf bedding Little Pinkie, Little Blanche, and Little Bright Eye; ground cover Polka Dot; and the standard bush varieties.
SOIL AND LIGHT: Vinca likes full sun if soil is kept moist. In hot areas, give plants some shade. Any soil will be tolerated, but a rich type is preferred.
PLANTING: Seeds are slow to germinate; start indoors 3 months before the last frost, or buy started plants. Set 8 to 10 inches apart.
SPECIAL HELPS: Borders, pots, tubs, and window boxes are all good spots for vinca. Shear plants if growth lags. Plants are perennial in warm areas, where they make a good ground cover.

W

WAX BEGONIA
see begonia

WINGED EVERLASTING
see ammobium

Z

ZINNIA

DESCRIPTION: This favorite annual comes in a variety of heights, colors, and flower shapes. The tallest may reach 3 to 4 feet, while the shortest are only 6 to 12 inches. Among the many types are 2-foot Scarlet Ruffles; 2½-foot green-flowering Envy; 3-foot large-blooming State Fair; cactus-flowered Blaze and Snow-Time; and miniature Thumbelina, Pink Buttons, and Cherry Buttons.
SOIL AND LIGHT: Zinnias like hot weather and full sun.
PLANTING: Sow seed outdoors when temperatures are warm; they should germinate in 4 to 5 days and grow quickly. Space 6 to 12 inches apart, depending on the type.
SPECIAL HELPS: There's a size and flower shape for nearly every sunny spot. Remove faded flowers.

Bright-colored portulaca thrives in dry, sunny spots, and tolerates even the poorest soil.

Annual Basics

To grow beautiful annuals well, you need friable soil or a nutritious soilless substitute. Friable soil crumbles in your hand, and is a combination of humus and minerals, mostly sand and clay. But *combination* is the key word. If a soil is all sand, it drains too quickly and retains too few nutrients. But if it is all clay, it holds water so well that it can drown your plants. Soil also contains incidental trace elements, fungi, and bacteria.

The quickest way to analyze your soil is to pick up a handful and squeeze it lightly. If it runs through your fingers too fast, it contains too much sand; if it remains in your hand as a sticky mass, it's heavy with clay. But if the soil falls apart in your hand in crumbling bits and pieces, it should be good to use. Improve any soil by incorporating humus materials annually.

SOIL PREPARATION

Most soils contain enough food elements to last for many years. But for one reason or another, some soils do not contain these elements in a form readily usable to plants. The natural processes that make these elements available can be accelerated by the addition of peat moss, compost, and other organic materials. But because this process may take considerable time, plant foods should be added periodically to supply nutrients for immediate plant needs.

If your soil is heavy with clay, you will need to improve the soil structure, either by adding a thin layer of leaves, grass clippings, and spent annuals, or by aerating the soil by spading or tilling. It's best to do both. Spread compost, peat, and other decomposed organic matter in a thin layer over the surface and work the materials into the soil. Rent a rotary tiller for a weekend to complete the job with less effort, breaking up remaining clods and leveling the ground as you go.

Apply your additives at the rate of 2 or more bushels per 100 square feet. Not only will these organic materials stimulate root development, but they also can help hold water and maintain a more even moisture level in the ground.

When breaking up the soil on a new annual bed, use a garden fork rather than a spade. The fork tines tend to break up clods vertically as well as horizontally, thereby eliminating one chore in the process.

Tilling the soil with the help of horsepower greatly cuts down on labor, and permits you to do a better job. Cross over your tracks for another run—it helps further.

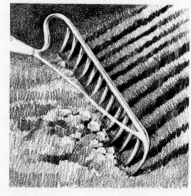

Rake beds repeatedly until you have leveled the ground and removed all weeds, twigs, and stones. Then level with final raking.

FERTILIZERS AND AMENDMENTS

A soil amendment is anything that makes up for deficiencies. Examples are organic matter, balanced plant foods, lime, manures, and other waste matter. Organic matter includes decomposed leaves, dried grass clippings, straw, sawdust and wood ashes, corn or cane stalks, fruit pomade, spent hops, seaweed, banana skins, cocoa hulls, cottonseed, wood chips, and even sludge. The last two, combined under forced aeration and cured for 30 days, produce a finished product that looks and smells like ground bark, and has a pH factor of 6 to 7.

Balanced plant foods include many commercial products that contain nitrogen, phosphorus, and potash. Most of these sacked fertilizers contain lesser amounts of calcium, sulfur, and magnesium. Of the chemical fertilizers, ammonium nitrate should be used exactly as per directions. Because it has a high nitrogen content (33%), it needs sufficient dilution to avoid burning plant material. Super-phosphate contains 20% phosphorus, and muriate of potash, 60% potassium. All should be applied with care.

Animal manures are good all-around fertilizers because of the humus they contain; dried manure is safer to use than fresh manure. Bone meal is a good additive for plants that prefer a slightly alkaline soil. It also contains some nitrogen and phosphoric acid, but no potash. Cottonseed meal helps acid-loving plants. Lime modifies both the physical and chemical properties of the soil. It pulls together small particles of clay, and thereby makes the soil more porous.

Perlite and vermiculite can be used to lighten soil and keep the particles apart. Urea formaldehyde is a synthetic organic fertilizer that contains a very high amount of nitrogen (38%). But since it has a built-in release control, the nitrogen is available to the plants over a longer period of time, virtually eliminating the danger of burning plant tissues. Other additives that should be widely available soon are wood and coal ashes.

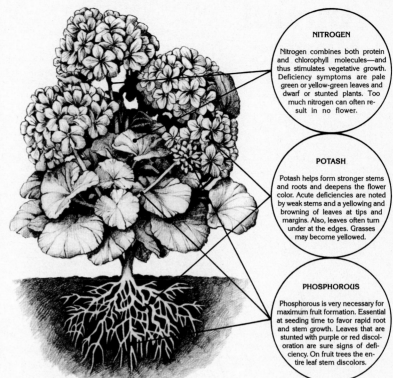

NITROGEN

Nitrogen combines both protein and chlorophyll molecules—and thus stimulates vegetative growth. Deficiency symptoms are pale green or yellow-green leaves and dwarf or stunted plants. Too much nitrogen can often result in no flower.

POTASH

Potash helps form stronger stems and roots and deepens the flower color. Acute deficiencies are noted by weak stems and a yellowing and browning of leaves at tips and margins. Also, leaves often turn under at the edges. Grasses may become yellowed.

PHOSPHOROUS

Phosphorous is very necessary for maximum fruit formation. Essential at seeding time to favor rapid root and stem growth. Leaves that are stunted with purple or red discoloration are sure signs of deficiency. On fruit trees the entire leaf stem discolors.

The importance of nitrogen, phosphorous, and potash to the growth of your new annuals cannot be overemphasized. The hyphenated numbers on a bag of fertilizer indicate the pounds of nitrogen, phosphorous, and potash per hundred pounds of fertilizer.

Nitrogen is necessary for the formation of new cells in all plant parts, and stimulates the growth of stems and leaves. It is the soil nutrient most often lacking, and hence, the one most often replaced.

Phosphorous strengthens both stems and roots. It also stimulates food storage and increases seed and fruit production. Next to nitrogen, phosphoric acid is the most valuable fertilizer constituent.

Potash, the third major element in fertilizer compounds, is needed for normal plant growth to protect plants from the ravages of disease. It also aids and stimulates the growth of sturdy roots, and is essential for good flower color. Potash is a soluble mineral found in several compounds, including potassium carbonate and potassium hydroxide.

Good fertilizers for annuals include manure, superphosphate, and mixed fertilizers in combinations such as 4-12-4 or 5-10-5. Apply manure at the rate of about 4 bushels per 100 square feet, and superphosphate at about 5 pounds per 100 square feet. With formula fertilizers, apply according to the manufacturer's directions. Work them into the top 6 inches of soil every other year.

For an added boost, you can apply inorganic fertilizer to your annuals just before they start flowering. Apply at the rate of 1 pound per 100 square feet. For flowers with a long blooming period, give beds a second treatment halfway through the season.

The best time to apply commercial fertilizers is a day or two before you put the seeds in the ground. Because the minerals are sacked with sand or some other inert and inexpensive material, they may not be thoroughly mixed. By raking them in, you ensure a more even distribution. Intermediate applications should be applied to rows as top-dressing. They will seep down with sprinkling. Keep the fertilizer 6 inches from the base of plants to avoid possible burning.

Annual Basics

COMPOSTING

Homemade compost is one of the most valuable soil builders you can use; it's inexpensive because you can make it from waste materials that would otherwise be carted away. Compost is vegetation that has been decomposed by bacteria and fungi. A compost pile is a kind of factory where millions of microbes are at work making a product that can yield virtually everything plants need.

Locate the pile on fairly level land in an out-of-the-way corner. A shady spot is best, as it won't require watering as often. Don't crowd it against a fence or the garage.

HOW TO BUILD A COMPOST PILE

For an average suburban lot, plan on a pile about 5-feet-square. If you have a lot of trees, make two piles. The pile may be started at ground level, or from a pit about 18 inches deep. A pit makes the pile somewhat less conspicuous and keeps the level of moisture more constant. You can erect side walls on two or three sides to better hold the pile within bounds. Two-inch planking makes good walls, as do brick or concrete blocks. Make walls about 3 feet high.

Fallen leaves probably will be your chief composting material, but grass clippings spread out in thin layers together with green weeds also should be included. The trick is to pull the weeds before they go to seed. Make a practice of saving vegetable and apple parings, dry bread crusts, lettuce, carrot tops—in fact, any kitchen discards that don't

contain fat or grease that might attract rodents.

However, do not include eggshells or citrus fruit rinds, which decompose too slowly and leave the pile looking untidy. Top the kitchen wastes with leaves or soil.

After the leaves fall in autumn, mow the lawn one more time, crushing the dried leaves as you go. Then dump these materials onto the pile in 4-inch layers, topped with thin layers of soil. The soil keeps the moisture in, prevents blowing, and adds bacteria to the stack. Soak the pile well after each major addition. Adding a pint of lime or plant food to the layer speeds decomposition.

The process of decomposition may take six months, a year, or longer, depending upon the moisture the pile receives and the air that reaches it. Techniques and methods vary from region to region. Californians have evolved a platform base surrounded by snow fencing to allow for the free flow of air and water. They turn or stir the pile frequently, and in some cases, compost is finished and ready to use in two months.

HOW TO USE COMPOST

It's fine to have a big pile of rich compost stashed away in a far corner of the garden—a stack so completely decomposed that you can't recognize any of its parts—but it does your garden no good at all unless it's spread around.

Compost is particularly useful when you're starting a new flowerbed. If you make your plans and diagram the bed in the fall, you can add a 2-inch layer before you turn the soil. Do this before winter and let the clods lie open to the snow and freezing rain. This will break down the lumps and freeze out some weed roots in the process. Then turn the soil once more in the spring, adding a second layer of compost if your soil is poor, and your bed will be ready to plant. As the annuals reach maturity and begin to bloom, you can add a top-dressing of compost around each plant. The extra nutrients will keep the flowers blooming longer, and will enrich the soil for subsequent plantings.

In the spring, combine compost with garden soil for your seedling plantings if you don't want to spend the money for a sterile mix. To make your concoction sterile, you need to bake it in an oven or barbecue along with a potato. When the potato is baked soft, the plant mix should also be sterile and free of weeds. If you are reusing old pots or planting trays, be sure they are clean and free of disease. A soapy scrubbing can work wonders. But if you value your time, potting mix bought sacked

and sterile costs much less.

Compost also can help in the renovation of an old garden or the making of a new one. Old gardens usually benefit from a grand cleanup, and the resulting heaps of leaves and other debris are often partially decomposed already. Pile these materials in a stack in the fall, water the pile well, and by spring, you should have compost good enough to scatter as a top-dressing around old trees and shrubs and new flowerbeds.

If you're starting with raw, bulldozed, suburban land, you may have to gather your compost materials elsewhere. Strike up an acquaintance with local tree-trimming crews and leaf rakers in older sections of town. Also, scrounge spent hops from the nearest brewery, pomace from a fruit-canning factory, or topsoil from a road construction crew. If your soil is mucky clay, add sand and gypsum sufficient to modify the problem, but not so much that you end up with something closely akin to concrete.

As you plant your garden, add the scrounged compost to each heap of soil as you return it to the ground with planting of trees and shrubs. If you crave privacy, plant castor beans and tithonia, the Mexican sunflower, in a boundary-line trench laced with compost. These two annuals will grow 4 to 5 feet high as a summer foliage barrier.

For overhead color, combine compost with perlite or vermiculite to fill hanging pots of petunias. Or fill containers with compost and soil to grow marigolds and zinnias beside

your doorstep. If you still have leftover compost, plant it with zucchini in a large-sized tub.

PESTS AND DISEASES

There are two ways to approach pest and disease control. First, you can make your annuals as strong and healthy as possible with good soil, protection from the elements, and a steady and assured water supply. It is the plants that have been weakened by wind, drought, and insufficient nutrients that fall prey to bugs and disease. And second, you can hand-pick and kill the bugs, caterpillars, beetles, and cutworms that show up to threaten your plants.

As long as you concentrate on annual flowers, pests and diseases are a small threat. Your best defense is to pull out and destroy any plant that becomes deeply infected with aphids or leaf-miner. Beetles and caterpillars can be pulled off one by one and dropped in a can of kerosene for quick extinction. Cutworms are most often a threat to new seedlings set out on open ground. They feed on young, succulent stems, sometimes felling several seedlings in a single night. Young pansies, cineraria, and geraniums are their most common prey. Unfortunately, tomato and cabbage starts are a cutworm delicacy. Wrap a 2-inch protective collar around these seedlings.

The aphid is perhaps the greatest pest for annual-growers. A sucking insect, it attacks dahlias, dianthus, ageratum, petunias, snapdragons, and zinnias, just to mention a few. Not only do aphids rob plants of vigor and deform buds and flowers, they also carry mosaic and other virus diseases. Small colonies should be cut out and destroyed. You can detect their presence by the accumulations of honeydew they secrete. Rotenone and pyrethrum, botanical poisons, are effective against these insects. Nicotine sulphate is an old-time remedy, and malathion is a modern help.

Diseases, on the other hand, afflict annuals less than trees and perennials. Powdery mildew, the mosaics, and ring spot are the most damaging. Your best bet is simply to plant disease-resistant varieties.

75

Annual Basics

Get the jump on summer color by starting your annuals indoors on a warm windowsill or under artificial lights. Whether you want many plants or just a few, you can get your summer beds growing early with the starter kits available at most nursery houses and supermarkets. The kits come complete with everything you need. Just follow the simple package instructions and, with a bit of diligence, you'll be setting out seedlings well ahead of your garden neighbors. As you watch the seedlings grow from day to day, you'll have time to plan their outdoor placements carefully.

These seed-starting kits are almost one-step affairs—quick, clean, and efficient. The individual planters are net-enclosed peat packets that swell to pot-size when soaked in water. Plant 2 or 3 seeds in each pot and return to the tray of moist peat or vermiculite, which is kept damp by a wick in a plastic reservoir. Only occasionally do the pots and plants need overhead watering. When the seedlings show their first true leaves, thin out the plants, leaving the strongest one to mature. You don't need to fertilize, because the growing medium contains enough plant food to sustain the seedlings until they are moved to their place in the garden.

If you grow your kits in a sunny window, you'll need to turn the flats occasionally to avoid developing spindly plants. Turn the trays every time the shoots start leaning toward the light. Most common bedding annuals now are available in kits.

COLD FRAMES

Want a part-time greenhouse to extend your gardening seasoning? With a cold frame, it's as easy as building a box. The same basic structure you use as a cold frame also can double as a hotbed with the addition of a soil-heating cable (see page 78). Some cables come equipped with built-in soil thermostats, preset for 70 degrees.

Both structures use the heat of the sun to warm the enclosed soil. The hotbed provides supplemental heat during the nighttime hours, a key requirement for easy seed-starting.

Locate the frame facing south and give it some shelter against harsh winds. Choose a level site and see that the soil has good drainage.

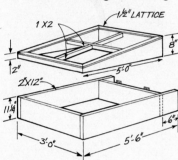

The sloping top of the frame will ensure easy runoff of rain. Turn the soil within the frame and rake even. If you plan to grow plants in pots, add sand as a top surface. If plants are to grow in the ground, add a top layer of good soil. The ideal temperature for seed-starting is 70 degrees, so buy an inexpensive thermometer to aid in maintaining the sufficient heat. When the frame temperature rises, prop the lid open. At night, if heavy frosts are due, add insulated covers to hold heat. Temperatures below 45 degrees can damage delicate seedlings. Water only with a sprinkling can; the excessive pressure from a garden hose can uproot the little plants.

Don't use fertilizer in the seedbed, as small seedlings can't tolerate plant foods. And water whenever the soil feels dry, or whenever you notice signs of plant-wilting. Be ready to plant seedlings in early spring.

For the base of a cold frame or hotbed, use 2x12 rot-resistant lumber, preferably redwood or cedar, to make a 36x66-inch box. If you use non-resistant wood, treat it with a wood preservative other than creosote, which is known to be hard on plants.

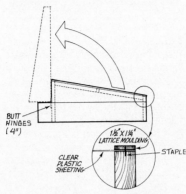

Build the top to measure 36x60 inches, and taper the sides from 2 to 8 inches. Inside the top, fasten a piece of 1x2 lumber side-to-side and flush with the top edge. Add another piece front-to-rear, also flush with the top. Use a lap joint where the strips cross. This grid supports the plastic sheeting. Hinge the top to the base with 4x4 butt hinges.

The top, fully open, is supported

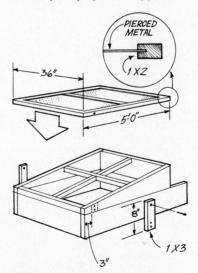

on the expansions of the side base boards. Stretch and staple clear plastic (6 to 8 mils thick) to the lid edge, and top with molding strips to prevent tearing in the wind. Also build a frame of 1x3s to hold a sheet of pierced metal for use as a sun filter. When freezes are due, cover lid with blankets or building boards

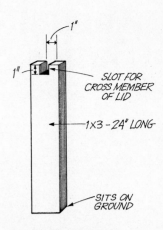

weighted with bricks.

A number of products are available that will insulate against cold air. A lid of rigid composition board that is impregnated with a tar-like substance works well. Cut a piece of 1x3 wood 24 inches long to serve as a prop for the lid. Stand it on the ground inside the frame and rest a crossmember of the lid into the notched top. Move prop to adjust for air.

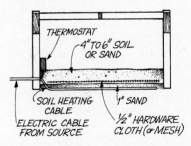

Use the cold frame for early crops of radishes, lettuce, and onions (all quick-growing), and for starting seedling vegetables or annuals.

Pot up cannas, dahlias, and tuberous begonias to start in the frame about 6 weeks before the last frost date. When the weather is frost-free, set the plants out for summer blooming. Use the frame with the sun filter to harden-off greenhouse-grown plants, or to condition small houseplants to an outdoor environment.

In late summer or fall, sow the seeds of biennials and perennials for use in the garden the following year. Or, as days cool, plant fall crops of parsley, radishes, and lettuce to harvest from the frame.

Annual Basics

COLD FRAME

In the fall, move plants that aren't reliably winter-hardy in your area into the cold frame. Chrysanthemums can be established in the frame in the fall, then saved for cuttings or divisions to use in the spring. Canterbury-bells, English daisies, foxgloves, and forget-me-nots also may be carried safely through the winter for early spring planting.

If you move some of your houseplants outdoors for the summer, use the frame (with the sun filter) for the more delicate plants that need protection from sun and wind during the hottest months.

Take advantage of the micro-climates in your garden when you locate your box. Place it against a south wall or a building where it's protected from the prevailing wind. The lower side of the box should face south to admit the most sunlight. For your own convenience, place it near the house for easy winter-tending, and near an outside faucet for the necessary watering year-round. During the bitterest winter months, cover the frame with blankets and an old tarpaulin; uncovering it only on bright sunny days. It's a privilege to harvest fresh parsley or crisp lettuce, or to grow flower seedlings for spring.

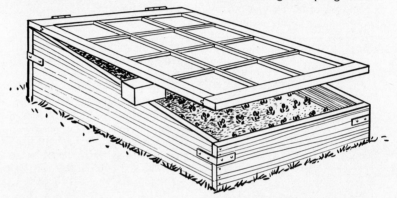

HOTBEDS

With a little bit of adjustment, the same cold frame can be used as a hotbed. Lay a coated soil cable on the ground in an even pattern, and then cover over with dirt. Next, spread a mesh layer across the entire box area, and cover with 4 to 6 inches of good garden loam.

In this little hothouse, you can plant seed and grow young plants that will be ready to set out in the garden as soon as the danger of frost has passed. To make your life easier, select a cable with a built-in thermostat so you don't have to tend the hotbed as often. In two or three months, this very small space can enable you to grow 20 or more trays of seedling varieties that otherwise might not be available.

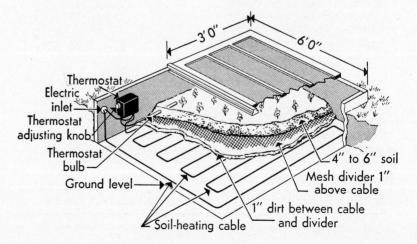

STARTING SEEDS OUTDOORS

The hardier annuals can be planted out as seeds—not as seedlings half-grown in a hotbed, on a windowsill, or under artificial lights. With the proper planting, good soil, and the right amount of moisture, you can go seed-to-bloom in just one step.

First, scatter seeds over a raked area. Do not cover with soil, but rather firm the seed in place with a board or your hand. Water the bed well by misting so as not to wash the seed away, and keep it moist until the seedlings show green.

Sow large seeds in shallow troughs to a depth of about three times the diameter of the seed. For climbing vines, install a trellis before you plant, raking soil over seeds.

Your main obligation for the next week or two is to keep the area just moist enough—and never soggy—while the sprouts are germinating and taking hold.

On a hot, windswept location, temporarily cover the seed with thin-mesh cloth—old window curtains or cheesecloth will do—and tie down the corners. As the seedlings start showing their second and third sets of little leaves, carefully thin out the weaker plants without damaging the select ones.

About one month after seed planting, pinch off the top shoots with your thumbnail and forefinger to encourage good branching. Some seed plants are bred for such branching; the pinching process will not be needed on these. Initially, weed the bed by hand to encourage plant growth. Do not endanger the young sprouts with hoe-cultivation.

Strive always for good foliage and bushy plant forms. The abundant show of flowers will follow naturally. Keep the blooms coming by proper watering whenever natural rainfall is not enough. And cut out all faded flowers as they appear to keep them from going to seed. This will result in the development of a new crop of flowers.

Add handfuls of compost or mulching material around the growing plants to keep them from suddenly drying out in the hot sun. When flower bloom slows, renew by cutting back leggy stems and adding fertilizer around the stalks. Then water in well.

Plant sweet peas in a freshly dug trench laced with nutrients. Backfill to 2 or 3 inches from the top, and place the seeds according to packet instructions. Return the surplus soil to the trench as needed to give cover. Keep the trench moist.

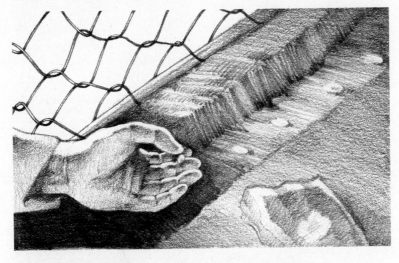

THINNING

The practice of thinning involves the sacrifice of some plants for the benefit of others, and should be practiced whenever quality is desired over quantity.

Some gardeners find the thinning process a bit disturbing, and prefer to salvage the plants they lift to use elsewhere. This operation is usually called pricking out, and it works better with sturdy vegetable starts than with flowers.

The hardier annuals are generally not offered in pots or flats by nursery houses or supermarkets since they grow easily from seed.

79

Annual Basics

SEEDLING KNOW-HOW

You can avoid a lot of fuss and muss by buying started plants in flats or trays at your local nursery supplier. These seedling plants also are available in individual peat pots.

The small expanding peat pots can be set out just as they are, or you can peel off the nylon net wrapping and quickly put them in the ground. If you use fiber mix containers, break off the pot rim before you set the plant in the ground. With large flats, break away one side of the box and lift out the individual plants with a putty knife.

Space the plants 6 to 8 inches apart—less for pansies and alyssum, more for tall marigolds. And pull up weeds when they first appear so they won't compete with the annuals for sun, space, water, and nutrients.

Water-in the seedlings with a soaker hose, or with a soft all-night rain, if you can schedule it. The object is to ease the garden soil closely around the young roots, leaving none exposed to the air. If the days are hot and sunny at planting time, stick a wooden shingle on the south side of each plant for a week or so to give the plant some shade and time to adjust to the brighter situation.

Gently sprinkle entire bed; if you just water the individual plants, dry soil nearby will leach away the moisture. As the plants mature, with some reaching heights of 3 to 4 feet, raise your sprinkler onto a stool so its stream will arc over plants, rather than hitting them full-force.

If you don't like to use your fingernails to pinch out young annuals, snip them out instead. But either way, trim leggy plants by removing three or four upper leaflets just above a leaf joint. Do this when the plants are about 6 inches tall, unless they are already branching well on their own. Information on seed packs usually indicates if the plant is self-branching.

For low plant maintenance, spread an inch or more of mulching material around bases.

The mulch insulates surface soil from the sun, protects against drying winds and beating rains, and also retains soil moisture.

80

MULTIPLICATION KNOW-HOW

To get more mileage out of certain garden plants, simply root cuttings that you clip in midsummer. But don't get carried away—take only as many cuttings as you can carry through the winter easily. Then you'll have new plants to enjoy indoors during cold weather, plus sizable starts for next spring. Such plants as coleus, geranium, and wax begonia are easy to manage.

Regardless of which of these plants you want to increase, the procedure is the same as shown here for coleus. Take about 4 inches of stem, making a cut just below a leaf stem. Remove lower leaves and insert in a rooting medium of peat and perlite or all sand. You can root cuttings in water, but later the transfer to soil may be tricky.

After you insert cuttings in the rooting medium, water well and put the container in a tightly closed plastic bag that's out of direct sun. In about ten days, check for roots by pulling gently on a cutting. When you are sure of roots, pot up the cuttings in a porous mix in 3-inch pots. Set in good light and water whenever surface soil dries.

With geraniums, you can shape your garden plants to smaller mounds in August for another surge of bloom. Use the cuttings to start new potted plants for winter bloom in your sunniest room. Come spring, you can return the plants to the frost-free garden beds to begin the cycle again.

Take cuttings from three or four of your favorite coleus plants and nurture them as above. They'll repay you with a showy display of color throughout the winter months. Then, ready new trays of bright cuttings in moist sand for eventual return to the garden.

Try the Victorian custom of planting a stand of cosmos in a big tub or container for a feathery accent on a summer terrace. Then when frosts threaten, bring the tub indoors to a sunny window and enjoy continuing bloom through Thanksgiving.

As summer ends, rescue wax begonias, verbena, and impatiens to use indoors.

A large planter full of soil weighs more than you might expect. Move such a load easily with three poles or lengths of broomstick. As the rear pole is uncovered, move it around to the front of the line.

TENDER BULBS

Gladiolus

Plant gladiolus and you'll soon know why they're garden favorites of beginners and experts alike. Their dramatic solid and two-toned flower spikes—in all colors but true blue—are just-right accents in any garden location. Use glads alone, or in perennial or annual borders.

The unique form and startling colors of gladiolus appear two to three months after the corms are planted. Set them out every two weeks from the last frost until midsummer for constant bloom, or plan your planting for concentrated color when the rest of the garden is not at its peak.

Gladiolus grows easily in slightly acid, well-drained soil that's in a sunny spot. Flowers range from the large, exhibition, florists'-type to the small, airy, less-formal miniature. Both make magnificent cut flowers, and their strong vertical lines and sword-like foliage are good garden accents.

1 Glads should be planted in rows or clumps of four, eight, or more, and set out about 6 inches apart. Plant jumbo corms 6 inches deep; medium-size (2-inch-diameter) corms are laid down 4 inches; and small ones are put 2 inches into the ground. New corms that form over the summer can be dug and stored. Few insects or diseases bother glads.

2 Staking may be necessary to prevent plants from falling over. Choose inconspicuous stakes, such as bamboo, and use string to support plants. Run it down each side of plants, or around clumps if you've planted in groups. For extra support, mound soil around plant bases. After flowers have bloomed, fertilize to encourage strong corms for next year.

3 Mulching is a good practice with all tender bulbs. Covering the ground with leaf mold, grass clippings, wood chips or other organic matter lessens the need for weeding and allows the ground to stay moist and cool. After blooms fade, leave foliage until it matures. Dig corms, cut off tops, and cure in a warm place. Store where it's cool and dry.

TENDER BULBS

Dahlia

Dwarf dahlias, above, border an entrance walk to brighten this garden with everblooming plants all summer long.

These dwarfs are ideal bedding plants—they're small-flowered, low-growing, and need no staking or disbudding.

Like their larger cousins, dwarf dahlias blossom in many forms and in every rainbow color but clear blue.

STARTING DWARF DAHLIAS FROM SEED

1 Bushy, dwarf dahlias, which grow only 1 to 2 feet tall, are commonly and easily started from seed. Sow three seeds per pot in sterile soil, then pull all but the largest seedling. It should grow rapidly, quickly setting flower buds and developing its fat, fleshy tuber. In addition to the dwarf dahlias, there are the larger single, anemone, peony, cactus, miniature, and pompon varieties. Blooms range from 1 inch to 1 foot across, while the plants themselves can stretch from 6 inches to 10 feet in height. Buy tubers for larger types.

2 When the soil is warm and all danger of frost is past, transplant tubers outdoors into a sunny spot. Soil should be rich and well-drained. Dahlias need lots of water and fertilizer to stay in bloom, and should be mulched to keep their roots cool and the ground moist and free of weeds. Dwarf dahlias should be spaced 18 inches on center; intermediate-sized miniatures and pompons, 2 feet apart; and the tall, exhibition varieties, 3 to 4 feet apart. Use dahlias for borders, in perennial beds, with annuals, and as screens.

STARTING STANDARD DAHLIAS FROM TUBERS

1 Before planting a tall tuber, push a stake in the ground to support the stem. Make holes 4 inches deep, set tubers horizontally, and fill in the holes as your plants grow.

2 Allow only one shoot per tuber to grow, and when two pairs of leaves form, pinch off the growing tip. The bared stem then should be tied to the stake to keep plant upright.

3 As each stem matures, cut off side flower buds as they form to produce large central blooms. Dahlias make magnificent cut flowers. Dig tubers in fall after frost darkens foliage.

TENDER BULBS
Tuberous Begonia

Choose upright plants for pots, edgings, and borders, and use trailing types atop low walls and in hanging baskets.

Elegant tuberous begonias belong on your "must-have" list if you want spectacular color for semi-shady spots.

A gorgeous palette of red, pink, yellow, orange, and white provides beauty from midsummer until frost.

Tuberous begonias display a colorful variety of flower forms—formal, ruffled, rose, carnation, and camellia.

How To Grow and Store Tuberous Begonias

1 Buy hard, round tubers in April or May and grow them indoors so they'll bloom earlier. In a shallow flat of barely moist sphagnum moss, sand, and vermiculite, plant the tubers, round side down. Don't overwater or the begonias may rot. Keep them warm (at least 65° F.) in bright light, but avoid burning sun. When roots are well-established and the tops near 3 inches tall, pot up tubers 1 inch below the surface of the soil. Shift outdoors after all danger of frost is past.

2 Outdoor tuberous begonias need rich soil and perfect drainage. Water frequently to keep surface roots moist. The foliage also benefits from frequent misting. Fertilize every week or two with soluble plant food for an array of vibrant color and good year-round growth. Before frost comes in the fall, dig plants and dry two weeks or until stems and soil easily drop from the tubers. Store dry, out of frost's way, in a holder of peat, sand, vermiculite, or sphagnum moss.

TENDER BULBS

Caladium

Let tropical-looking caladiums brighten up a shady corner of your patio or garden with their jewel-like, heart-shaped foliage of vivid red, green, pink, white, and silver. You can use them in planters on terraces and patios, plant them directly in the garden, or sink potted tubers into the ground. Their bright colors make them increasingly popular.

Caladiums like well-drained soil that's rich in organic matter. Water them frequently to keep the soil damp, and treat the foliage to a misting on hot days. Caladiums may be grown in full shade, although a little sunlight gives them a more intense color. They thrive in warm temperatures and high humidity, and should be fed every month. Three weeks before frost in fall, stop watering. Dig when foliage dies.

1 For fewer plant losses, start caladiums indoors four to six weeks before moving outside. A good rooting mixture is half-and-half peat and perlite. Space tubers round side up 1 inch apart in a shallow box. Cover lightly with mixture, water, and place in a warm spot draped with clear plastic.

2 Transplant from flats to 4-inch pots when rooted, whether you'll bed them or use in containers. Firm a loose potting mix around the plants, allowing ½ inch at the tops for water. After watering, locate plants in a bright, warm spot. Transfer outdoors when all danger of frost is past.

Canna Lily

If you still think of cannas as tall Victorian plants, you're in for a nice surprise. The new dwarf cannas grow to just 2 or 3 feet, but bloom with spectacular color in sunny locales.

Cannas like a rich, moist soil, and should be fed several times during the growing season. Start them inside one month before the last frost in spring, or plant horizontally in the ground 1 inch deep after frost is past. Dig rhizomes in the fall after tops blacken.

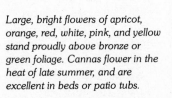

Large, bright flowers of apricot, orange, red, white, pink, and yellow stand proudly above bronze or green foliage. Cannas flower in the heat of late summer, and are excellent in beds or patio tubs.

TENDER BULBS
Calla Lily

The calla lily's spathe-shaped flowers of pink, yellow, and white bloom 2 feet above its arrow-shaped and often spotted foliage. Callas are perfect in pots or beds.

Known primarily as a greenhouse or indoor plant, the calla lily deserves more recognition as a tender outdoor bloomer, happy in full sun or light shade.

Start calla lilies indoors in March or April to fill the garden with delicate flowers by May and June. Or plant outdoors 3 inches deep when soil warms.

Calla lilies need rich, organic soil, lots of water, and liquid feeding every two weeks. Dig rhizomes after frost has darkened the foliage and store for next year.

Exotics

Aptly called the pineapple lily, the eucomis sends up flower spikes that mimic the fruit—complete with topknots. The spikes of cream-and-green star-shaped flowers appear less than two months after bulbs are started. Give them rich soil and feed monthly.

The climbing gloriosa lily presents exotic red and yellow blooms starting in July, and makes an excellent cut flower. Give the lily a trellis to climb on, or provide support stakes. Plant tubers 4 inches deep in good soil. Dig both plants and store before hard frosts.

For a touch of the very unusual, try eucomis, the pineapple lily, left, or the gloriosa lily, above. Both need full sun and do equally as well in beds or containers.

TENDER BULBS

Exotics

Flowers of orange, red, yellow, or copper and narrow, sword-shaped leaves adorn the montbretia from late summer until frost. For best effect, plant in clumps of twelve, with corms 4 inches deep and 4 inches apart in a light, sandy soil.

Fragrant white flowers with black centers sit atop the acidanthera two months after they are set out. Also called sweet-scented gladiolus, they should be planted 2 inches deep and 5 inches apart in coarse soil. Lift both in fall.

Corms of montbretia, left, and acidanthera, above, grow into 2-foot plants filled with graceful flowers. Both need full sun and should be watered freely.

Perfect double-flowers of ranunculus bloom in many colors in early summer. Lift them after they flower.

Intermingle blue agapanthus with hardy daylilies to achieve a burst of midsummer color in sun or light shade. Plant agapanthus 2 inches deep in rich, moist soil.

Summer Bulb Storage

If you plant recommended varieties of summer bulbs "by the book" and you still don't reap the promised glorious harvests of color, you should check your bulb quality. Examine your storage area first, because quality usually depends on correct storage more than on any other factor. Just as dampness, extreme temperature, and pests can make your dinner inedible, the same factors render these bulbs' carefully-built reserves of "food" unusable for starting new blooms.

Gladiolus Dig corms anytime after foliage begins to yellow. You can wait until frost to dig late plantings, but don't wait until a hard freeze. Leave about 1 inch of growth on corms, then cure for two to four weeks at 75 to 80 degrees in a well-ventilated room.

Before placing the corms in winter storage, dust them lightly with an all-purpose garden or rose dust. The best storage temperatures range from 35 to 45 degrees. Make certain that the temperature never drops below freezing. Break off the 1 inch of the top growth left on the corm for curing, then store corms in old nylon hose or onion bags hung from a ceiling or wall. You also can store them in shallow flats with screen wire bottoms.

You'll probably want to save the smaller corms—called cormels—for propagation of some of your favorite varieties. Some are as small as buckshot, so dig carefully to avoid losing them in the soil. Separate them immediately from large corms and store in barely dampened sand or peat moss. Examine them every few weeks to make sure they're still healthy, but not sprouting. If sprouting occurs, your storage medium is too moist.

Dahlia Wait until after a light frost, then cut plants back to 4 to 6 inches above the soil. Dig carefully to avoid damaging or breaking off the tubers. Hose off as much soil as possible,

and allow to dry only slightly in a shady area before storing. Do not divide at this time—wait until spring when bud growths show you where to cut.

Ordinary cartons make good storage containers. Place the still-moist tubers in the boxes and cover with dry vermiculite, sawdust, or sphagnum moss. Tie a label to each clump or write the name on the stem with an indelible pencil. Check monthly and sprinkle on more packing material if the roots begin to shrivel. Store at 35 to 45 degrees.

Tuberous begonia A light frost is not too harmful, but dig the tubers before frost, if possible. Leave about 4 inches of top attached. Then dry for several days in the sun—long enough so that stem stubs detach easily. Store tubers as you do dahlia roots, but at a slightly higher temperature—45 to 60 degrees. Keep the packing dry to avoid decay.

Canna After the first killing frost, cut off tops to within 14 inches of soil level. Dig roots and dry in a warm room for two to three weeks. Dust the undivided clumps with a fungicide, and store, stem side down, at a temperature of 45 to 50 degrees. Packing material is optional, but roots must be kept dry during storage.

Caladium Tubers are very sensitive to frost, so dig them in early fall while weather is still warm. Carefully remove most of the clinging soil, then dry for a week or so in a warm, dry place. Store as you would dahlias, but at 60 degrees, and never at temperatures over 80 degrees.

Ismene Dry the bulbs, with fleshy roots attached, in an inverted position for two weeks. Store at 60 degrees.

Calla lily Store rhizomes just as you would dahlias, but keep the packing medium-dry, since callas are prone to rot. Store at 45 to 55 degrees.

Galtonia Lift bulbs anytime before frost. Dry, and store at 60 degrees.

Gloriosa Dig in the fall before frost, then store at 45 to 50 degrees.

Hymerocallis Bulbs should be lifted before frost and dried upside down. Store at 60 degrees.

Tigridia Treat the same as

gladiolus, although they are somewhat more hardy. In some areas, they can be mulched and left outdoors through the winter. Or, store indoors in a dry place at 40 to 50 degrees.

Tritonia Also similar to gladiolus, these bulbs should be dug before frost. They, too, can be left to winter outdoors in warmer climates after they have been mulched. Store indoors at 45 to 50 degrees.

Coraldrops In northern climes, dig up after foliage dies back and store at temperatures of 55 to 60 degrees for the winter.

Tuberose In the North and South, dig up bulbs in the fall and replant in the spring when both days and nights are warm. Cut off frost-nipped stems and dry thoroughly. Store in peat at 55 to 65 degrees.

Oxalis In warmer climates, leave the Chilean variety in the ground through the winter, with at least a 2-inch layer of soil and some mulch in wind-plagued areas. Other varieties serve well indoors as winter pot plants.

Sprekelia Also known as Aztec lily and as a form of amaryllis, this bulb should be lifted before frost and dried fully. Then take off dried foliage and store in perlite or vermiculite through the winter at a steady 55 to 60 degrees.

Achimenes After flowers fade, pack rhizomes in vermiculite and store in a cool place through winter.

Allium Leave in the ground and mulch each year until they overcrowd. Then dig up and replant in the spring or fall.

Anemone Leave poppy anemone in the ground, but in northern states, lift and store Greek (blanda) and apennine varieties in the fall.

Freesia Bulbs remain in the ground in the South, but elsewhere, they must be lifted and stored in a dry place until time for replanting.

Foxtail lily This tuberous-rooted plant prefers to remain in the ground, and should not be disturbed. Mulch it each fall with straw or wood chips.

Ranunculus Dig bulbs in the fall after foliage dies back and store through the winter in peat or perlite at 50 to 55 degrees.

Lilies This is a large family, but most prefer to remain in the ground.

INDEX

A

Achimenes, 94
Acidanthera, 92
Acroclinium, 43
Ageratum, 6, 9, 16, 40, 43, 75
Allium, 94
Alyssum, 9, 16, 21, 22, 23, 27, 28, 30, 39, 40, 41, 43-44, 80
Amaranth, 9, 12, 20, 23, 41, 44
   globe, 38, 40, 56
Ammobium, 44
Anchusa, 44-45
Anemone, 94
Antirrhinum. *See* Snapdragon
Arctotis. *See* African daisy
Aster, 14, 16, 18, 23, 32, 40, 45

B

Baby-blue-eyes, 16, 40, 62
Baby's-breath. *See* Gypsophila
Bachelor's button, 9, 16, 40
Balsam, bush, 45
Bean
   castor, 9, 41, 49, 75
   scarlet runner, 27, 36, 40
Begonia
   Reiger, 28
   tuberous, 77, 86-87, 94
   wax, 16, 24, 26, 28, 30, 32, 40, 41, 46, 81
Bells-of-Ireland. *See* Moluccella
Black-eyed Susan, 24, 36, 41, 65
Blanket flower. *See* Gaillardia
Bluebonnet, Texas, 59
Blue lace flower, 40, 46
Brachycome. *See* Swan River Daisy
Browallia, 16, 24, 30, 40, 47
Burning bush, 47
Butterfly flower, 40, 47

C

Caladium, 20, 32, 88, 94
Calendula, 9, 10, 14, 16, 18, 22, 38, 40, 41
Calliopsis. *See* Coreopsis
Callistephus. *See* Aster
Candytuft. *See* Iberis
Carnation, 21, 41, 49
Celosia, 59, 9, 12, 16, 21, 23, 38, 40, 49
Centaurea, 16, 40, 51-52, 53-54
Chinese-lantern, 38, 41
Chrysanthemum, 21, 50, 78

Cigar plant. *See* Cuphea
Clarkia, 16, 40, 41, 50, 56
Cleome, 9, 12, 16, 22, 23, 40, 41, 50-51
Cobaea, 12, 36, 40, 41
Cockscomb. *See* Celosia
Coleus, 9, 16, 20, 24, 51, 81
Coneflower, 41, 65
Convolvulus. *See* Morning glory
Coraldrops, 94
Coreopsis, 9, 14, 16, 22, 40, 41, 51
Cornflower, 9, 23, 40, 41, 51-52
Cosmos, 6, 9, 14, 16, 18, 20, 23, 32, 40, 41, 52, 81
Cup-and-saucer vine, 24, 36, 40, 41
Cupflower, 30, 62
Cuphea, 52
Cynoglossum, 52-53
Cypress, summer, 47

D

Dahlia, 6, 14, 16, 38, 41, 53, 77, 84-85, 94
Daisy
   African, 16, 41, 43
   cape, 48
   dahlberg, 53
   English, 78
   gloriosa, 12, 16, 41
   painted, 41
   shasta, 14, 38
   Swan River, 16, 41, 68
   tahoka, 41, 69
Delphinium. *See* Larkspur
Devil-in-a-bush. *See* Nigella
Dianthus, 9, 16, 18, 20, 21, 24, 40, 49, 64, 69, 75
Dimorphotheca, 48
Dusty miller, 20, 39, 40, 41, 53-54
Dyssodia, 53

E

Eschscholzia, 9, 40, 41, 48, 64
Eucomis, 91
Euphorbia, 16, 54
Everlasting, 40, 67

F

Farewell-to-spring. *See* Godetia
Feverfew, 38, 40, 41, 54
Fire bush, 47
Firecracker plant. *See* Cuphea
Fire-on-the-mountain, 16, 54

Flax, 9, 54-55
Flossflower. *See* Ageratum
Forget-me-not, 9, 22, 38, 40, 44-45, 52, 78
Four-o'clock, 9, 12, 16, 18, 21, 40, 41, 55
Foxglove, 27, 78
Freesia, 94

G

Gaillardia, 9, 16, 40, 41, 55
Galtonia, 94
Gazania, 5, 9, 18, 41, 55
Geranium, 14, 16, 20, 21, 23, 24, 27, 30, 41, 55-56, 75, 81
Ghost weed. *See* Euphorbia
Gladiolus, 83, 94
Godetia, 9, 41, 50, 56
Gomphrena. *See* Globe amaranth
Gypsophila, 9, 16, 40, 41, 56-57

H

Helianthus. *See* Sunflower
Helichrysum. *See* Strawflower
Heliotrope, 16, 21, 41, 57
Helipterum, 43
Hollyhock, 9, 16, 32, 57
Hymenocallis, 94

I-J

Iberis, 16, 18, 21, 28, 40, 41, 48
Ice plant, 57-58
Impatiens, 12, 16, 20, 24, 26, 28, 32, 41, 58, 81
Ismene, 94

K

Kale, flowering, 20, 21
Kochia, 16, 47

L

Lantana, 41, 58
Larkspur, 9, 16, 18, 38, 39, 40, 41, 58-59
Lathyrus. *See* Sweet Pea
Liatris, 14, 16, 18
Lily
   Aztec, 94
   calla, 90, 94
   canna, 77, 89, 94
   foxtail, 94

gloriosa, 91, 94
  pineapple, 91
Limonium, 67
Linaria, 59
Linum, 54-55
Lobelia, 9, 14, 16, 21, 23, 24, 27, 28, 30, 39, 40, 41, 59
Love-in-a-mist. See Nigella
Love-lies-bleeding, 12, 44
Lupine, 9, 27, 41, 59-60

M

Marigold, 5, 6, 9, 12, 14, 16, 20, 21, 38, 40, 41, 60, 75
Matricaria, 38, 54
Matthiola. See Stock
Mesembryanthemum. See Ice plant
Mexican fire plant, 54
Mignonette, 16, 21, 60
Mirabilis. See Four-o'clock
Moluccella, 16, 38, 40, 41, 46
Montbretia, 92
Moonflower, 36, 40, 41
Morning glory, 12, 18, 24, 27, 36, 40, 41, 51
Moss. See Portulaca
Myosotis. See Forget-me-not

N

Nasturtium, 9, 16, 21, 22, 24, 30, 32, 36, 40, 41, 61
Nemesia, 9, 16, 40, 61
Nemophila, 16, 41, 62
Nicotiana, 9, 12, 16, 21, 40, 41, 62
Nierembergia, 30, 52, 62
Nigella, 9, 16, 62-63

O

Oxalis, 94
Oxypetalum, 16

P-Q

Painted tongue. See Salpiglossis
Pansy, 6, 9, 16, 22, 23, 28, 30, 38, 39, 40, 41, 63, 75, 80
Papaver, See Poppy
Patient lucy. See Impatiens
Pelargonium. See Geranium
Periwinkle. See Vinca
Petunia, 5, 6, 9, 10, 12, 14, 16, 20, 21, 22, 24, 26, 28, 30, 40, 41, 63, 75
Phlox, 9, 14, 40, 41, 64

Pincushion flower. See Scabiosa
Pinks, 16, 40, 64
Plumosa. See Celosia
Poppy
  Alpine, 64
  California, 9, 40, 41, 48, 64
  Iceland, 9, 22, 41, 64
  Shirley, 24, 64
Portulaca, 40, 65
Primrose, 16, 22, 28

R

Ranunculus, 38, 94
Reseda. See Mignonette
Ricinus. See Castor bean
Rocky Mountain garland, 50
Rudbeckia, 12, 14, 16, 24, 36, 40, 65

S

Sage, scarlet, 40, 66
Salpiglossis, 5, 16, 65-66
Salvia, 5, 16, 38, 66
Satinflower. See Godetia
Scabiosa, 5, 66
Schizanthus, 47
Sea lavender. See Statice
Sedum, 23
Snapdragon, 6, 9, 12, 14, 16, 18, 20, 38, 40, 66-67, 76
Snow-on-the-mountain, 16, 54
Solidago, 14, 16
Spiderflower. See Cleome
Spiderplant. See Cleome
Sprekelia, 94
Statice, 12, 22, 38, 40, 41, 67
Stock, 16, 21, 41, 67
Strawflower, 38, 40, 67
Sunflower, 12, 18, 32, 40, 41, 68
  Mexican, 9, 32, 69, 75
Sweet pea, 18, 21, 36, 40, 41, 68, 79
Sweet sultan, 21, 41, 68-69
Sweet William, 16, 24, 41, 69

T-U

Tagetes. See Marigold
Thrift. See Statice
Tigridia, 94
Tithonia, 9, 32, 40, 69, 75
Toadflax, 59
Tobacco, flowering or ornamental. See Nicotiana
Torenia, 40, 69-70
Touch-me-not, 45-46

Trachymene. See Blue lace flower
Tritonia, 94
Tropaeolum. See Nasturtium
Tuberose, 94

V

Velvet flower. See Salpiglossis
Verbena, 9, 16, 21, 30, 39, 40, 41, 81
Vinca, 16, 18, 70
Viola sp. See Pansy

W-Y

Wax begonia. See Begonia, wax
Wishbone flower, 40, 69-70

Z

Zinnia, 5, 6, 9, 12, 14, 16, 18, 20, 21, 22, 30, 32, 38, 40, 41, 70, 75

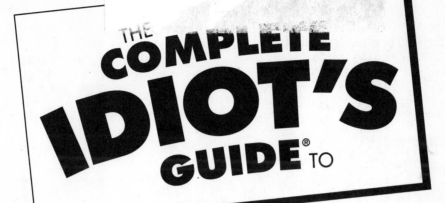

Rock Guitar Songs

A copublication of Alfred Publishing Co., Inc. and Penguin Group (USA) Inc.

Alfred Publishing Co., Inc.

Alpha Books
Publisher: *Marie Butler-Knight*
Editorial Director/Acquiring Editor: *Mike Sanders*
Managing Editor: *Billy Fields*
Senior Development Editor: *Phil Kitchel*
Senior Production Editor: *Janette Lynn*
Design and Layout: *Becky Harmon, Brian Massey*
Proofreader: *Aaron Black*

Alfred Publishing
Publishers: *Steven Manus and Ron Manus*
Editor-in-Chief: *L. C. Harnsberger*
Project Managers: *Aaron Stang and Kate Westin*
Senior Editor: *Kate Westin*
Instructional Text: *Jack Allen and Aaron Stang*
Biographical Text: *Jon Senge and Donny Trieu*
Engraving Manager: *Al Nigro*
Music Arrangers: *Jack Allen, Danny Begelman, Aaron Stang*

Contents

Reviewing the Basics

Getting to Know Your Guitar 1

The Parts of the Guitar 1

Using Your Right Hand 2

Using Your Left Hand 3

Tuning Your Guitar 4

The Basics of Music Notation 6

Reading Guitar Tablature (TAB) 11

Songs

After Midnight, Eric Clapton 14

All Along the Watchtower, Jimi Hendrix 18

American Idiot, Green Day 22

Back in Black, AC/DC 28

Bad Company, Bad Company 34

Bad to the Bone, George Thorogood and the Destroyers 38

Boulevard of Broken Dreams, Green Day 42

Casey Jones, Grateful Dead 46

China Grove, The Doobie Brothers 50

Dirty Deeds Done Dirt Cheap, AC/DC 54

Dr. Feelgood, Mötley Crüe 58

Europa (Earth's Cry Heaven's Smile), Santana 66

For What It's Worth, Buffalo Springfield 70

Gimme Some Lovin', The Spencer Davis Group 74

The House of the Rising Sun, The Animals 78

How You Remind Me, Nickelback 82

In-A-Gadda-Da-Vida, Iron Butterfly 86

Jump, Van Halen 90

Layla, Derek & the Dominos 96

Long Train Runnin', Doobie Brothers 104

Mama Told Me Not to Come, Three Dog Night 110

Panama, Van Halen 116

Peter Gunn, Duane Eddy 122

The Reason, Hoobastank 126

Sunshine of Your Love, Cream 132

Sweet Child O' Mine, Guns N' Roses 136

Truckin', Grateful Dead 142

Welcome to the Jungle, Guns N' Roses 148

When I Come Around, Green Day 156

Wild Night, Van Morrison 162

Appendixes

Appendix A: Chord Theory 169

Appendix B: Guitar Fingerboard Chart 179

Appendix C: Glossary 181

Artist Index

AC/DC
Back in Black 28
Dirty Deeds Done Dirt Cheap 54
The Animals
The House of the Rising Sun 78
Bad Company
Bad Company 34
Buffalo Springfield
For What It's Worth 70
Eric Clapton
After Midnight 14
Cream
Sunshine of Your Love 132
Derek & the Dominos
Layla 96
Doobie Brothers
China Grove 50
Long Train Runnin' 104
Duane Eddy
Peter Gunn 122
George Thorogood and the Destroyers
Bad to the Bone 38
Grateful Dead
Casey Jones 46
Truckin' 142
Green Day
American Idiot 22
Boulevard of Broken Dreams 42
When I Come Around 156
Guns N' Roses
Sweet Child O' Mine 136
Welcome to the Jungle 148
Jimi Hendrix
All Along the Watchtower 18
Hoobastank
The Reason 126
Iron Butterfly
In-A-Gadda-Da-Vida 86
Mötley Crüe
Dr. Feelgood 58
Nickelback
How You Remind Me 82
Santana
Europa (Earth's Cry Heaven's Smile) 66
The Spencer Davis Group
Gimme Some Lovin' 74
Three Dog Night
Mama Told Me Not to Come 110
Van Halen
Jump 90
Panama 116
Van Morrison
Wild Night 162

Introduction

We all play guitar for pretty much the same reason—to play our favorite songs. It's so easy to get caught up in mastering technique, learning to read music, or understanding music theory that we can spend hours at the instrument and still not have a good song to play. Note reading, technique, and theory are all great tools—but that's all they are. This is your chance to put all those tools together to play songs!

Learning all your favorite songs is the single most important musical learning experience you can have. All the songs in this book use related chords, scales, techniques, and other elements, so as you learn your favorite songs, you are actually learning the skills you need to play other favorites as well.

Everything is included to help you play every song. First, there is a review of the basics, like holding the guitar and reading music and TAB. Every song is then presented with a short introduction that explores the tricks to making it easy to play. All the music is shown in standard music notation, TAB, and guitar chords so you can choose which is best for you.

We suggest getting the recordings to all the songs in this book that you plan to learn. Listen to them often, and keep them handy as you learn each song. It's not important that you master every aspect of every song. You can focus on the parts that grab your attention the most—a lick you like, the melody, the chords, or just anything you *want* to play. As you gain experience, technique, and knowledge, putting the pieces together and learning the complete songs will get easier and easier.

Be sure to check out the other books in this series to see if there are other favorites you'd like to learn. If you want more information on playing the guitar, reading music, or even writing your own music, there are lots of other *Complete Idiot's Guides* to help you along.

Now tune your guitar, crank up the music, and dig in.

How to Use This Book

Some people approach learning an instrument by isolating all the technical skills and, through years of study and practice, develop a command of those skills and tools. Others learn simply by having a friend show them a simple song, and then proceed to learn on a song-by-song basis. Some combination of the two methods is probably the best, but you should always spend a good portion of your music time learning songs that you would really love to perform for your friends and family—or for yourself.

In this book, each song is written in full music notation and TAB (tablature). Reading music is a skill acquired through diligent practice, and it has many benefits. TAB offers a quick way of knowing what to play without having to be an accomplished music reader. We believe that providing TAB in conjunction with standard music notation is the ideal way to get you up and playing right away. All the guitar parts include TAB to show exactly where to fret each note. Guitar chord grids indicate chord fingerings for strumming and fingerpicking accompaniment parts.

Start by picking a song you really want to play. If you don't already have one, get a copy of the recording and listen to it carefully as you learn the song. Music is an aural art, so always have the sound of the song clearly in your head before you attempt to learn to play it on the guitar.

Read through the lesson that precedes each song and practice the music examples before attempting to play the whole song. Each lesson is broken into various sections. We've also included some sidebars along the way to point out things that are particularly important, interesting, or helpful.

Key Thoughts A brief introduction to the song.

 Take Note The main body of the lesson, with tips, pointers, excerpts, examples, and other helpful information.

 ## Guitar Gods

A thumbnail biography of the artist.

 ## Fun Fact

Interesting trivia about the artist or the song.

 ## Tip

Additional help, insight, and advice on topics in the lessons.

 ## Definition

Definitions of key terms used in the text.

If you want to know more about chords, be sure to read Appendix A. It will teach you about the different kinds of chords, how they are constructed, and what the symbols mean.

Appendix B is a diagram of the guitar fretboard, showing every note on every string up to the twelfth fret.

Finally, we've provided a glossary in Appendix C that covers all the music terms used throughout this book.

Acknowledgments

Special thanks to the Alfred Publishing writing, editing, and arranging team of Jack Allen, Danny Begelman, Al Nigro, Jon Senge, Aaron Stang, Donny Trieu, and Kate Westin. Thanks also to James Grupenhoff and Marcus Thomas for licensing, and to Steve Manus, Ron Manus, and Link Harnsberger for initiating and supporting this project.

Trademarks

All terms mentioned in this book that are known to be or are suspected of being trademarks or service marks have been appropriately capitalized. Alpha Books/Penguin Group (USA) Inc. and Alfred Publishing Co., Inc. cannot attest to the accuracy of this information. Use of a term in this book should not be regarded as affecting the validity of any trademark or service mark.

Reviewing the Basics

Getting to Know Your Guitar

You may or may not be able to name all the parts of your guitar, and you may or may not need to. If you ever get into a conversation with another guitarist, however, it will probably go better if you know what is being referred to as "the nut" or "the bridge."

The Parts of the Guitar

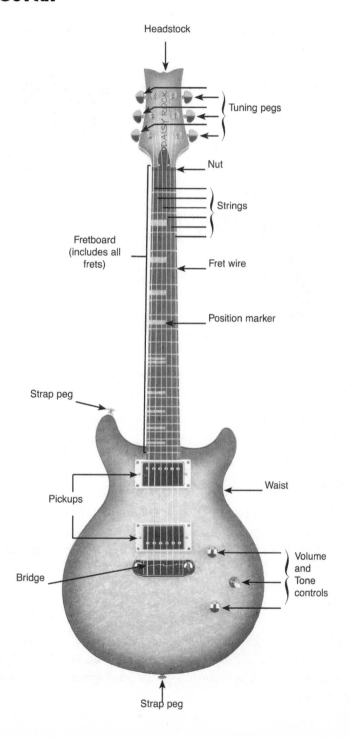

Headstock

Tuning pegs

Nut

Strings

Fretboard
(includes all
frets)

Fret wire

Position marker

Strap peg

Pickups

Waist

Bridge

Volume
and
Tone
controls

Strap peg

How to Hold Your Guitar

Below are two typical ways of holding your guitar. Pick the one that is most comfortable for you.

Sitting.

Standing with a strap.

Using Your Right Hand

Sometimes your right hand will play individual notes on a single string, and sometimes it will play chords using many strings. To *strum* means to play several strings by brushing quickly across them, either with a pick or with your fingers. This is the most common way of playing a chord.

Tip

Strumming is done mostly from the wrist, not the arm. Use as little motion as possible. Start as close to the string as you can, and never let your hand move past the edge of the guitar.

Strumming with a Pick

Hold the pick between your thumb and index finger. Hold it firmly, but don't squeeze too hard.

On a *down-stroke*, strum from the lowest note of the chord to the highest note of the chord. Move mostly your wrist, not just your arm. For an *up-stroke*, strike the strings from highest to lowest.

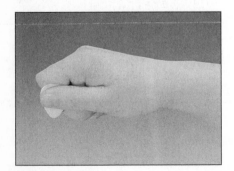

Holding the pick.

Starting near the lowest string.

Finishing near the highest string.

Using Your Left Hand

Your left hand needs to be relaxed when you play. It's also important to keep your fingernails neat and trim so that your fingers will curve in just the right way, otherwise you'll hear lots of buzzing and muffling.

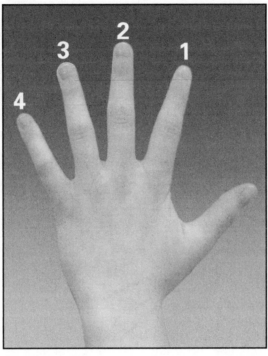

The left hand finger numbers.

Proper Left Hand Position

Your left hand fingers will work best when your hand is correctly shaped and positioned. Place your hand so your thumb rests comfortably in the middle of the back of the neck and your wrist is away from the fingerboard. Position your fingers on the front of the neck as if you are gently squeezing a ball between them and your thumb. Keep your elbow in and your fingers curved.

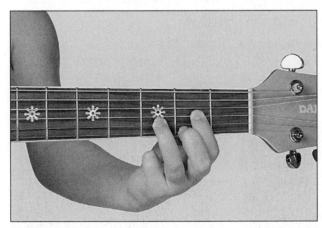

Front view.

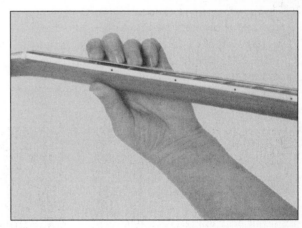

Top view.

3

Placing a Finger on a String

When you press a string with a left hand finger, make sure you press firmly with the tip of your finger and as close to the fret wire as you can without actually being right on it. This will create a clean, bright tone. If your finger is too far from the fret wire, the note will buzz. If it is on top of the fret wire, you'll get a muffled, unclear sound. Also, make sure your finger stays clear of neighboring strings.

Right! The finger is close to the fret wire.

Wrong! The finger is too far from the fret wire.

Wrong! The finger is on top of the fret wire.

Tuning Your Guitar

Every musician knows the agony of hearing an instrument that is not in tune. Always be sure to tune your guitar every time you play, and check the tuning every now and then between songs.

About the Tuning Pegs

First, make sure your strings are wound properly around the tuning pegs. They should go from the inside to the outside as shown in the illustration. Some guitars have all six tuning pegs on the same side of the headstock. If this is the case, make sure all six strings are wound the same way, from the inside out.

Turning a tuning peg clockwise makes the pitch lower. Turning a tuning peg counter-clockwise makes the pitch higher. Be sure not to tune the strings too high, or you run the risk of breaking them.

Tip

Always remember that the thinnest, highest-sounding string, the one closest to the floor, is the *1st* string. The thickest, lowest-sounding string, the one closest to the ceiling, is the *6th* string. When guitarists say "the top string," they are referring to the highest-sounding string, and "the bottom string" is the lowest-sounding string.

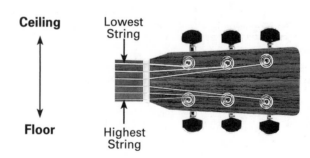

4

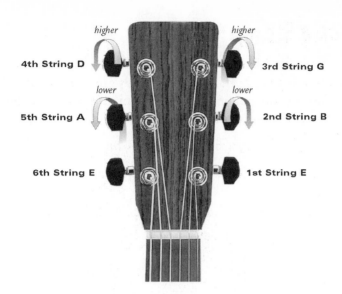

Tuning the Guitar to Itself

When your 6th string is in tune, you can tune the rest of the strings using the guitar by itself. The easiest way to tune the 6th string is with a piano. If you don't have a piano available, consider buying an electronic tuner or pitch pipe. There are many types available, and a salesperson at your local music store can help you decide which is best for you.

The 6th string is tuned to the E below middle C.

If you have access to a piano, tune the 6th string to the note E below middle C.

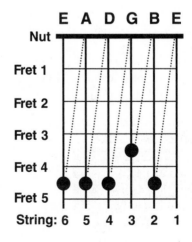

To tune the rest of the strings, follow this sequence:

- ◆ Press 5th fret of 6th string to get pitch of 5th string (A).
- ◆ Press 5th fret of 5th string to get pitch of 4th string (D).
- ◆ Press 5th fret of 4th string to get pitch of 3rd string (G).
- ◆ Press 4th fret of 3rd string to get pitch of 2nd string (B).
- ◆ Press 5th fret of 2nd string to get pitch of 1st string (E).

5

The Basics of Music Notation

Standard music notation contains a plethora of musical information. If you don't already read notation, you will probably benefit from studying the following fundamental concepts. Understanding even a little about reading notation can help you create a performance that is true to the original.

Notes

Notes are used to indicate musical sounds. Some notes are held long and others are short.

Note Values

whole note	𝅝	4 beats
half note	𝅗𝅥	2 beats
quarter note	𝅘𝅥	1 beat
eighth note	𝅘𝅥𝅮	½ beat
sixteenth note	𝅘𝅥𝅯	¼ beat

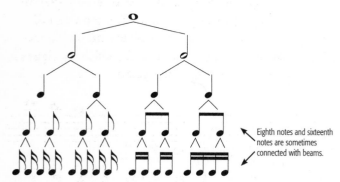

Eighth notes and sixteenth notes are sometimes connected with beams.

Relative note values.

When a *dot* follows a note, the length of the note is longer by one half of the note's original length.

Dotted Note Values

dotted half note	𝅗𝅥.	3 beats
dotted quarter note	𝅘𝅥.	1½ beats
dotted eighth note	𝅘𝅥𝅮.	¾ beat

A *triplet* is a group of three notes played in the time of two. Triplets are identified by a small numeral "3" over the note group.

Quarter-note triplet.

Rests

Rests are used to indicate musical silence.

Rest Values

whole rest	▬	4 beats
half rest	▬	2 beats
quarter rest	𝄽	1 beat
eighth rest	𝄾	½ beat
sixteenth rest	𝄿	¼ beat

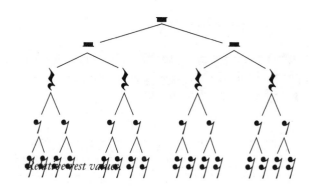

Relative rest values.

The Staff

Music is written on a *staff* made up of five lines and four spaces, numbered from the bottom up. Each line and space is designated as a different pitch.

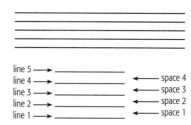

line 5 ⟶ _____ ⟵ space 4
line 4 ⟶ _____ ⟵ space 3
line 3 ⟶ _____ ⟵ space 2
line 2 ⟶ _____ ⟵ space 1
line 1 ⟶ _____

The staff is divided into equal units of time called *measures* or *bars*.

Measure.

A *bar line* indicates where one measure ends and another begins.

Bar line.

A *double bar line*, made of one thin line and one thick line, shows the end of a piece of music.

Double bar line.

Notes on the Staff

Notes are named using the first seven letters of the alphabet (A B C D E F G). The higher a note is on the staff, the higher its pitch.

E F G A B C D E F

The *treble clef*, also called the *G clef*, is the curly symbol you see at the beginning of each staff. The treble clef designates the second line of the staff as the note G.

Here are the notes on the lines of the treble staff. An easy way to remember them is with the phrase "Every Good Boy Does Fine."

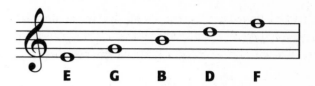

E G B D F

Notes on the lines.

Here are the notes on the spaces. They are easy to remember because they spell the word FACE.

F A C E

Notes on the spaces.

The staff can be extended to include even higher or lower notes by using *ledger lines*. You can think of ledger lines as small pieces of additional staff lines and spaces. The lowest note in the following figure is the open low E string of the guitar.

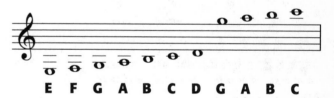

E F G A B C D G A B C

Notes on ledger lines.

Accidentals

An *accidental* raises or lowers the sound of a note. A *sharp* ♯ raises a note one *half step*, which is the distance from one fret to another. A *flat* ♭ lowers a note one half step. A *natural* ♮ cancels a sharp or a flat. An accidental remains in effect until the end of the measure, so if the same note has to be played flat or sharp again, only the first one will have the accidental. See the Guitar Fingerboard Chart on page 180 for all the flat and sharp notes on the guitar up to the 12th fret.

HALF STEPS • NO FRET BETWEEN

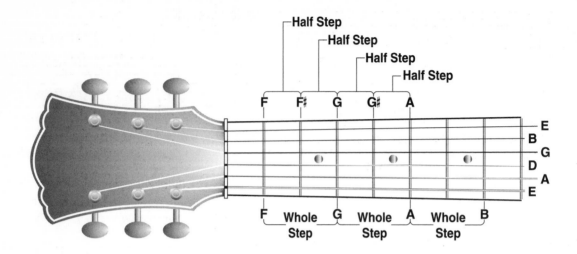

WHOLE STEPS • ONE FRET BETWEEN

Key Signatures

Sometimes certain notes need to be played sharp or flat throughout an entire song. In this case, it's easier to put the sharps or flats in the *key signature* instead of putting an accidental on each individual note. If you see sharps or flats at the beginning of a staff just after the treble clef, that means to play those notes sharp or flat throughout the music. The key signature can change within a song as well, so be sure to keep an eye out. Below are two examples of key signatures.

Play each F, C, and G as F♯, C♯, and G♯.

Play each B and E as B♭ and E♭.

Time Signatures

The *time signature* is a symbol resembling a fraction that appears at the beginning of the music. The top number tells you how many beats are in each measure, and the bottom number tells you what kind of note gets one beat. Most songs have the same number of beats in every measure, but the time signature can also change within a song. It's important to notice each time signature and count correctly, otherwise you could end up getting ahead in the song or falling behind.

4/4 Time

Count: 1 2 3 4   1 2 3 4   1 2 3 4

4 (top) = 4 beats to a measure

4 (bottom) = quarter note ♩ gets 1 beat

C is a time signature that means the same as 4/4.

3/4 Time

Count: 1 & 2 & 3 &   1   2   3   1   2   3   1   2   3

3 = 3 beats to a measure
4 = quarter note ♩ gets 1 beat

6/8 Time

Count: 1 2 3 4 5 6   1 2 3 4 5 6   1 2 3 4 5 6   1 2 3 4 5 6

6 = 6 beats to a measure
8 = eighth note ♪ gets 1 beat

9/8 Time

Count: 1 2 3 4 5 6 7 8 9   1 2 3 4 5 6 7 8 9

1 2 3 4 5 6 7 8 9   1 2 3 4 5 6 7 8 9

9 = 9 beats to a measure
8 = eighth note ♪ gets 1 beat

12/8 Time

Count: 1 2 3 4 5 6 7 8 9 10 11 12   1 2 3 4 5 6 7 8 9 10 11 12

1 2 3 4 5 6 7 8 9 10 11 12   1 2 3 4 5 6 7 8 9 10 11 12

12 = 12 beats to a measure
8 = eighth note ♪ gets 1 beat

Ties

A *tie* is a curved line that joins two or more notes of the same pitch, which tells you to play them as one continuous note. Instead of playing the second note, continue to hold for the combined note value. Ties make it possible to write notes that last longer than one measure, or notes with unusual values.

Hold B for five beats.

The Fermata

A *fermata* ⌒ over a note means to pause, holding for about twice as long as usual.

Pause on notes with a fermata.

Repeat Signs

Most songs don't start and then ramble on in one continuous stream of thought to the end. They are constructed with sections, such as verses and choruses, that are repeated in some organized pattern. To avoid having to go through pages and pages of duplicate music, several different types of *repeat signs* are used to show what to play over again. Repeat signs act as a kind of roadmap, telling you when to go back and where to go next, navigating you through the song.

Repeat Dots

The simplest repeat sign is simply two dots on the inside of a double bar. It means to go back to the beginning and play the music over again.

Go back and play again.

When just a section of music is to be repeated, an opposite repeat sign at the beginning of the section tells you to repeat everything in between.

Repeat everything between facing repeat signs.

1st and 2nd Endings

When a section is repeated but the ending needs to be different, the *1st ending* shows what to play the first time, and the *2nd ending* shows what to play the second time. Play the 1st ending, repeat, then skip the 1st ending and play the 2nd ending.

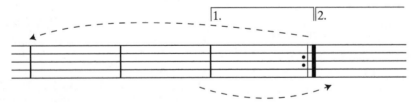

Play the 1st ending, repeat, then skip to the 2nd ending.

Other Repeat Signs

D.C. al Fine	Repeat from the beginning and end at ***Fine***.
D.C. al Coda	Repeat from the beginning and play to the coda sign ✛, then skip to the ***Coda*** and play to the end.
D.S. al Fine	Repeat from the sign 𝄋 and end at ***Fine***.
D.S. al Coda	Repeat from the sign 𝄋 and play to the coda sign ✛, then skip to the ***Coda*** and play to the end.

Reading Guitar Tablature (TAB)

Tablature, or *TAB* for short, is a graphic representation of the six strings of the guitar. Although standard notation gives you all the information you need to play a song, the TAB staff tells you quickly where to finger each note on the guitar. The bottom line of the TAB staff represents the 6th string, and the top line is the 1st string. Notes and chords are indicated by the placement of fret numbers on each string.

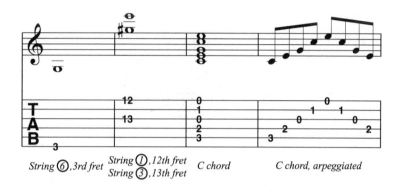

String ⑥,3rd fret   String ①,12th fret   C chord   C chord, arpeggiated
String ③,13th fret

The following are examples of various guitar techniques you might come across in the notation of the songs. Unless otherwise indicated, the left hand does the work for these.

Bending Notes

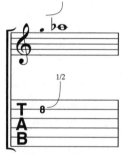

Half step: Play the note and bend the string one half step (the sound of one fret).

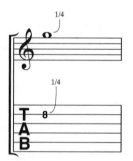

Slight bend/quarter-tone bend: Play the note and bend the string slightly sharp.

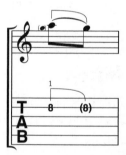

Prebend and release: Play the already-bent string, then immediately drop it down to the fretted note.

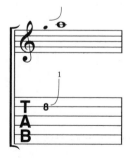

Whole step: Play the note and bend the string one whole step (the sound of two frets).

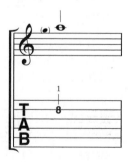

Prebend (ghost bend): Bend to the specified note before the string is plucked.

Unison bends: Play both notes and immediately bend the lower note to the same pitch as the higher note.

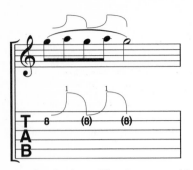

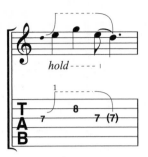

Bend and release: Play the note and bend to the next pitch, then release to the original note. Only the first note is attacked.

Bends involving more than one string: Play the note and bend the string while playing an additional note on another string. Upon release, relieve the pressure from the additional note, allowing the original note to sound alone.

Bends involving stationary notes: Play both notes and immediately bend the lower note up to pitch. Return as indicated.

Articulations

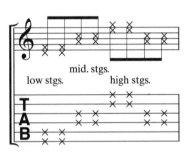

Hammer-on: Play the lower note, then "hammer" your left hand finger onto the string to sound the higher note. Only the first note is plucked.

Muted strings: A percussive sound is produced by striking the strings with the right hand while laying the fret hand across them.

Pull-off: Play the higher note with your first finger already in position on the lower note. Pull your finger off the first note with a strong downward motion that plucks the string, sounding the lower note.

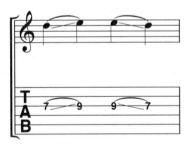

Palm mute: The notes are muted (muffled) by placing the palm of the right hand lightly on the strings, just in front of the bridge.

Legato slide: Play the first note, and with continued pressure applied to the string, slide up to the second note. The diagonal line shows that it is a slide and not a hammer-on or a pull-off.

Harmonics

Natural harmonic: Lightly touch the string with the fret hand at the note indicated in the TAB and pluck the string, producing a bell-like sound called a harmonic.

Artificial harmonic: Fret the note at the first TAB number, then use a right hand finger to lightly touch the string at the fret indicated in parentheses (usually 12 frets higher than the fretted note), and pluck the string with an available right hand finger or your pick.

Tremolo Bar

Specified inteval: The pitch of a note or chord is lowered to the specified interval and then returned as indicated. The action of the tremolo bar is graphically represented by the peaks and valleys of the diagram.

Unspecified interval: The pitch of a note or chord is lowered, usually very dramatically, until the pitch of the string becomes indeterminate.

Pick Direction

Down-strokes and up-strokes: The down-stroke is indicated with this symbol ⊓, and the up-stroke is indicated with this one ∨.

Rhythm Slashes

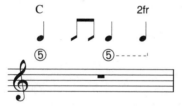

Strum marks with rhythm slashes: Strum with the indicated rhythm pattern. Strum marks can be located above the staff or within the staff.

Single notes with rhythm slashes: Sometimes single notes are incorporated into a strum pattern. The note name is given, with the string number in a circle and the fret number indicated.

After Midnight

Key Thoughts

At the tender age of 25, with a stellar career behind him that included playing with the Yardbirds, John Mayall, Cream, and Blind Faith, Eric Clapton announced his arrival as a solo artist with the crashing F chord at the beginning of "After Midnight."

Take Note

"After Midnight" features a fast, funky rhythm. Keep your wrist loose and relaxed. Be prepared to give your right arm a little bit of a workout due to relentless strumming interspersed with an occasional hammer-on flourish.

Note the pick directions in the following rhythm pattern. Maintain a constant sixteenth-note down-and-up rhythm, and make sure your pick only contacts the strings on the indicated beats.

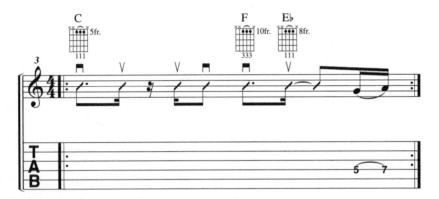

Tip

If you've ever heard J. J. Cale's recording of "After Midnight," you know that he wrote the song at a much slower tempo. It might behoove you to start learning the song at J. J. Cale's laid-back-boogie speed and gradually accelerate up to Slowhand's not-so-slow version.

Guitar Gods

Though internationally revered as one of the greatest guitarists of a generation, **ERIC CLAPTON** was surprisingly reluctant to break out as a solo artist. In 1970, his self-titled solo debut peaked at No. 13 with the hits "After Midnight," "Let It Rain," and "Blues Power," but before the record even hit store shelves, Clapton took himself out of the spotlight to form Derek & the Dominos. Four years and a kicked drug addiction later, he made his permanent return as a solo artist, reaching No. 1 with *461 Ocean Boulevard*.

This song is in the key of C and contains the chords C, E♭, F, and G. This chord progression is a perfect vehicle for improvising a solo using the *minor pentatonic scale*, which is a five-note scale. The notes of the C minor pentatonic scale are C, E♭, F, G, and B♭.

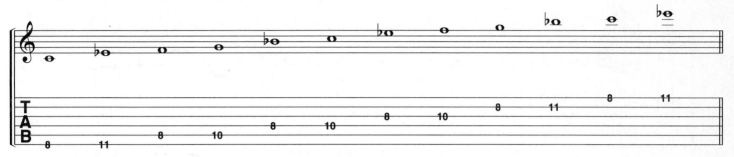

C minor pentatonic scale.

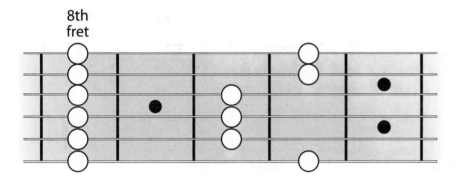

Use the notes in the scale above to create your own solo on "After Midnight." In the bluesy style of the song, some of the notes are characteristically bent to a higher pitch. In particular, experiment with bending the F note on the tenth fret of the 3rd string up a whole step to G, and bend the B♭ note on the eleventh fret of the 2nd string up a whole step to C. Yeah! Now you're jamming. "It's all gonna be peaches and cream."

AFTER MIDNIGHT

Words and Music by
JOHN CALE

Lyrics:
1. Af - ter mid - night,_____ we gon' let it all_____ hang_____ down.
2. Af - ter mid - night,_____ we gon' shake your tam - bou - rine.

All Along the Watchtower

Key Thoughts

"All Along the Watchtower" marries the incomparable lyrical genius of Bob Dylan and the undisputed instrumental prowess of Jimi Hendrix. It features a minimalist chord progression of C#m–B–A–B throughout, but Jimi maintains your interest by varying the style of his solos with electric blues riffs; Hawaiian-influenced slide glissandos (played with a cigarette lighter); jazzy, Wes Montgomery-style octaves; and a funky wah-wah workout.

Take Note

The intro opens the song with a bang. A reverb-drenched 12-string acoustic guitar, thunderous drums, booming bass guitar, and even a Vibra-Slap lead us into Jimi's slinky, melodic opening solo.

Watch yourself with the syncopated rhythm. The "off" accents on the drums will do their best to fool you into believing you're playing "on the beat," until the verse comes and shows you're half a beat off. Count and follow the notation, and you'll be alright.

With four full guitar solos in fewer than four minutes, "All Along the Watchtower" is a lead guitarist's tour de force. Our transcription only contains the intro guitar solo, so we'll show you some key elements to play during the other solos in the examples that follow. Use these examples as starting points for creating your own solos. Live recordings reveal that Jimi Hendrix rarely copied his own studio solos note-for-note when he performed, so feel free to improvise your own and perhaps soon you'll experience how "the wind begins to howl."

The first example is a trademark Jimi Hendrix line derived from a minor pentatonic scale. This occurs at the end of the second solo (about 1:05 on the original recording).

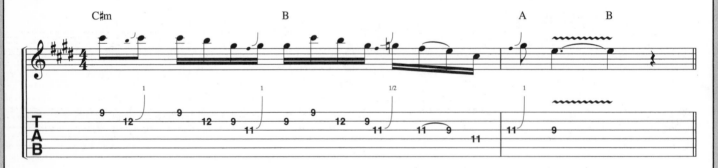

☆ Fun Fact ☆

Bob Dylan originally recorded "All Along the Watchtower" with a sparse folk accompaniment. Jimi Hendrix chose to redefine the song as an electrified exploration of a chilly, fog-enshrouded landscape. The Hendrix cover has become such a definitive version that Bob Dylan himself usually performs the song in a style more akin to Jimi's than his own.

The next example is halfway through the third solo (at 1:59 on the recording). Jimi picks up a cigarette lighter and uses it as a slide for these graceful glissandos.

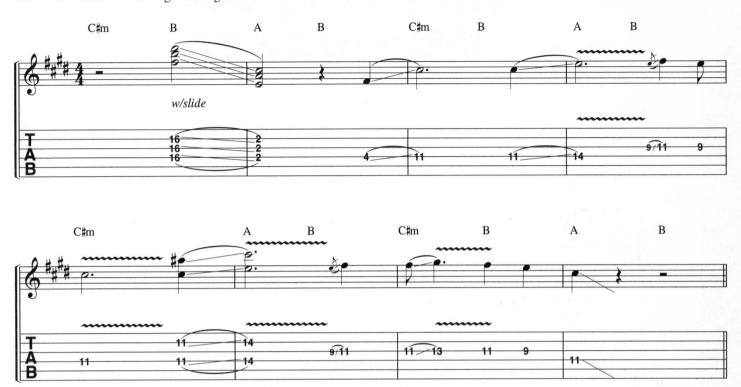

Octaves ascending up the C♯ minor pentatonic scale come immediately after the slide part. Use your left hand index finger on the 3rd string and your little finger on the 1st string. The fleshy part of your index finger should come across the 2nd string to mute it; that way you can use your pick in broad rhythmic strokes across all top three strings without getting extraneous notes.

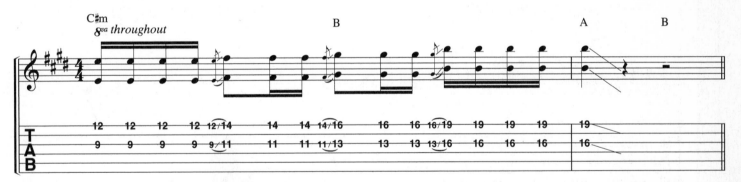

The last example is a groovy pattern that Jimi brings in at 2:33. To recreate the feel of his rhythm, it helps to slide your left hand up into each position. On the first two chords, Jimi simply adds his little finger to create an "add 9" chord for just an instant. This tasty embellishment is finished off with dissonant double stops.

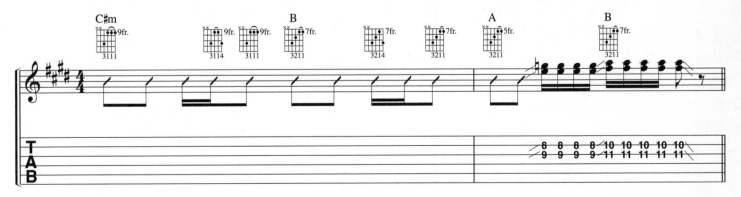

19

ALL ALONG THE WATCHTOWER

To match recorded key, tune guitar down one half step.

Words and Music by
BOB DYLAN

1. "There must be some kind of way   out of here,"   said the jok - er   to the   thief.___
2. "No   rea-son   to   get   ex - cit - ed,"   the thief, he   kind - ly   spoke.
3. *See additional lyrics*

"There's too much con - fu - sion,   I   can't   get   no   re - lief.___
"There are man - y   here   a - mong   us   who feel that life   is but   a joke,___   but,

All Along the Watchtower - 2 - 1

Verse 3:
All along the watchtower,
Princes kept the view.
While all the women came and went,
Barefoot servants, too.
Well, outside in the cold distance,
A wild cat did growl.
Two riders were approaching
And the wind began to howl.
(To Outro:)

American Idiot

Green Day's multiple Grammy Award-winning album *American Idiot* brought classic three-chord rock and roll to a new level of artistry, refinement, and social expression. The title track is based on a driving power-chord riff. Grab your electric guitar, crank up the overdrive on your amp, and let loose!

The first thing you might notice is that the song is in the key of A♭, having four flats in the key signature. Part of Green Day's writing process for this album involved exploring new keys, so although we could have simplified the key to G or A, we decided to leave it intact in recognition of the band's intent to break away from traditional guitar keys. Hopefully it will help you do the same!

The opening guitar part is straight-ahead, power-chord rock. We've indicated the full barre chord fingerings because many people find it easier to hold the full barre chord while striking just the bottom strings (as shown in the TAB). Also, if some extra strings get hit, they're part of the chord and will still sound okay.

Here is the opening riff. It forms the basis for most of the song, so once you have it down, you're ready to rock.

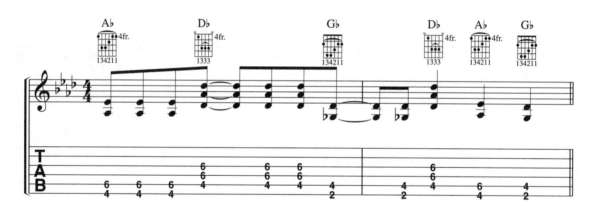

Guitar Gods

Rising from the northern-California underground punk scene, **GREEN DAY** found mainstream success in the 1990s with albums heavily rooted in the brand of punk created by the Ramones and Buzzcocks. Their 2004 release, *American Idiot*, came as quite a surprise from a band that had established itself on catchy three-chord punk-pop songs. A lyrically aggressive and politically charged rock opera, the album was the group's biggest critical success and established Green Day as much more than just a punk band.

AMERICAN IDIOT

Words by BILLIE JOE
Music by GREEN DAY

American Idiot - 5 - 1

Back in Black

You've got to love AC/DC. These guys literally define cool guitar riffs, and "Back in Black" features several of them.

Take
Note
In the first two bars of the intro, the guitar just counts off time with the hi-hat, then the main riff for the intro and verse kicks off in bar 3. The phrase starts with simple 1st-position E, D, and A chords. Listen to the recording and imitate the rhythm; strike the chords aggressively and cut each one short. The chords are followed by an E minor pentatonic scale riff in 1st position. After playing the open B, strike the A on the 3rd string, immediately bend it up, return, and release to open G. The first two bars of the phrase are shown below.

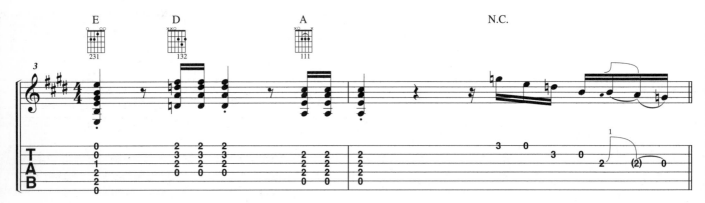

Now, let's try the second half of the intro/verse figure. It starts exactly like the first half, but ends with a highly *syncopated* (off-beat) pattern. The left hand fingers to use are shown in the following example. Notice that the ascending notes on the 6th string have both *staccato* (·) and *accent* (>) marks, telling you to play them cut short and with emphasis. Listen to the recording for guidance, and work on this passage until you can play it in your sleep. It is the key to playing the interlude guitar part that comes later.

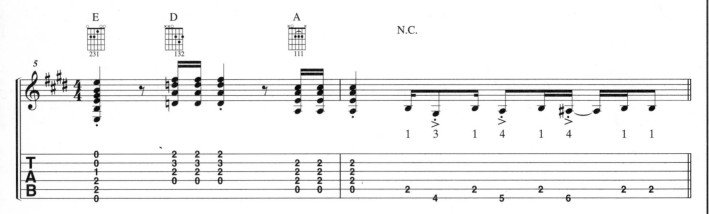

Below is the interlude figure, which is really just an expanded version of the previous riff. In the intro, the ascending notes G#–A–A# are cut short, but in the interlude, they are sustained. Also, the ascending line in the intro begins on a G#, but in the interlude it is a G♮ that is then pulled sharp, almost to G#, with a large vibrato action.

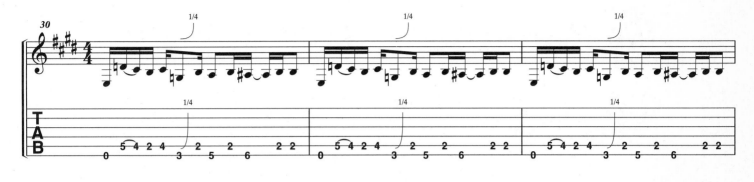

The chorus is straightforward rhythm guitar shown with rhythm slashes above the melody. Notice the indication in bars 17 and 18 to play the 6th string at the third fret. To clarify this part, we've written it below in notation and TAB so you can compare it to the rhythm slash notation. They both tell you to play the same thing.

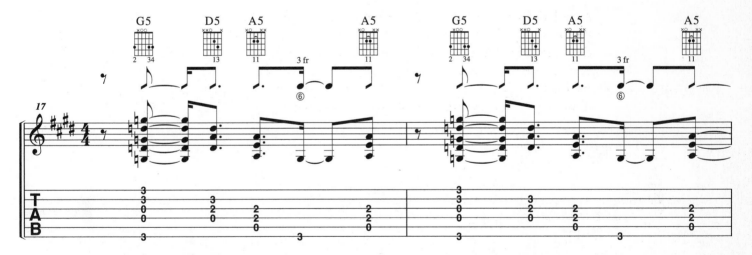

Guitar Gods

AC/DC was formed in 1973 by rhythm guitarist Malcolm Young in Australia. The AC/DC sound is minimal, but thunderous. It features a tight, steady rhythm section (anchored by Malcolm's stellar rhythm playing); screaming, melodic, blues-based vocals; and fluid, scorching guitar solos courtesy of Malcolm's brother, Angus. The band lost their original singer, Bon Scott, after the release of their most successful album to date, *Highway to Hell* (1979). Remarkably, the band regrouped and immediately recorded a follow-up with a new singer, Brian Johnson. The album *Back in Black* was released in 1980 and proved to be the band's career-defining album. In 2003, AC/DC was inducted into the Rock and Roll Hall of Fame.

BACK IN BLACK

Words and Music by
ANGUS YOUNG, MALCOLM YOUNG
and BRIAN JOHNSON

Moderate rock ♩ = 94

Intro:

1. Back in black,__ I hit the sack, I've been too long, I'm glad__ to be back, yes, I
2. *See additional lyrics*

am. Let loose from the noose that's kept me hang-in' a-bout.__ I keep

look-in' at the sky 'cause it's get-tin' me high, for-get the hearse 'cause I'll nev-er die. I got

Back in Black - 4 - 1

Chorus:

back,_____ back,_____ well, I'm

back,_____ yeah, back,_____ yeah.

Back,_____ back._____

Back in black,___ yes, I'm back in___ black._____ I wan-na say___ it.

Guitar Solo 2:
(w/ad lib. lead guitar based on E minor pentatonic scale)

Repeat and fade

w/Rhy. Fig. 2 *(Elec. Gtr.)*

Verse 2:
Back in the back of a Cadillac,
Number one with a bullet, I'm a power pack.
Yes, I'm in a band, with the gang,
They got to catch me if they want me to hang.
'Cause I'm back on the track and I'm beating the flack,
Nobody's gonna get me on another rap.
So, look at me now, I'm just makin' my play,
Don't try to push your luck, just get outta my way.
'Cause I'm back,…
(To Chorus:)

Bad Company

Bad Company was formed in 1973 by four former members of Free, Mott the Hoople, and King Crimson. Though the record company wanted to call the band the Heavy Metal Kids, singer Paul Rodgers insisted on naming the band after a 1972 Robert Benton film, *Bad Company*.

Though the signature instrumental figure to "Bad Company" is really played on piano, we've arranged the introduction and verse here for guitar. It is best to perform this section fingerstyle, handling the down-stem notes with your thumb and playing the up-stem notes with your fingers. You'll need your pick for the chorus, though, so keep it close by *palming* it.

Definition

Palming the pick means holding it in the palm of your hand with your ring finger, while keeping your index and middle fingers free.

In measure 25, the piano figure is taken over by a guitar playing power chords, starting with a pickup on beats 3 and 4 that leads into the chorus at measure 26. These power chords are best played full force with a pick. (See "Dirty Deeds Done Dirt Cheap" for an explanation of power chords.)

That's it! Probably the most challenging part of playing this song is mastering the transition from fingerstyle to pick and back again.

☆ Fun Fact ☆

Bad Company recorded their debut album at Headley Grange, a seventeenth-century three-story manor house in southern England that bands such as Led Zeppelin, Fleetwood Mac, and Genesis often used as a retreat for writing and rehearsing new material. The track for "Bad Company" was recorded using Led Zeppelin's mobile studio in a field outside Headley Grange under a full moon.

BAD COMPANY

To match recorded key, tune guitar down one half step.

Words and Music by
PAUL RODGERS and SIMON KIRKE

Bad to the Bone

When George Thorogood set out to emulate the giants of blues, he set his sights particularly on the primitive blues of the "Boogie Man" John Lee Hooker. He nailed John Lee's raw, one-chord, blues-boogie sound perfectly with "Bad to the Bone."

"Bad to the Bone" is played in *Open G tuning* with a slide bar (though you can play it without a slide). Open G tuning is a very popular alternate tuning that allows slide guitarists to play full chords simply by placing the slide bar across all the strings. To tune to open G, tune the 6th string down to D, an octave below the open 4th-string D. Then, tune the 5th string down to G, an octave below the open 3rd-string G. Do not change the tuning of the 4th, 3rd, and 2nd strings, but tune the 1st string down to D, an octave above the open 4th-string D.

The song is written in $\frac{12}{8}$. Technically, this means there are twelve beats per measure and an eighth note gets one beat. From a practical point of view, what you'll really feel is four strong beats per measure (where you tap your foot), and each beat is subdivided into three eighth notes.

This whole song is based on a signature riff of only three chords: G, C, and B♭. If you're using a slide, use it for the chords at the fifth and third frets. To play without a slide, use a 3rd-finger barre at the fifth fret, and a 1st-finger barre at the third fret. Play with an aggressive blues feel, and you've got it made.

☆ Fun Fact ☆

George Thorogood was originally a minor-league baseball player, but turned his life toward music after seeing John Paul Hammond perform in 1970.

🎼 Tip

Slides come in all shapes and sizes. The lighter your strings, the thinner and lighter your slide needs to be so that the weight of it won't press the strings down to the frets. The reverse is also true: the heavier your strings, the heavier the slide needs to be to dig tone out of the guitar. Most guitarists wear the slide on either the little finger or the ring finger.

BAD TO THE BONE

Open G tuning:
⑥ = D ③ = G
⑤ = G ② = B
④ = D ① = D

Words and Music by
GEORGE THOROGOOD

Moderately ♩. = 98   *Intro:*

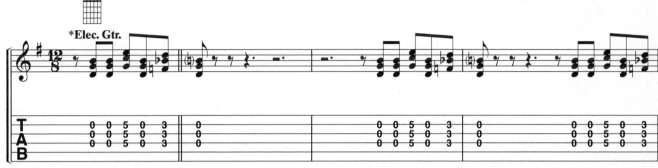

Chord shapes are played with slide worn on pinky or with fingers 3 and 1.

Band enters

w/slide

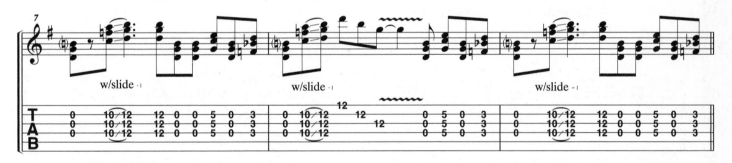

w/slide   w/slide   w/slide

𝄉 *Verses 1, 2, & 4:*

Cont. rhy. simile

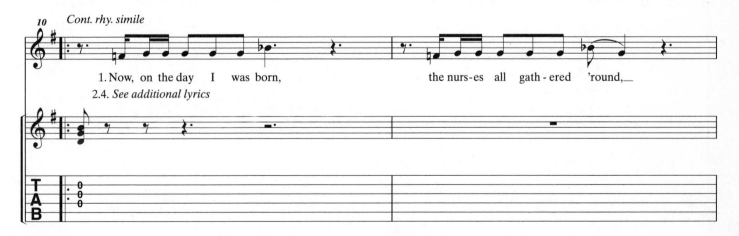

1. Now, on the day I was born,   the nurs-es all gath-ered 'round,__
2.4. *See additional lyrics*

Bad to the Bone - 3 - 1

and they gazed in wide won - der   at the joy they had found.__

The head nurse spoke up,   said, "Leave this one a - lone."__

She could tell right a - way__   that I was bad to the bone.

1.

Bad__ to the bone.   Bad__ to the bone.

B - b - b - b - b - b - b - bad,__   b - b - b - b - b - b - b - bad.__

B - b - b - b - b - b - b - bad,__   bad__ to the bone.

2.3.

B - b - b - b - b - b - b - bad,__   b - b - b - b - b - b - b - bad.__

To Coda ⊕

B - b - b - b - b - b - b - bad,__   bad__ to the bone.

Guitar Solo 1:
(ad lib., use intro as a model for improv.)   *Repeat as necessary*   *Last time*

Verse 3:
Cont. rhy. simile

I'll make a rich wom - an beg,__   and I'll make a good wom - an steal.

Bad to the Bone - 3 - 2

Verse 2:
I broke a thousand hearts
Before I met you.
I'll break a thousand more, baby,
Before I am through.
I wanna be yours, pretty baby,
Yours and yours alone.
I'm here to tell ya, honey,
That I'm bad to the bone,
Bad to the bone.
B-b-b-b-b-b-b bad,
B-b-b-b-b-b-b bad.
B-b-b-b-b-b-b bad,
Bad to the bone.
(To Guitar Solo 1:)

Verse 4:
Now, when I walk the streets,
Kings and Queens step aside.
Every woman I meet, heh, heh,
They all stay satisfied.
I wanna tell you, pretty baby,
What I see I make my own.
And I'm here to tell ya, honey,
That I'm bad to the bone,
Bad to the bone.
B-b-b-b-b-b-b bad,
B-b-b-b-b-b-b bad.
B-b-b-b-b-b-b bad,
Whoo, bad to the bone.
(To Outro:)

Bad to the Bone - 3 - 3

Boulevard of Broken Dreams

No, this is not the old jazz standard from 1934. It is Green Day's biggest hit to date, though the lyrics of the two songs bear a remarkable similarity: "I walk along the street of sorrow ..." (1934); "I walk a lonely road ..." (2004).

"Boulevard of Broken Dreams" was originally performed in the key of F minor, which requires the guitar player to use barre chords throughout the song. Since this might make you feel like it's the "Boulevard of Broken Hands," we've arranged it a half step lower, in the key of E minor. If you want to play along with the recording, you'll need to put a capo at the first fret.

The rhythm pattern for the verse is transcribed below. Follow the strumming directions, and notice there is a muted stroke (indicated by an "x" notehead) just before each chord transition. This muted stroke gives your hand a moment to change position.

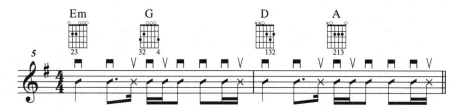

For the chorus at bar 19, the rhythm changes to straight eighth notes. Use all down-strokes in this section.

The outro figure at bar 52 takes an unexpected turn in the form of the D♯5 chord, which acts as a leading tone back to the Em chord. The song's abrupt ending on the D♯5 is jarring and leaves the listener waiting for a resolution that never comes.

Guitar Gods

GREEN DAY's *American Idiot* earned great critical acclaim. The album touched on timely issues of the day and featured singles like "American Idiot," "Boulevard of Broken Dreams," "Holiday," and "Wake Me Up When September Ends." *American Idiot* received seven Grammy nominations, eventually winning the Best Rock Album award. With over 15 million copies sold worldwide, it trails just behind the 1994 album *Dookie* as the best-selling release in the Green Day catalog.

BOULEVARD OF BROKEN DREAMS

This arrangement is transposed from the original key.
To match recording, capo at 1st fret.

Words by BILLIE JOE
Music by GREEN DAY

Casey Jones

Key Thoughts

Although "Casey Jones" is often misinterpreted as some sort of pro-drug statement because of its opening line "Driving that train, high on cocaine," it is actually an anti-drug song. Hence the answering second line: "Casey Jones, you better watch your speed."

Take Note

The first two measures contain the signature guitar part to this song. It's a simple lick based off the C and F chord shapes. Here's how to play it:

1. Barre your 1st finger across the top two strings at the eighth fret (G and C).

2. Strike the G and C, and immediately hammer your 3rd finger down on the A note at the tenth fret.

3. To play the little sliding lick on beat 3, place your 3rd finger on the ninth-fret E, play the note, and immediately slide down to the seventh-fret D. Pull off from D to C so all three notes are on one string.

Remember that a diagonal line means to slide your finger from one note to the next.

Guitar Gods

One of the most beloved and closely followed jam bands from the '60s to the '80s, **GRATEFUL DEAD** spread a message of peace and love through music everywhere they went. In 1967, they released their self-titled debut on the Warner Bros. Records label, which mysteriously gained nowhere near the expected acclaim given the legions of "Deadheads." Some varying experimentation on how to present Grateful Dead on a record resulted in three more albums in the late 1960s. Then, in 1970 came the release of *Workingman's Dead* and *American Beauty*, which contained what would be several of the Dead's most popular songs including "Casey Jones," "Truckin'," "Sugar Magnolia," and "Uncle John's Band." These albums also served to establish bluegrass as a part of mainstream rock music.

The chorus and verses use a basic "choppy" rhythm strum. Remember that the staccato dots tell you which chords to cut short. If there is no staccato mark, let the chord sound for its full value. The basic strum part to the first four measures is shown below.

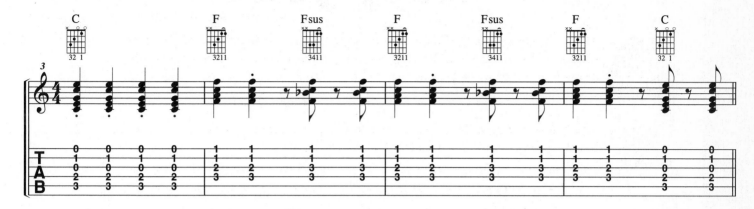

CASEY JONES

Words by
ROBERT HUNTER
Music by
JERRY GARCIA

Chorus:
Driv-ing that train,___ high on co - caine,___ Ca - sey Jones,___ you'd bet - ter

watch your speed.___ Trou - ble a - head,___ trou - ble be - hind,___

and you know that no - tion just crossed my mind._____

Verse:
1. This old en - gine makes it on time,___ leaves Cen - tral Sta - tion 'bout a
2. Trou - ble a-head, the la - dy in red,___ take my ad - vice___ you'd be
3. *Instrumental*
4. *See additional lyrics*

quar - ter to nine.___ Hits Riv - er Junc - tion at sev - en - teen to,___ at a quar -
bet - ter off dead.___ Switch-man's sleep - ing, Train Hun - dred and Two___

Casey Jones - 2 - 1

Verse 4:
Trouble with you is the trouble with me,
Got two good eyes but you still don't see.
Come 'round the bend, you know it's the end,
The fireman screams and the engine just gleams.
(To Chorus:)

China Grove

"China Grove" is a classic rock staple by the Doobie Brothers. Its rhythmic groove requires some deft chord work on the guitar.

The intro riff starts off with two quarter-note E5 chords, followed by four muted eighth-note strokes. The muted chords appear with "x" noteheads in the notation. Play the two E5 chords at the seventh fret with down-strokes. Now, after a quick downward slide, return your hand to the seventh-fret position and slightly lift your fingers from the fretboard while continuing to make contact with the strings. This will muffle the strings to produce a dull, percussive sound without a distinct pitch when you strum. You'll need to raise your index finger up a little from the E5 chord to mute the 6th string as well.

In bar 3, your left hand moves down to a D5 chord at the fifth fret. Keep your pick hand moving up and down in a constant eighth-note motion for this measure. Strike D5 on beat 1, play muted strokes on the "&" of 1 and the downbeat of 2, then catch the A/C♯ chord with the up-stroke on the "&" of 2. Play two more muted strokes on 3 &, then move to the open-position A5 chord and play a down-stroke on beat 4 and a muted up-stroke on the "&," then quickly move back up the neck to the seventh fret in preparation for a return to the E5 chord. This rhythmic motif carries through both the verse and chorus.

 Tip

The "&" of a beat is the second half of the beat, as when counting eighth notes: 1 & 2 & 3 & 4 &.

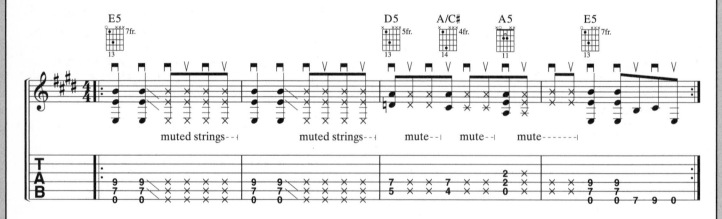

The next example shows the rhythm from the two-beat pickup into the bridge.

Continue this rhythm until the C–D–E progression that leads back to the verse pattern. We've thrown in an optional lead guitar fill after the first E chord, but if you prefer, you can let the E chord sustain across the measure instead.

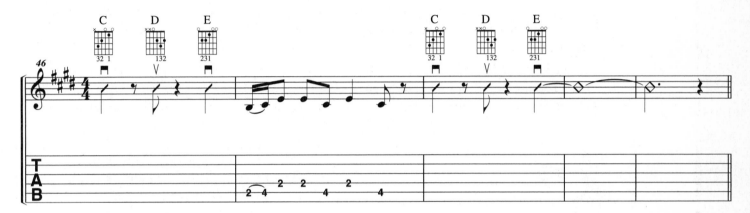

Guitar Gods

The **DOOBIE BROTHERS** recorded some of the biggest hits of the 1970s, giving us classic rock staples like "Black Water," "Long Train Runnin'," and "What a Fool Believes." Starting out as a Northern California country-boogie band, they were a constantly evolving bunch and covered lots of musical ground in their career, crafting songs that melded rock, country, boogie, R&B, light funk, pop, and jazz. Interestingly, among their staunchest supporters in the early days was outlaw biker gang the Hell's Angels. But as the band's sound evolved, so, too, did its fan base. The Doobie Brothers's breakthrough album was *Toulouse Street*, released in 1972. It included the classics "Rockin' Down the Highway," "Jesus Is Just Alright," and "Listen to the Music." Their 1973 follow-up album, *The Captain and Me*, was an even bigger success and featured the top-ten hit "China Grove."

CHINA GROVE

Words and Music by
TOM JOHNSTON

Dirty Deeds Done Dirt Cheap

AC/DC electrified the rock scene in the late 1970s as the quintessential, hard-driving, power-chord riff band of the era. "Dirty Deeds Done Dirt Cheap" is an aggressive song, so play it aggressively! Use all down-strokes, and play with authority and attitude. If you're really bold, don a British schoolboy uniform with shorts and do the Angus duck walk across the room while you jam.

The guitar part for "Dirty Deeds Done Dirt Cheap" uses "*5 chords*" exclusively: E5, G5, A5, D5, and B5. Also called *power chords*, "5 chords" have only two notes: the *root* and the *fifth*. The root is the first note of the corresponding major scale and gives the chord its letter name. The fifth is, quite simply, the fifth note of the scale. For example, the E5 chord contains the notes E and B, derived from the E major scale like this:

E Major Scale

E	F#	G#	A	B	C#	D#	E
1	2	3	4	5	6	7	8

Power chords are characteristic of hard rock music because when distortion is applied, they produce a "heavy" sound without the harmonic dissonance that occurs with chords of three or more notes.

Fun Fact

The sight of AC/DC lead guitarist Angus Young flailing around onstage in his trademark schoolboy outfit is one of the most memorable and iconic in rock music.

The intro establishes the tone of the song with rhythmic stabs. The verse is basically a single E5 chord sustained for four measures at a time beneath the vocals. The chorus moves up to an A5 chord and breaks the pattern in half, with quarter-note accents punctuating the end of each two-measure phrase.

DIRTY DEEDS DONE DIRT CHEAP

Words and Music by
ANGUS YOUNG, MALCOLM YOUNG
and BON SCOTT

Dirty Deeds Done Dirt Cheap - 3 - 1

Verse 3:
If you got a lady and you want her gone,
But you ain't got the guts.
She keeps naggin' at you night and day,
Enough to drive you nuts.
Pick up the phone, leave her alone.
It's time you made your stand.
For a fee, I'm happy to be
Your back door man, hey.
(To Chorus:)

Dr. Feelgood

Key Thoughts

To prepare to play this like the recording, you'll need an electric guitar (a nice, fat-sounding Les Paul with humbucker pickups would be ideal) and a good heavy metal distortion pedal. The full-on "crunch" rhythm you hear in this track requires a lot of overdrive and bottom end. You might want to warn the neighbors first.

Take Note

On the recording, the guitar is tuned down one whole step. If you want to play along, tune your low E string to the repeated low E note that kicks off the recording, then tune the rest of your guitar to your low E string. Your guitar will be in standard tuning, but down a half step.

The song opens with a pounding, repeated E note in the guitar and bass. To get the correct effect, you'll need to carefully mute the strings using a *palm mute* technique. To create the palm mute effect, lay the palm of your pick hand lightly on the strings, just in front of the bridge. If you can't hear the notes when you strike them, you are muting too much. You should hear the notes clearly, but muffled and with no sustain.

Tip

The **palm mute** is used extensively in rock rhythm guitar. By muffling the sound of the guitar, you can create a very percussive, driving sound. It will feel much better than allowing the strings to ring.

The intro starting at bar 5 is the signature guitar part, which is also played in the choruses throughout the song. It opens with a double-picked line (each note played twice) on the low E string. Start with an up-stroke because it begins on the off beat. This line leads to a two-note D chord that moves to a two-note A chord with C♯ in the bass A/C♯. Just lower your 1st finger one fret from D to C♯ to play the A/C♯. The second measure of the lick starts with the same double-picked line, but this time leads to an E7(♯9) chord. (Incidentally, this form of the E7(♯9) is often called the "Purple Haze" chord because it is the central chord Jimi Hendrix plays in his signature guitar part to "Purple Haze.")

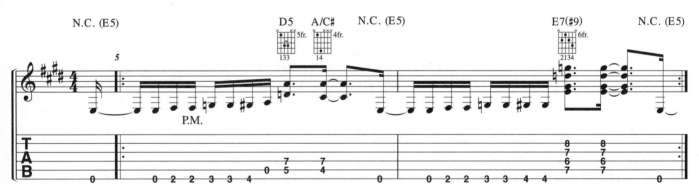

The verse is classic, hard-driving, rock rhythm guitar with just two simple power chords: A5 and E5. (See the lesson for "Dirty Deeds Done Dirt Cheap" for an explanation of power chords.) On the A5, barre the 3rd and 4th strings with your 1st finger and stay in this position throughout the whole riff. The low G note that follows is under your 2nd finger. Release the pressure on your 1st-finger barre as you play the low G, but don't actually let go of the chord. Bar 2 of the riff resolves to E5 after the low G—just slide your barre from the 3rd and 4th strings to the 4th and 5th strings. Be sure to mute throughout and use lots of crunch from your amp or distortion pedal. In the song, these two measures are played again, then again, but with additional open notes filling the space (mostly open A and open E). The basic riff is shown below.

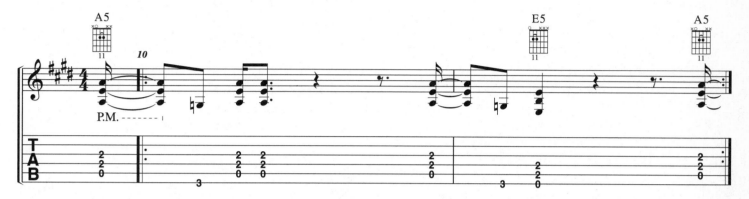

To get the correct "crunch" rhythm sound from your amplifier, first scoop out the mid-range and boost your treble and bass controls. Then, lower your master volume to a listenable level and boost your pre-amp volume until you get the right amount of overdrive.

Guitar Gods

MÖTLEY CRÜE started in 1981 when bassist Nikki Sixx, drummer Tommy Lee, guitarist Mick Mars, and vocalist Vince Neil came together. They were arguably the most influential band of the Sunset Strip hair-metal scene, leading a crowd that included Guns N' Roses, Cinderella, Ratt, and Poison. The band's history reads like the ultimate chronicle of rock and roll notoriety, complete with deadly, alcohol-fueled automobile accidents, near-fatal drug overdoses, and a long-standing reputation for dating supermodels and actresses. The Crüe's 1989 best-seller, Dr. Feelgood, was recorded when the band was finally clean and sober, and subsequently became their career highlight. The album included the poignant hits "Kickstart My Heart" and "Without You," and its menacing title track became the group's first top-ten single.

DR. FEELGOOD

To match recorded key, tune guitar down one whole step.

Music by MICK MARS and NIKKI SIXX
Lyrics by NIKKI SIXX

Moderate shuffle ♩ = 102

Intro:

Play 6 times

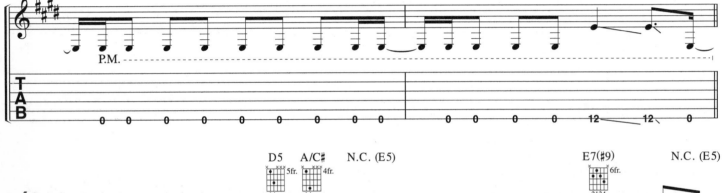

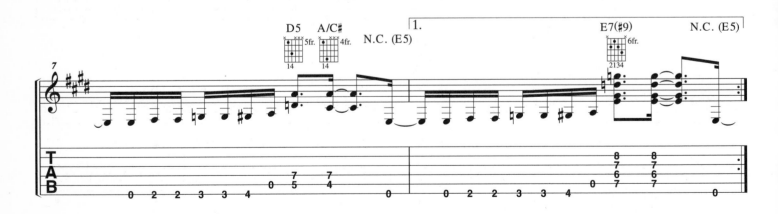

pack - ag - es of can - dy - cane.___ He's___ the one they call Doc - tor Feel - good.___ He's___

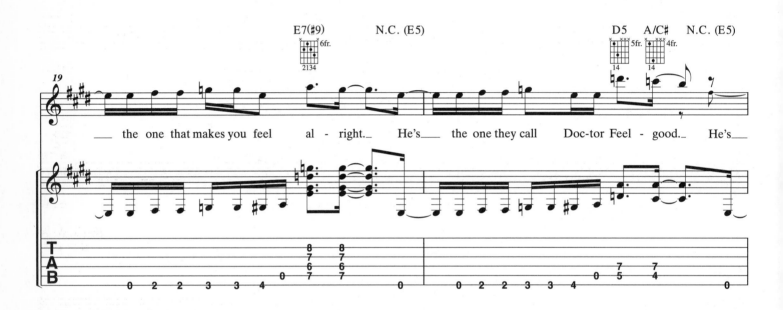

___ the one that makes you feel al - right.___ He's___ the one they call Doc - tor Feel - good.___ He's___

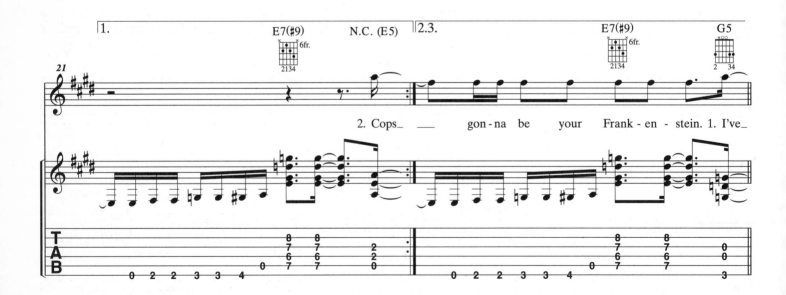

2. Cops___ ___ gon - na be your Frank - en - stein. 1. I've___

Verse 2:
Cops on the corner always ignore.
Somebody's getting paid.
Jimmy's got it wired, law's for hire;
Got it made in the shade.
Got a little hide-away,
Does his business all day,
But at night he'll always be found
Selling sugar to the sweet people on the street.
Call this Jimmy's town.
(To Chorus:)

Verse 3:
He'll tell you he's the king of these barrio streets
Moving up to Shangri-La.
Came by his wealth as a matter of luck.
Says he never broke the law.
Two-time loser, running out of juice,
Time to move out quick.
Heard a rumor goin' 'round,
Jimmy's goin' down.
This time it's gonna stick.
(To Chorus:)

Bridge 2:
Let him soothe your soul,
Just take his hand.
Some people call him an evil man.
Let him introduce himself real good.
He's the only one they call "Feel-good."
(To Guitar Solo:)

Europa (Earth's Cry Heaven's Smile)

Gato Barbieri's huge instrumental hit "Europa" is actually a song by Carlos Santana, and our arrangement is based on the Santana version. While most of the songs in this book focus on guitar accompaniment parts, this song is a guitar instrumental, so it's the melody we'll be looking at here.

The original key of "Europa" is C minor. To make it a little easier, we've arranged it in A minor. If you want to match the recorded key, you can capo your guitar at the third fret. Once you have the patterns memorized in A minor, though, you can easily just slide them up three frets to play in C minor without a capo.

The main melody (labeled A) is in 5th position. Listen to a recording of the song, and follow the music and TAB. The B section is a passionate improvisation on the main melody. This section is more challenging, with lots of bends and slurs. You'll absolutely need an electric guitar with light gauge strings to do these bends. When you're reading the music for a bend, the cue-size note (the very small note next to the full-size note) and corresponding TAB number is what you play; then, you immediately bend the string until the note sounds like the next indicated pitch. Most of the bends then slur back down to the starting pitch.

The B section uses a soaring, overdriven guitar tone. Use your lead pickup with the tone control rolled down about half way, and try to achieve a smooth, silky overdriven sound either from your amp or with a good overdrive effect pedal.

Guitar Gods

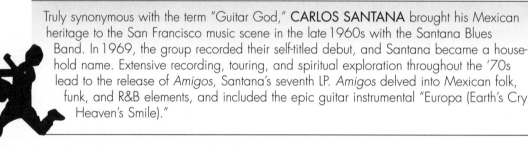

Truly synonymous with the term "Guitar God," **CARLOS SANTANA** brought his Mexican heritage to the San Francisco music scene in the late 1960s with the Santana Blues Band. In 1969, the group recorded their self-titled debut, and Santana became a household name. Extensive recording, touring, and spiritual exploration throughout the '70s lead to the release of *Amigos*, Santana's seventh LP. *Amigos* delved into Mexican folk, funk, and R&B elements, and included the epic guitar instrumental "Europa (Earth's Cry Heaven's Smile)."

EUROPA
(Earth's Cry Heaven's Smile)

This arrangement is transposed from the original key.
To match recording, capo at 3rd fret.

Music by
CARLOS SANTANA and TOM COSTER

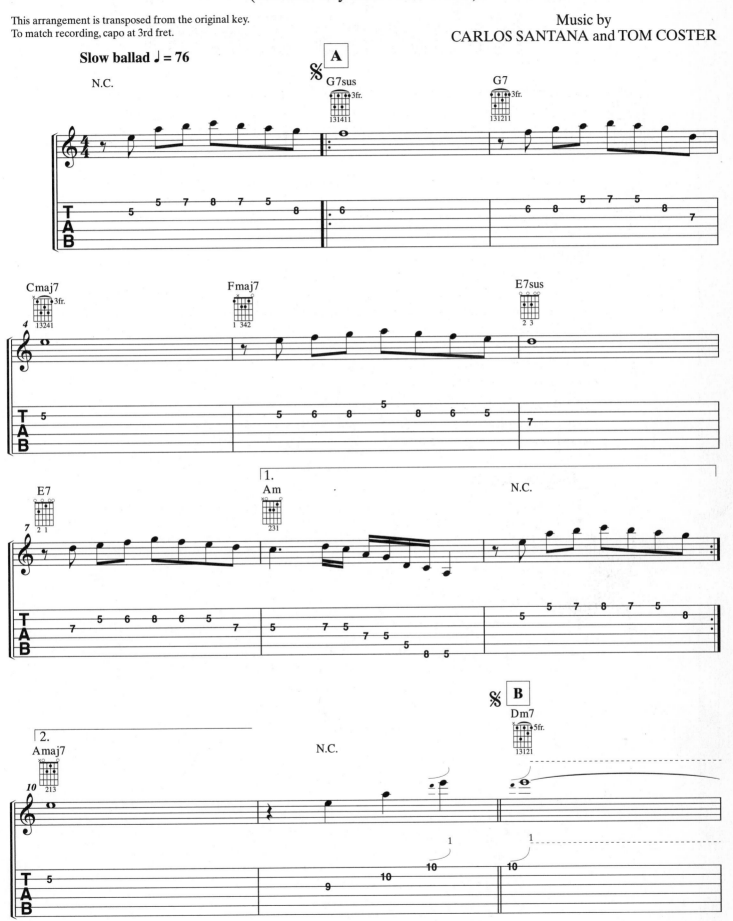

Europa - 3 - 1

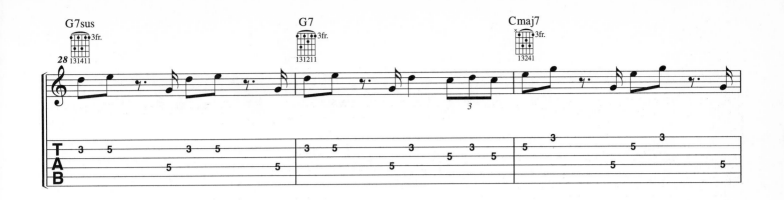

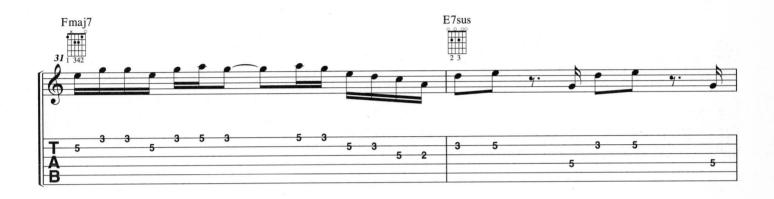

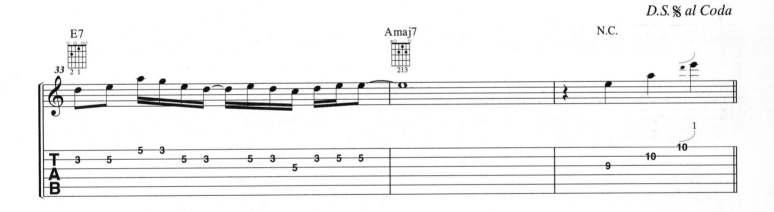

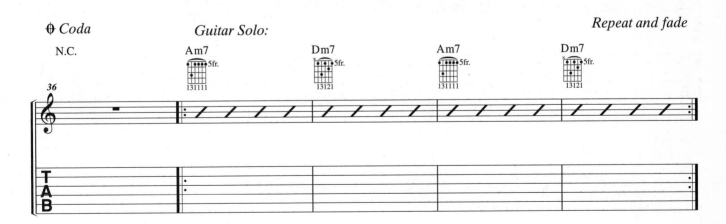

Europa - 3 - 3

For What It's Worth

Buffalo Springfield produced one of the most iconic songs of the '60s with "For What It's Worth," using just a handful of basic chords, a simple melody, and the distinctive chime of harmonics.

"For What It's Worth" begins with the chiming sound of natural *harmonics*. A harmonic is a frequency that vibrates above the fundamental pitch of a note. Individual harmonics may be isolated on the guitar by lightly touching a string over certain frets. The resulting sound is a pure, bell-like tone.

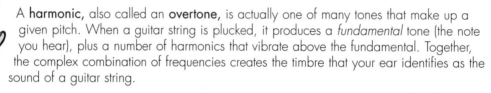

Definition

A **harmonic**, also called an **overtone**, is actually one of many tones that make up a given pitch. When a guitar string is plucked, it produces a *fundamental* tone (the note you hear), plus a number of harmonics that vibrate above the fundamental. Together, the complex combination of frequencies creates the timbre that your ear identifies as the sound of a guitar string.

The first note in "For What It's Worth" is a harmonic played at the twelfth fret of the 1st string. It appears in the notation as a diamond-shaped note on the space of the staff where the open 1st-string E would normally be written. The diamond-shaped notehead tells you that this is a harmonic, not a standard note. The indication *8va* above the staff is shorthand for "sounds an octave higher than written" and is used to keep the pitches within range of the staff, which is easier to read than using lots of ledger lines way above the staff.

The harmonics at the twelfth, fifth, and seventh frets are the easiest to produce on the guitar. Lightly touching the string directly over the twelfth fret produces a harmonic one octave higher than the pitch of the open string, the harmonic at the fifth fret sounds two octaves higher than the open string, and the harmonic at the seventh fret sounds an octave and a fifth above the open string. The diagram below shows these three harmonics on the first string.

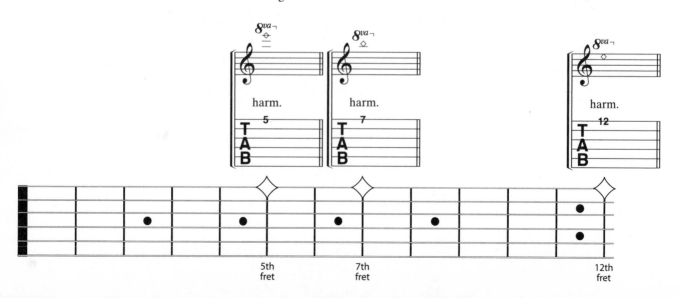

The guitar rhythm for the verses is a basic strum pattern. Feel free to add a muted down-stroke on the second beat of each measure.

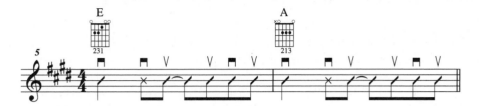

Practice changing back and forth between the E and A chords until your left hand can make a smooth transition without interrupting the beat. Notice how the index finger stays on the 3rd string for both chords; to minimize the motion of your fingers, simply slide it from one fret to the other without completely lifting off the string. Use the same technique to change from the E to the D chord, and from the D to the A chord. When changing from the A to the C chord, the 2nd finger remains on the second-fret, 4th-string E note. Use these types of common tones between chords as anchors around which you pivot your other fingers whenever possible.

Tip

The trick to making a harmonic sustain is the opposite technique you'd use for a fretted note. Instead of keeping the finger pressure on the string as normal, you must immediately lift the fretting finger off the string after the string is plucked to make the harmonic ring.

Guitar Gods

BUFFALO SPRINGFIELD is considered, by most, to be one of the most influential folk-rock groups of our time. Their '60s anthem "For What It's Worth" was inspired by a 1966 confrontation between police and young club goers on the Sunset Strip in Los Angeles, but it assumed much broader significance against the backdrop of the Vietnam War, the civil rights movement, and other events in those tumultuous times. The chorus of "Stop, children, what's that sound? Everybody look what's goin' down" has become standard musical background for any documentary film footage of 1960s-era demonstrations.

FOR WHAT IT'S WORTH

Words and Music by
STEPHEN STILLS

For What It's Worth - 2 - 1

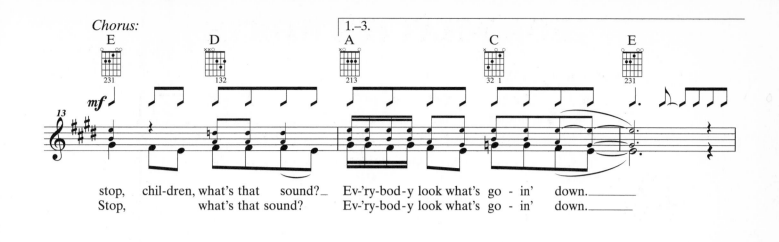

stop,   chil-dren, what's that   sound?_   Ev-'ry-bod-y look what's go - in'   down._____
Stop,   what's that sound?   Ev-'ry-bod-y look what's go - in'   down._____

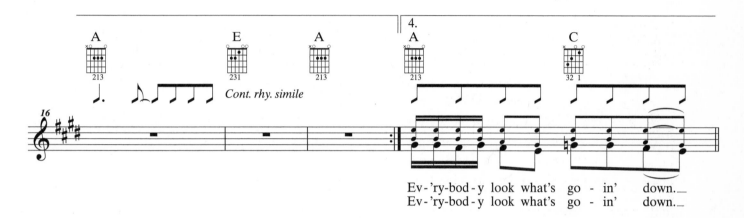

Ev-'ry-bod-y look what's go - in'   down._
Ev-'ry-bod-y look what's go - in'   down._

Repeat ad lib. and fade

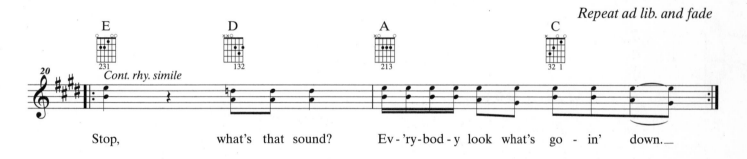

Stop,   what's that sound?   Ev - 'ry-bod - y look what's go - in'   down._

Verse 2:
There's battle lines being drawn,
Nobody's right if everybody's wrong.
Young people speaking their minds,
Getting so much resistance from behind.
I think it's time we stop,...
(To Chorus:)

Verse 3:
What a field day for the heat,
A thousand people in the street.
Singing songs and carrying signs,
Mostly say "Hooray for our side."
It's time we stop,...
(To Chorus:)

Verse 4:
Paranoia strikes deep,
Into your life it will creep.
It starts when you're always afraid,
Step out of line, the man come and take you away.
We better stop,...
(To Chorus:)

Gimme Some Lovin'

"Gimme Some Lovin'," by the Spencer Davis Group, prominently showcases 18-year-old Stevie Winwood's vocal talents alongside the blue-eyed-soul wunderkind's aggressive Hammond B-3 organ riffing. In this transcription, the signature organ part is arranged for guitar. Because there are only a few chords, the song may at first appear easy, but as with most blues-based music, the apparent simplicity can be deceptive. Listen to the record and try to infuse your performance with the same groove, energy, and dynamics.

The intro is a driving *octave* figure. An octave is two notes with the same letter name that are at half or double the frequency. For example, the open A string (the 5th string) on a guitar has a frequency of 220 *Hertz* (Hz), which means it vibrates 220 times per second. An octave above the open A string is the second fret of the 3rd string, which is an A note with a frequency of 440 Hz.

The octave notes in "Gimme Some Lovin'" are G notes. If you're playing a guitar without easy access to the upper register, you may transpose the riff down one octave by subtracting 12 from each TAB number.

The verse is played with the following two-bar strum pattern:

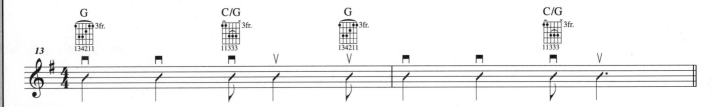

Guitar Gods

At the height of the British Invasion, guitarist **SPENCER DAVIS** and lead singer Stevie Winwood brought their R&B quartet across the pond. Their first hit, 1965's "Keep on Running," was a smashing success in the U.K., but barely made the top 100 in America. The group finally won favor in America with "I'm a Man" and their hottest seller "Gimme Some Lovin'," peaking at No. 7 on the charts. Despite the success of such top-ten songs, the Spencer Davis Group never performed in the United States. In 1967, Winwood left the group to form Traffic and later Blind Faith (with Eric Clapton). Davis later went on to produce other acts, including the Canadian group the Downchild Blues Band.

GIMME SOME LOVIN'

Words and Music by
**STEVE WINWOOD, MUFF WINWOOD
and SPENCER DAVIS**

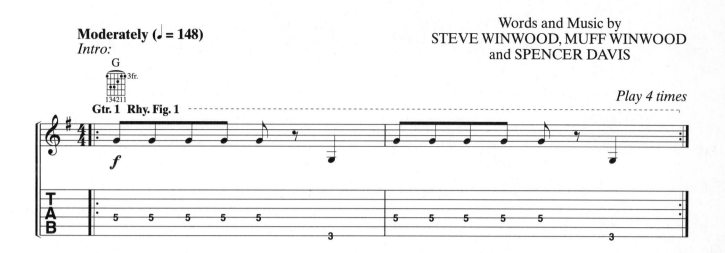

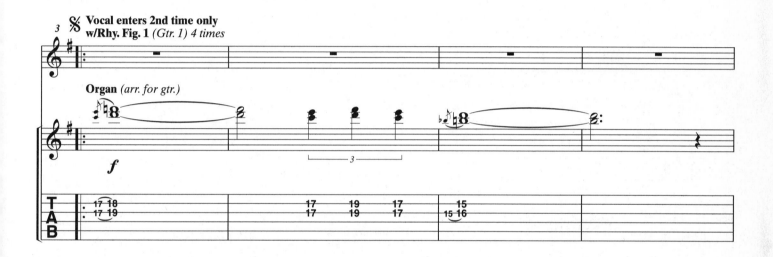

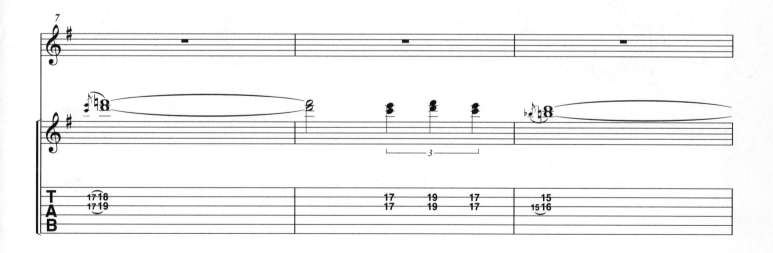

Gimme Some Lovin' - 3 - 1

The House of the Rising Sun

 Key Thoughts
The Animals rode the wave of the British Invasion to the top of the charts in 1964 with their gritty electric reinvention of the traditional American folk standard "The House of the Rising Sun."

 Take Note
The guitar part for "The House of the Rising Sun" consists of a series of *arpeggios*. An arpeggio consists of the notes of a chord played one after another instead of simultaneously.

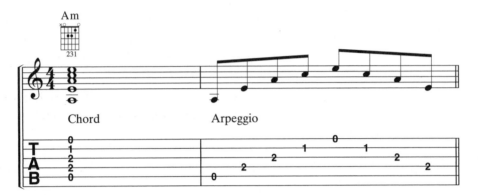

Guitar Gods

THE ANIMALS, along with the Rolling Stones, were standouts among the pack of R&B-influenced bands in England during the 1960s. The band recorded many hit songs during this period, but it was "The House of the Rising Sun" that became their signature recording. Their arrangement gave the song a new guitar riff and a soulful organ accompaniment, and it shot to the top of the charts in both the U.K. and the United States during the summer of 1964.

At first, many believed the band got "The House of the Rising Sun" from Bob Dylan's first album, but later it was revealed that the song came to them courtesy of the blues/folk singer Josh White. Alan Price, the original keyboard player with the Animals, claimed sole arrangement credit on the recording, a matter that is presently in dispute with the surviving members of the band.

Though the electric guitar on the original recording is played with a pick, these kinds of arpeggios lend themselves just as well to being played fingerstyle on either an electric or acoustic guitar. Notice that the pattern is very consistent, with an ascending group of notes (taking a slight stumble in the middle) followed by an even descending figure. If you are using a pick, perform the first five notes of each arpeggio with a single down-stroke, and play the last two notes with up-strokes.

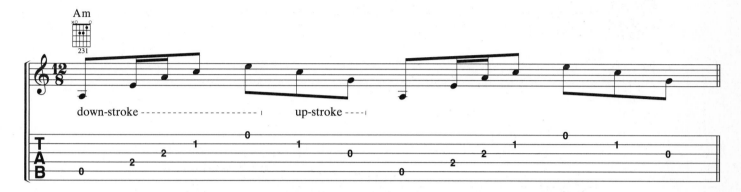

Note that the coda of the song employs a little harmonic variation. Until the ending, all of the D chords are D major chords. The coda alternates between Am and Dm chords, finally resolving on a jazzy Am9.

THE HOUSE OF THE RISING SUN

Words and Music by
ALAN PRICE

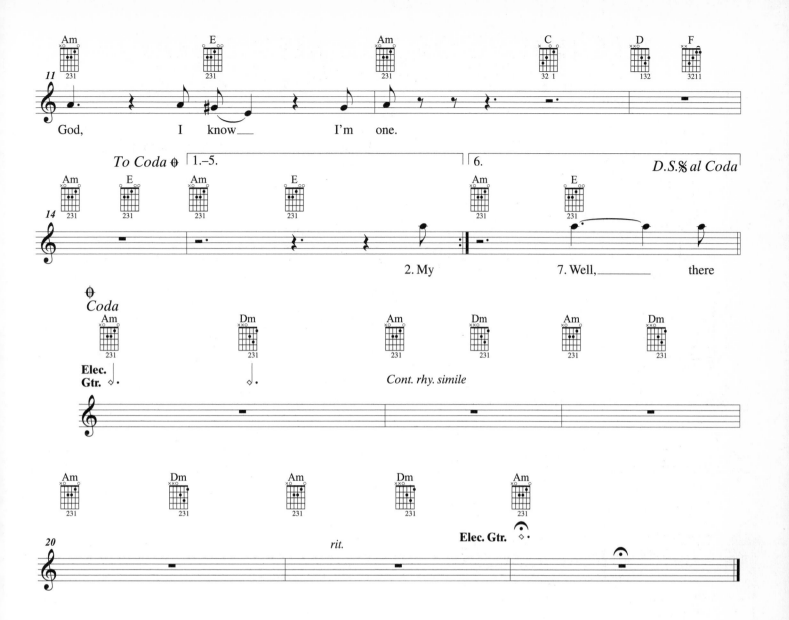

Verse 2:
My mother was a tailor,
She sewed my new blue jeans.
My father was a gambling man
Down in New Orleans.

Verse 3:
Now, the only thing a gambler needs
Is a suitcase and a trunk.
And the only time he's satisfied
Is when he's on a drunk.
(To Organ Solo:)

Verse 5:
Oh, mother, tell your children
Not to do what I have done.
Spend your life in sin and misery
In the house of the Rising Sun.

Verse 6:
Well, I got one foot on the platform,
The other foot on the train.
I'm going back to New Orleans
To wear that ball and chain.

How You Remind Me

Key Thoughts Canadian band Nickelback achieved commercial nirvana in 2001 with the pop/grunge blend of "How You Remind Me." The band's distinct style has led to a remarkable string of successes in the mold established by this song.

Take Note This song is in *Drop D tuning*. Drop D tuning is identical to standard tuning, except the 6th string is tuned down a whole step from E to D.

In the verse, note the similarity between the chord frames for Csus2 and Fsus(9), and between B♭sus2 and E♭sus(9). The chords of each pair are actually the same, but with a shift of the bass note from the 5th string to the 6th string. When playing the first measure, hold your 1st-finger barre at the third fret and your 3rd and 4th fingers at the fifth fret for Csus2. At the change to Fsus(9), simply move your index finger up from the 5th string to the 6th string. The change from B♭sus2 to E♭sus(9) is done the same way, but at the first fret.

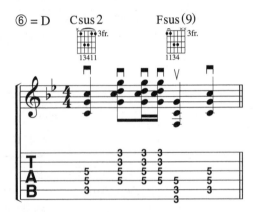

To emulate the strumming style in the verse that you hear on the recording, emphasize the bass strings of each chord on the first beat and try to strike the higher strings on the following beat. On the straighter eighth-note rhythm of the chorus, strike all the strings evenly with down-strokes, as shown below.

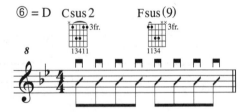

Fun Fact

The band's name is derived from the five cents change that bass player Mike Kroeger's brother often had to give customers in his job at a coffee shop, in which he would say, "Here's your nickel back."

HOW YOU REMIND ME

Lyrics by
CHAD KROEGER
Music by
NICKELBACK

How You Remind Me - 3 - 1

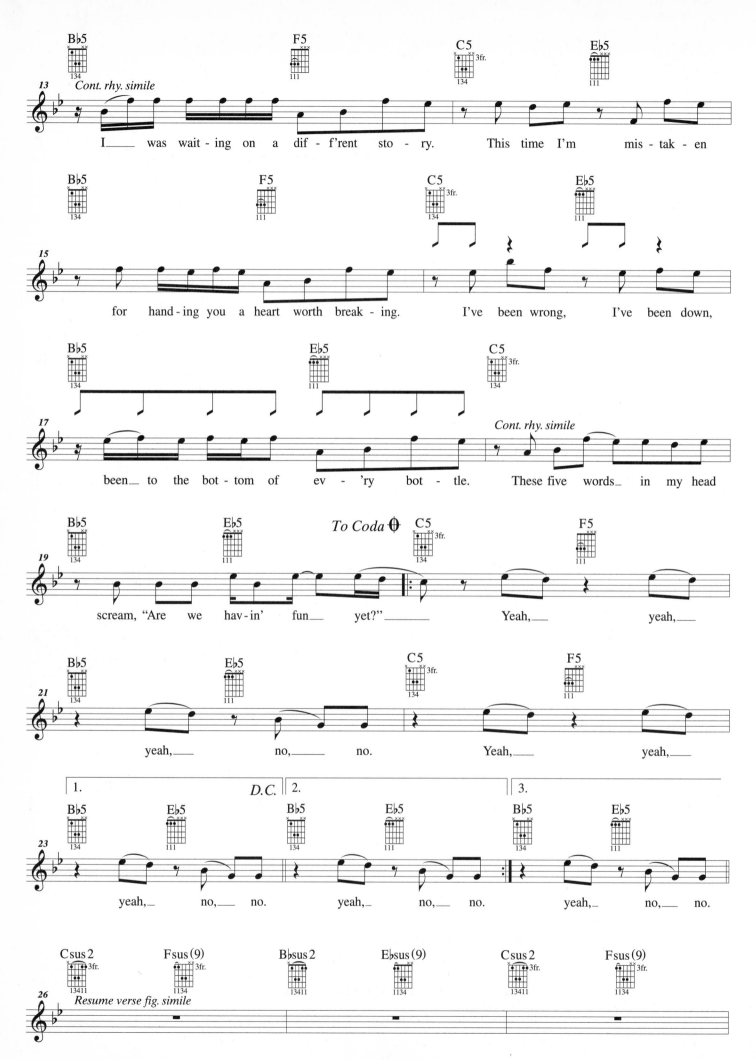

Verse 2:
It's not like you didn't know that.
I said I love you and I swear I still do.
And it must have been so bad.
'Cause livin' with me must have damn near killed you.
(To Chorus:)

In-A-Gadda-Da-Vida

Key Thoughts

When singer Doug Ingle seriously slurred the opening lyric to his song "In the Garden of Eden," the effect was so perfect that the band decided to go with the slurred version: "In-A-Gadda-Da-Vida." Iron Butterfly helped lay the foundation for heavy metal with this 17-minute guitar anthem.

Take Note

The entire song is guitar-riff driven. The chord grids shown over the music indicate the rhythm guitar part, but the primary guitar riff is shown in the notation and TAB. To get the right effect when playing the riff, you may want to find an old *fuzz box*. Fuzz boxes were the original distortion effects. They add a lot of distortion to the sound, as you can hear on the original recording.

The intro opens with the most famous guitar riff from the song, and the same riff continues throughout most of the verse. Listen to the recording to get the correct rhythm in your head. To get the right feel, try using down-strokes only—they produce a more powerful, driving rhythmic sound than alternate picking.

While the lead guitar plays the riffs, the rhythm guitar plays a percussive rhythm with an accented strum on beat 2 of every other measure. At the "x" noteheads, hold your hand in the chord shape, but don't press the strings fully, so you'll get a percussive "click" when you strike the strings.

Tip

Distortion is a different effect than over-drive. Compare the sound of distortion in this song to the overdriven guitar in a song like "Dirty Deeds Done Dirt Cheap," and you will see why distortion is also called "fuzz tone."

The example below shows the transition from the verse to the chorus. This is a cool little riff played at bar 13 of the song.

The chorus figure is a nice little pattern that outlines each chord before leading into the next. The first two beats of each measure outline the chord. Notice that the notes of the G chord (G–F–D–G) and those of the A chord (A–G–E–A) follow the same pattern of *root–seventh–fifth–root*. Similarly, the notes of the E chord (E–B–D–E) and the F♯ chord (F♯–C♯–E–F♯) both follow the pattern root–fifth–seventh–root. In the second half of each measure, a *chromatic* line (meaning the notes don't skip frets) leads into the root of the next chord. The chorus figure from bars 17–20 is shown below.

Definition

The **root** is the first note of a scale and the note that gives a chord its name. Counting up the notes of the scale, a chord's **fifth** is simply five notes above the root, and a **seventh** is seven notes above the root.

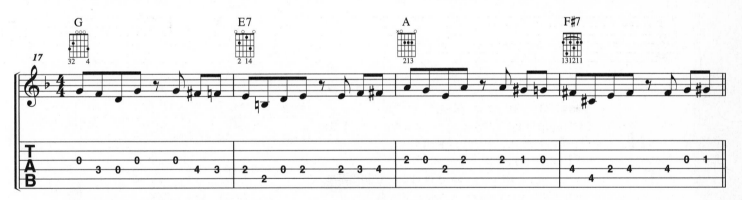

Guitar Gods

IRON BUTTERFLY emerged in 1966 as one of psychedelia's most iconic groups. Originating in San Diego, the band quickly moved to Los Angeles to play the local club circuit. It wasn't long before they had secured a recording contract and were teamed up to play acid-rock tours with Jefferson Airplane and the Doors. The band's debut LP, *Heavy* (1968), achieved modest top 100 success, but after a personnel shakeup, the group recorded their magnum opus, *In-A-Gadda-Da-Vida* (1969). The 17-minute title track saw extensive radio play, which helped the record to sell four million copies.

IN-A-GADDA-DA-VIDA

Words and Music by
DOUG INGLE

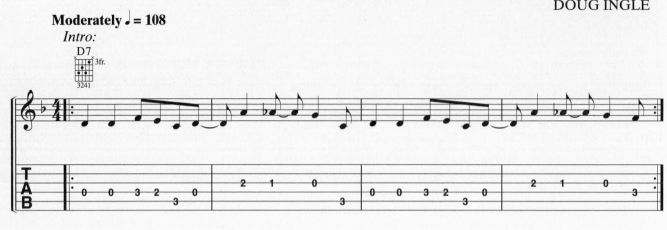

Jump

Key Thoughts

"Jump" marked Van Halen's crossover from hard rock superstars to '80s pop icons. Surprisingly, the song featured guitar virtuoso Eddie Van Halen on keyboards. Our version features his signature keyboard part arranged for guitar.

Take Note

The intro is a fingerstyle arrangement of Eddie's keyboard chords. It's actually a combination of the bass and keyboard parts: the thumb plays the bass notes (shown with down-stems in the notation), and the fingers pluck the chords (shown with up-stems). To prepare for this, first play the example below, which shows just the chord part without the bass line.

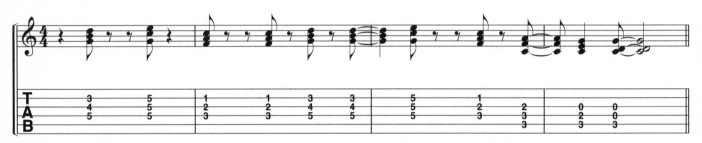

Now let's put the chords and the bass together. Play this very slowly. Count carefully, playing the bass notes with your thumb and the chords with your index, middle, and ring fingers. In the second measure, move your left hand to the G/C chord *before* playing the C note on beat 3.

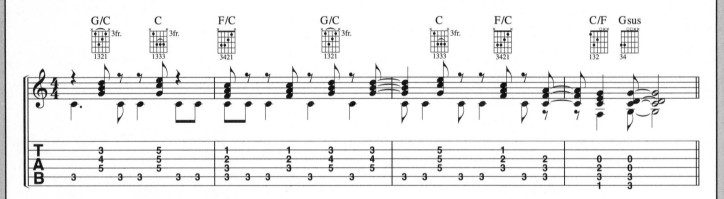

Guitar Gods

VAN HALEN featured two of the most charismatic figures in rock history: Eddie Van Halen, with his virtuosic, Paganini-meets-Eric Clapton guitar playing, and singer "Diamond" David Lee Roth, with his Robert-Plant-by-way-of-Frank-Sinatra showmanship. The band strung together one rock-radio hit after another in the 1980s, culminating in the band's breakthrough album, *1984*, which included the hit singles "Jump," "Hot for Teacher," and "Panama" and catapulted the band from hard-rock icons to pop-rock superstars. "Jump," the biggest single in the band's career, showcased Eddie's keyboard prowess and proved that he was more than just a guitar god. Van Halen was recently inducted into the Rock and Roll Hall of Fame.

The guitar fill shown below happens in the pre-chorus at measure 24. Notice how it is based on arpeggios of the F and C chords.

JUMP

Words and Music by EDWARD VAN HALEN, ALEX VAN HALEN,
MICHAEL ANTHONY and DAVID LEE ROTH

Jump - 4 - 1

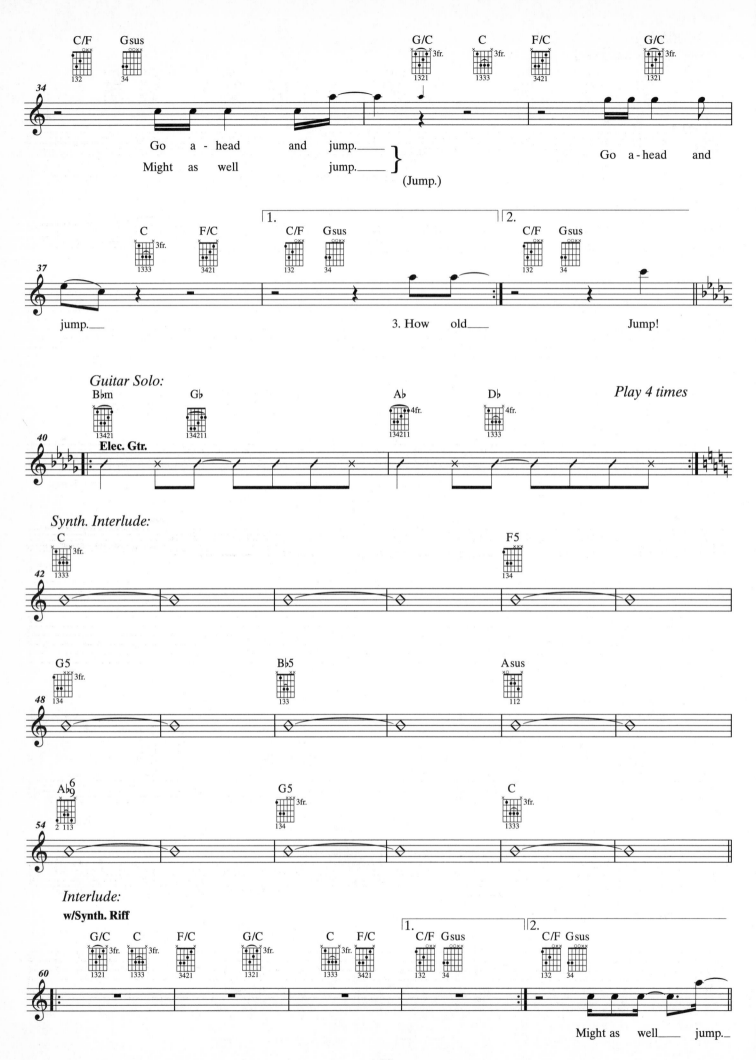

Layla

With passionate lyrics inspired by an ancient Persian love poem, music composed to express unrequited love for a best friend's wife, a fiery riff borrowed from an old blues song, a vocal sung with heart-wrenching desperation, and a piano coda created by a matricidal drummer, "Layla" boasts a pedigree like no other. With all its disparate elements, it was destined to become Eric Clapton's signature song, and is a standard by any measure.

Eric Clapton initially conceived "Layla" as a slow blues shuffle, but Derek & the Dominos decided the song was better served at a moderate tempo.

The intro is in the key of D minor. The signature riff was added at the suggestion of guest guitarist Duane Allman. It's a sped-up variation of the vocal line from Albert King's "As the Years Go Passing By." The riff is first established in a lower octave and in open position, combined with some double stops, defining the intro/chorus chord progression.

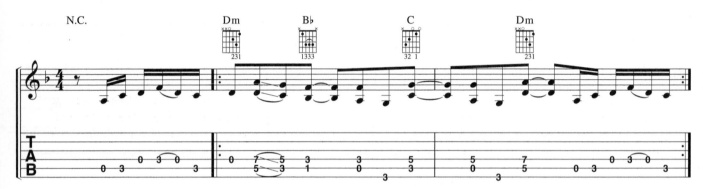

At measure 4, a second guitar introduces the riff two octaves higher, at the tenth-fret position. Notice there is a slight variation at the end of each alternating phrase. On the first pass, the 1st-string F at the thirteenth fret is bent up a whole step to G. On the next, the G at the fifteenth fret is bent up a whole step to A. This change will require you to shift your left hand momentarily out of the tenth-fret position. When bending these notes, support your little finger with the other fingers of your left hand to help push up the string.

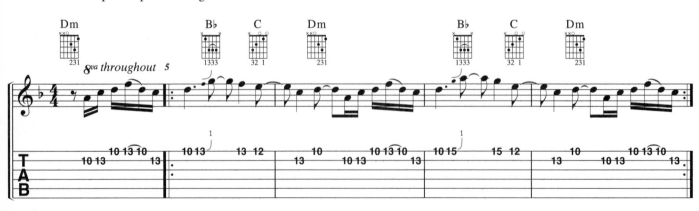

The verse modulates to the key of E major. The rhythm pattern may look complicated, but—as with most new things—if you break it down and take your time, you'll find it's actually not difficult at all. Try to strum it using the down-strokes and up-strokes shown in the example below. The two muted sixteenth notes at the end of the measure give your left hand a chance to reposition for the next chord.

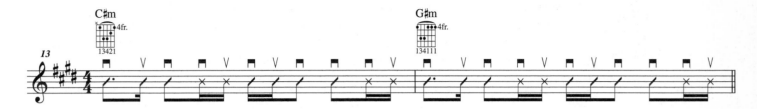

The song's beautiful outro was composed (and performed on the piano on the recording) by Jim Gordon, the drummer for Derek & the Dominos. Like a mini-symphony, this section features another modulation, this time to the key of C major. You may either play the melody, which is transcribed in the notation as a piano part, or you may strum the chords. The chord progression features an unexpected, yet lovely, twist with the inclusion of a B♭9(♭5) chord.

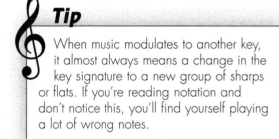

Tip

When music modulates to another key, it almost always means a change in the key signature to a new group of sharps or flats. If you're reading notation and don't notice this, you'll find yourself playing a lot of wrong notes.

☆ *Fun Fact* ☆

Eric Clapton devised the name Derek & the Dominos as a way for him to shy away from the fame and hype generated by his "Clapton is God" days with Cream. When the album *Layla and Other Assorted Love Songs* was released in December 1970 without a photo of Clapton on the cover, it received a lackluster public response. When

LAYLA

Words and Music by
ERIC CLAPTON and JIM GORDON

Moderately ♩ = 116

Intro:

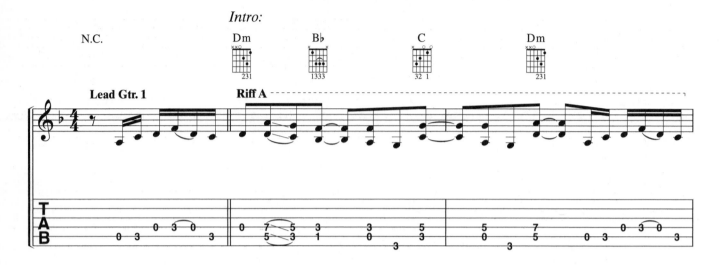

w/Riff A *(Lead Gtr. 1) 4 times*

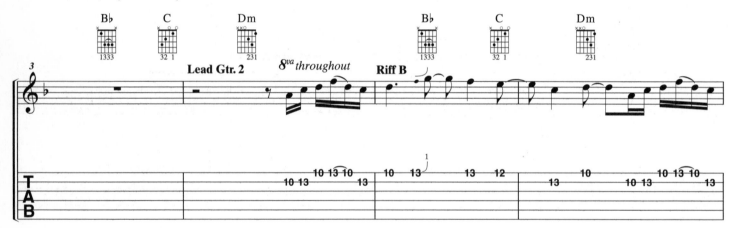

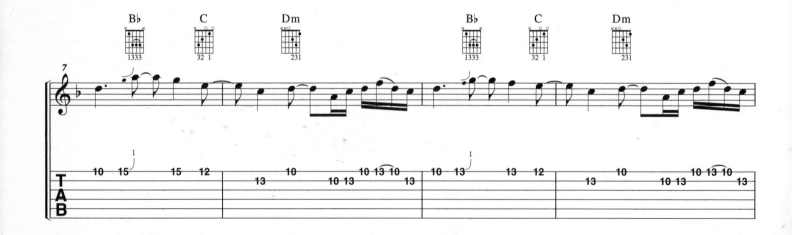

Layla - 6 - 1

Long Train Runnin'

Key Thoughts

The guitar part to "Long Train Runnin'" is quintessential Doobie Brothers. This is the song that had every young guitarist in the '70s trying to learn how to play that "killer strum"—the fast, fluid, funky, constant sixteenth-note groove that drives the entire band.

Like so many other songs, the signature guitar part of "Long Train Runnin'" is the intro. To play this rhythm groove, you first need to *listen to the music* (whoops! wrong Doobie Brothers song, but still very true). Sorry about the pun, but be sure to listen carefully to the recording so you know how this is supposed to sound. Music notation can only give you so much information, and the rest comes from listening.

Take Note

The secret to playing this guitar part is to strum a constant stream of sixteenth notes combined with some muted percussive strums. A few well-placed hammer-ons create an inside melody within the constant strum. The intro rhythm figure is played with a barre at the tenth fret, striking all strings but the 6th string. Strum the notes at the tenth fret, and immediately hammer your 2nd and 3rd fingers down on the eleventh and twelfth frets to form the Gm7 chord. Then, the trick is to release the left hand's pressure on the chord while maintaining the constant sixteenth-note strum to create a strong percussive part. Reapply the pressure so that the chord is sounded as shown in the following example; the muted chords are shown with "x" noteheads. After you've played it for a bit, see the additional tips that follow.

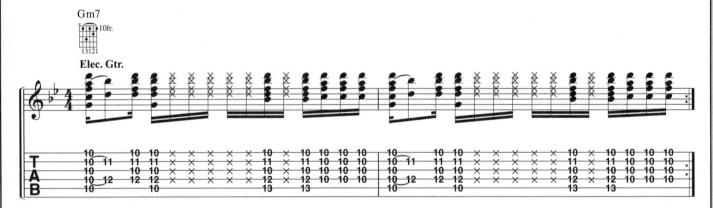

Here are some more tips for getting the correct feel:

- As you play the constant sixteenth-note strum pattern, be sure to strum from your wrist and keep a loose hold on the pick.

- Listen to the recording to hear the effect of the muted strums intermingled with the full chords. Use your ear as a guide for when to mute the strings.

- Once you get the pattern under your fingers, close your eyes and listen to yourself play. Again, use your ear to guide you. Your hands will automatically begin to bring out the melodies and percussive parts by responding to your ear.

While the electric guitar plays the part shown in the preceding example, an acoustic guitar plays the fairly simple line shown below.

The electric and acoustic guitars continue throughout the song. An interesting "crossing" of the parts occurs on the change to the Cm7 chord, which is first shown at bar 9. At this point, the acoustic guitar plays Rhythm Figure 2A, which sounds essentially like a continuation of what the electric guitar plays over the Gm7 chord. Meanwhile, the electric guitar plays a classic funk-style groove on Cm7 to Cm13. It is very common for guitarists to combine the Gm7 groove of the electric guitar with the Cm7 groove of the acoustic guitar. Learn all the parts and see what you prefer.

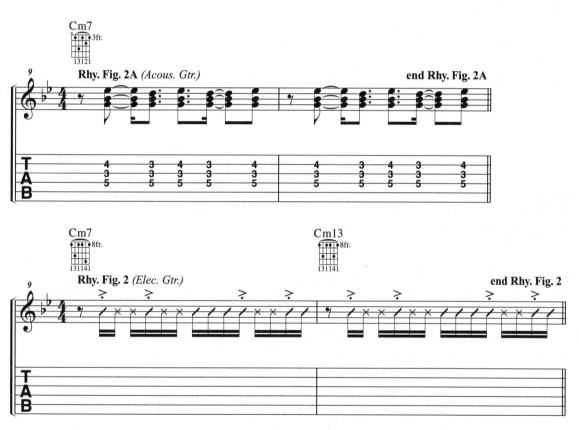

☆ Fun Fact ☆

This song, and most of the rest of the Doobie Brothers catalog, was produced by Ted Templeman. Templeman was with the group Harper's Bizarre in the '60s. (Remember "Feelin' Groovy"?) In 1977, he brought a then-unknown group, Van Halen, to Warner Bros., and produced their first six albums. In the Van Halen song "Unchained," his is the voice that pleads, "Come on Dave, gimme a break," to which Diamond Dave replies, "One break, coming up!"

LONG TRAIN RUNNIN'

Words and Music by
TOM JOHNSTON

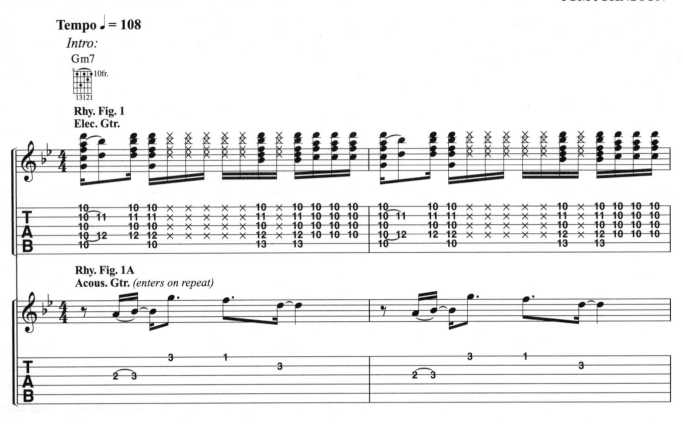

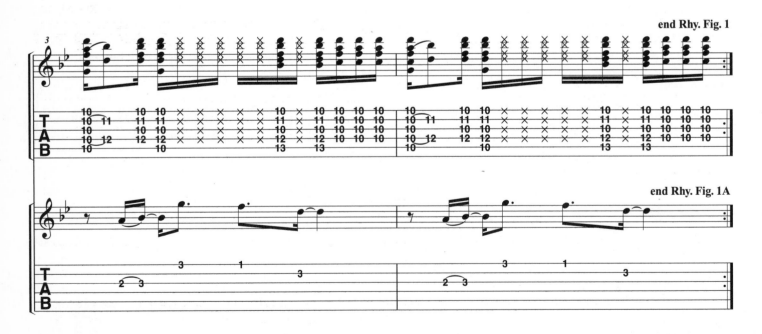

Long Train Runnin' - 4 - 1

Verse:

1. Down a - round__ the cor - ner, half a mile__ from here,__ you
2.–6. *See additional lyrics*

see them old trains run - nin' and you watch them dis - ap - pear.__ With - out

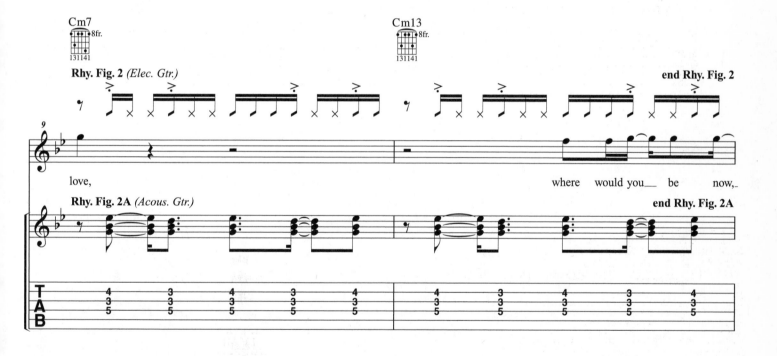

love, where would you__ be now,__

__ with-out

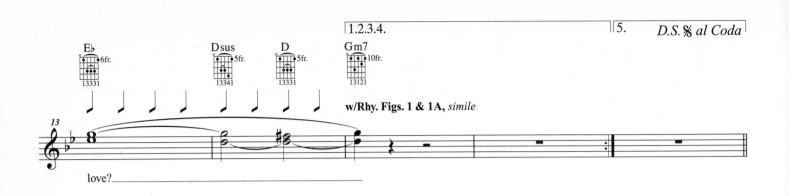

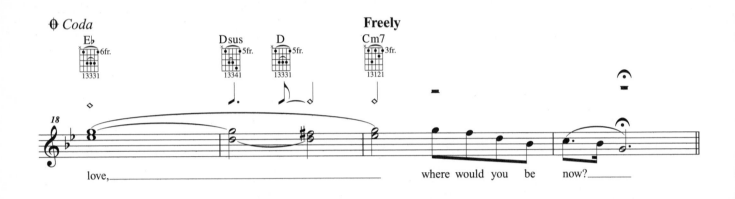

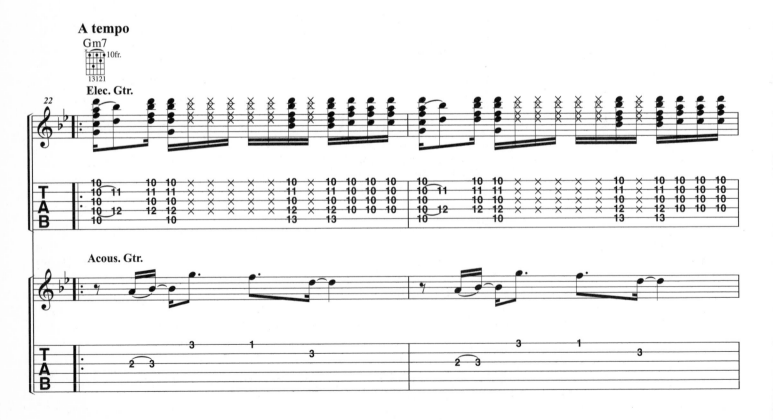

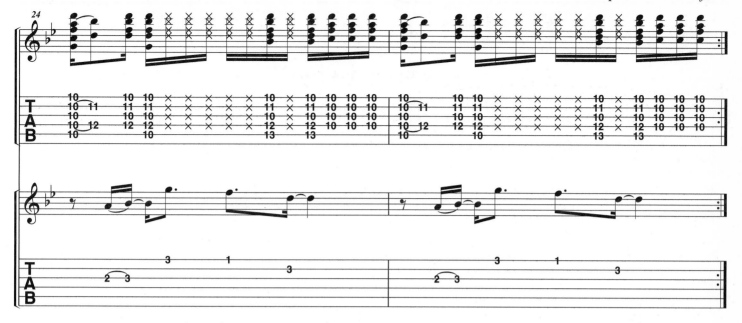

Verse 2:
You know I saw Miss Lucy,
Down along the tracks;
She lost her home and her family,
And she won't be comin' back.
Without love, where would you be right now,
Without love?

Verses 3 & 5:
Well, the Illinois Central
And the Southern Central freight,
Gotta keep on pushin', mama,
'Cause you know they're runnin' late.
Without love, where would you be right now,
Without love?
(1st time to Verse 4:)
(2nd time to Verse 6:)

Verse 4:
Harmonica Solo
(To Verse 5:)

Verse 6:
Where pistons keep on churnin'
And the wheels go 'round and 'round,
And the steel rails are cold and hard
For the miles that they go down.
Without love, where would you be right now,
Without love?
(To Coda)

Mama Told Me Not to Come

Key Thoughts
Written by Randy Newman, "Mama Told Me Not to Come" became Three Dog Night's first chart topper in 1970.

Take Note
The electric piano figure in the intro and verse reflects the offsetting, chaotic party scene depicted in the lyrics. Arranged for guitar in our transcription, it is a disorienting sequence of six eighth notes that cycle within a measure that's supposed to fit eight. Until the drum and bass enter to establish the beat, it's impossible to tell what meter you're in.

Characteristic of a Randy Newman composition, there's some interesting counterpoint on the chorus. While the bass ascends G–B–C–E♭, there is an internal voice that descends G–F–E–E♭ within the chord progression.

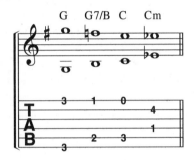

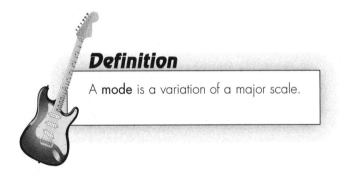

Definition

A **mode** is a variation of a major scale.

Within this counterpoint, the guitar plays a funky line (along with the bass) based on a Mixolydian *mode* with a key chromatic note thrown in for a bluesy inflection. That extra C♯ note is borrowed from the G blues scale (G–B♭–C–C♯–D–F).

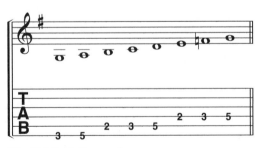

The G Mixolydian mode.

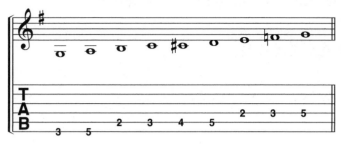

The G Mixolydian mode with the added bluesy note.

Note that, on the second pass of the chorus chord progression, the guitar player jumps the octave and then inverts the riff with a descending guitar line against the ascending bass part. Simple variations can add a lot.

Guitar Gods

In 1967, singers Danny Hutton, Cory Wells, and Chuck Negron formed **THREE DOG NIGHT,** and after a few early unsuccessful singles, the group hired backing musicians Jimmy Greenspoon (keyboards), Mike Allsup (guitar), Joe Schermie (bass), and Floyd Sneed (drums). Although the group didn't do much in the way of writing original material, they arguably released some of the best interpretations and arrangements of others' works. They scored their first top-ten hit in 1969 with Harry Nilsson's "One." A year later, the song "Mama Told Me Not to Come," written by the legendary composer/songwriter Randy Newman, was their first to make it to No. 1. The group's biggest hit, Hoyt Axton's "Joy to the World," spent six weeks at the top of the pop charts in 1971. Three Dog Night enjoyed huge success until 1976, when internal disagreement led to the group's breakup the following year.

MAMA TOLD ME NOT TO COME

Capo at 1st fret to match original recording.

Moderately ♩ = 112

Words and Music by
RANDY NEWMAN

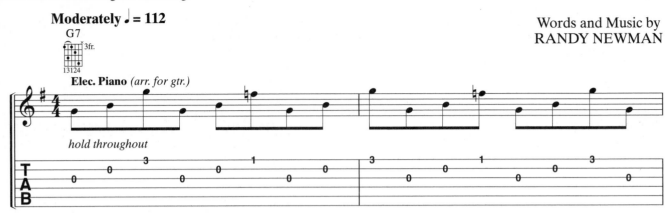

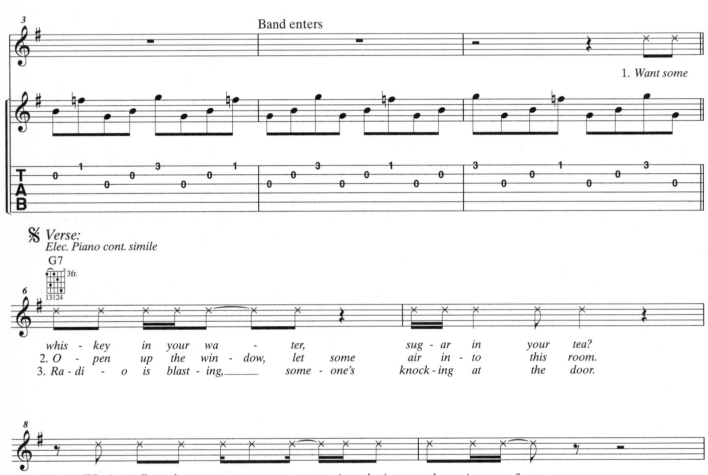

Band enters

1. *Want some*

℠ Verse:
Elec. Piano cont. simile

whis-	key	in	your	wa-	ter,	sug-	ar in your tea?

whis - key in your wa - ter, sug - ar in your tea?
2. *O - pen up the win - dow, let some air in - to this room.*
3. *Ra - di - o is blast - ing,___ some - one's knock - ing at the door.*

What's all these cra - zy ques - tions they're ask - ing me?___
I think I'm al - most chok - ing from the smell of stale per - fume.
I'm look - ing at my girl and___ she's passed out on the floor.

This is___ the cra - zi - est par - ty there could ev - er be.
And that___ cig - a - rette you're smok - in' 'bout scared me half to death.
I seen so man - y things I ain't nev - er seen be - fore.

Mama Told Me Not to Come - 4 - 1

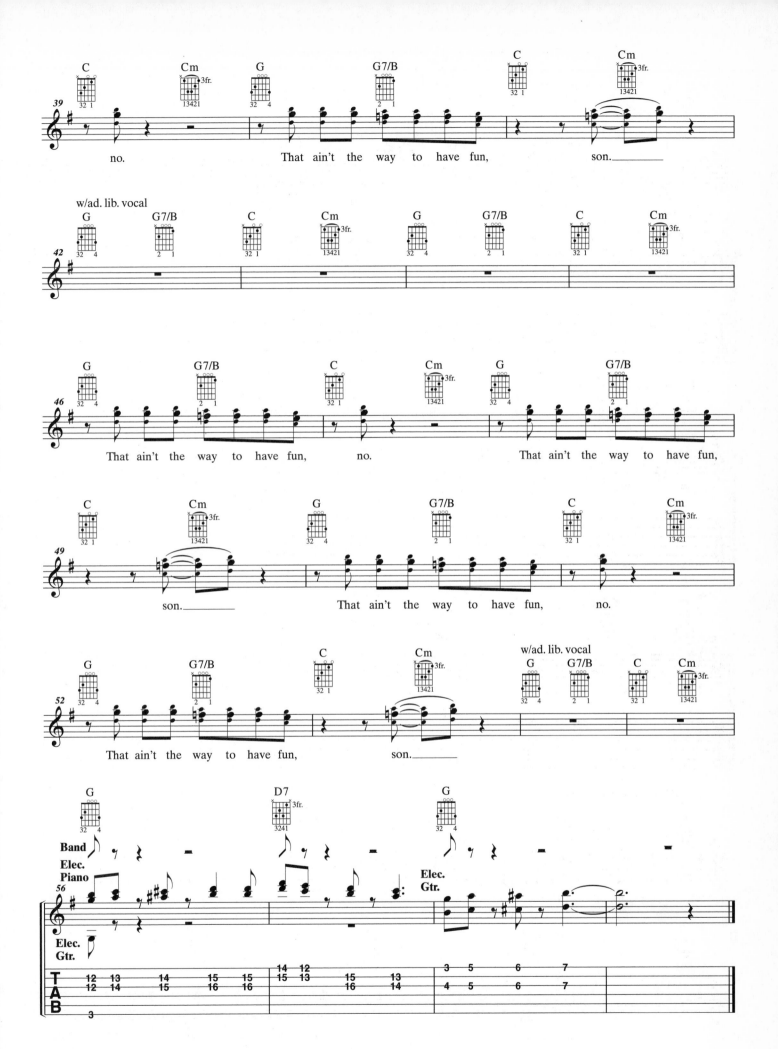

Panama

Key Thoughts

"Panama" features lots of Eddie Van Halen's signature rhythm and lead style. The intro is challenging, but we've simplified it enough so that with careful practice, a little hard work, and some of Eddie's "go-for-it" attitude, this is within your reach.

Take Note

The recording is a half step low, so you'll need to tune your guitar down a half step if you want to play along.

We're going to focus on the four-bar introduction. If you can master this much, most of the rest is related, so you'll be well on your way to playing the whole thing. Listen carefully to the recording before you try to play this. Listen in small pieces and try to relate what you see in the notation and TAB to what you hear. Even though this arrangement is simplified, pretty much everything Eddie does is here for you. The main thing missing is his signature whammy-bar dive-bomb sounds that you hear on the recording, where he drops the A chord in the fourth measure.

The first two measures are played in an E barre chord at the seventh-fret position. Hold the barre down the entire time; don't lift your 1st finger until measure 3. Measures 3 and 4 are very similar to the first two measures, but dropped two frets to the fifth position. Use down-strokes the whole time.

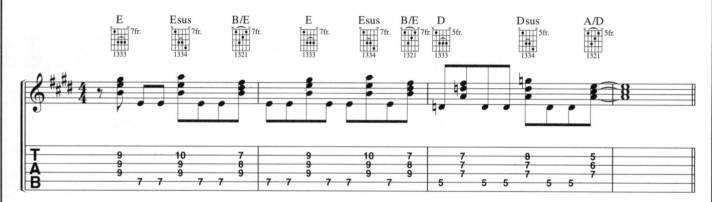

☆ Fun Fact ☆

The guitar solo in Michael Jackson's smash hit "Beat It" was played by Eddie Van Halen. Eddie was so thrilled when producer Quincy Jones invited him down to play on the project that he refused to be paid for his work. The song turned out to be one of the biggest hits of the '80s.

PANAMA

To match recorded key, tune guitar down one half step.

Words and Music by
EDWARD VAN HALEN, ALEX VAN HALEN,
MICHAEL ANTHONY and DAVID LEE ROTH

Panama - 5 - 1

Verse 2:
Ain't nothin' like it, her shiny machine,
Got the feel for the wheel, keep the moving parts clean.
Hot shoe, burnin' down the avenue,
Got an on-ramp comin' through my bedroom.
Don't you know she's comin' home to me?
You'll lose her in the turn.
I'll get her!
(To Chorus:)

Panama - 5 - 5

121

Peter Gunn

Henry Mancini's score to the popular late '50s TV show *Peter Gunn* introduced the world to his own smoky brand of blues-based jazz. The theme song was an immediate hit and spawned many cover versions. We based our arrangement on Duane Eddy's hit guitar instrumental version.

If you've listened to Duane Eddy play this song, you've heard how cool his guitar sounds. To imitate that killer tone, you need a hollow-body electric guitar (an old Gretsch would be perfect), a *tremolo bar*, and heavy-gauge flat-wound strings. Use your lead pickup, and put plenty of reverb on the amp.

Definition

The **tremolo bar** (or trem bar) is found on some electric guitars, attached to the bridge. Using the handle, you can affect the strings of the guitar to create vibrato, or even drop them down to a lower pitch and bring them back up again.

Despite the fact that this song is written in the key of F—not a very common guitar key—everything lies pretty nicely on the instrument. Duane opens the song with a tremolo bar effect. Don't worry—if you don't have a tremolo bar, you can still play this song.

- ◆ If you have a tremolo bar, here's what you do. Fret the F at the first fret. Push down on the bar enough to drop the F down one half step to E (do this *before* you play the note). Play the note, and let the bar return back up, raising the note from E to F.

- ◆ If you don't have a tremolo bar, you can still simulate the effect. Play the open low E string, then hammer-on to the first-fret F. Yes, the tremolo bar effect is very cool, but this is easier if you don't have the gear.

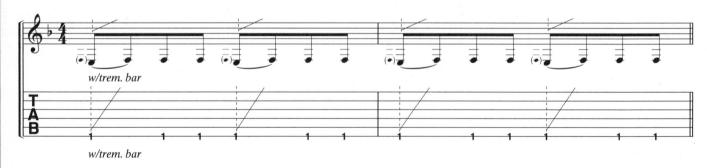

Now let's try the famous signature bass line riff. Use a small barre with the 1st finger at the first fret to play from the starting F to the B♭ on beat 4. To get the right sound, use a palm mute to mute the strings, and use all down-strokes. (See the lesson for "Dr. Feelgood" for an explanation of the palm mute technique.)

That covers the whole guitar part, but the melody is also fun to play. Just follow the TAB to find the right positions for the melody notes.

Guitar Gods

In 1958, *Peter Gunn*, a stylish, gritty, private-eye drama, debuted in black and white on NBC. Starring Craig Stevens as the dapper and sophisticated private eye, the series was set to an infectious, jazz-driven soundtrack, written by none other than **HENRY MANCINI**, one of the greatest and most successful film score writers in Hollywood. Blake Edwards, the series creator, came up with the idea to integrate jazz with the action, fusing score and storyline together. The idea worked beautifully. Mancini's film and TV scores blended cool, West-coast jazz with hip driving bass lines and lots of slick blues inflections, and established the standard for all detective and spy genre soundtracks to come in the '60s, including the "James Bond Theme" and "Secret Agent Man."

PETER GUNN

By HENRY MANCINI

The Reason

Key Thoughts

Playing the main guitar riff from the verses of this song will do wonders for your pick technique. The riff is such an obvious good technical exercise that, like the riff to "Sweet Child O' Mine," it may have started life as a technical study.

Take Note

This riff has wide string skips. We suggest you use a pick because it will teach you tremendous pick control, but you have the option of using your fingers if that is much easier. If you do use your fingers, use your thumb to play all the bottom notes and your middle finger to pluck the top melody. You could also use a "hybrid" pick and finger technique, where your pick plays the bottom bass note and either your middle or ring finger plucks the top melody line.

Essentially, the riff consists of a bass note (always the root of the chord) that constantly alternates with a simple melody drawn from the chord shape. The riff moves from the E chord to C#m, A, and B chords. Below are the fingerings for each pattern, isolated so you can practice them slowly. In these examples, the chord frame above the music shows the basic hand position required to play the riff, and the left hand fingers are given below the notes. In the song arrangement, the chord frames show you the strumming chords.

Here is the pattern for the E chord.

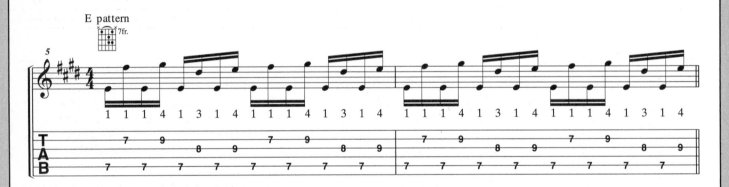

The next example is the pattern for the C#m chord. Notice that the fingering is basically parallel to the E chord pattern, just moved down to the fourth fret and altered to work over a minor chord instead of a major chord.

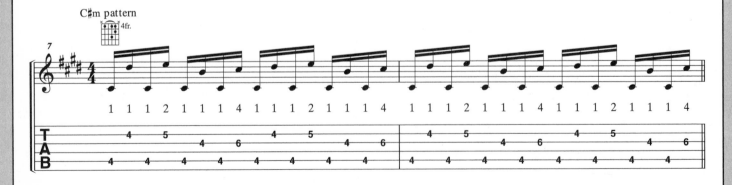

The A chord pattern is exactly the same as the pattern for C#m, only using an open A as the bass note instead of a C#.

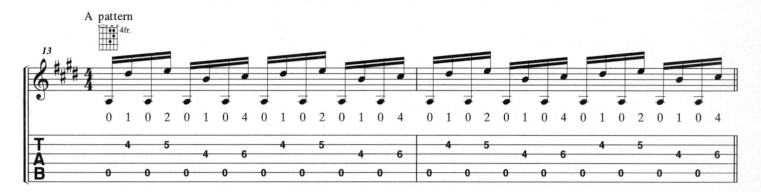

Here, the pattern slides down to the second fret to work over the B chord.

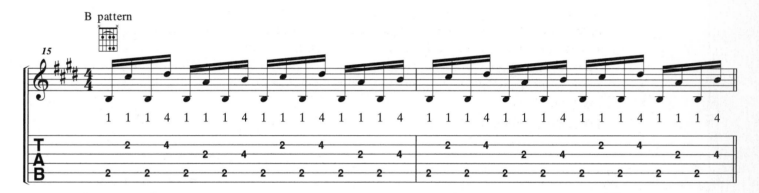

Guitar Gods

Playing an emotional, melodic brand of grunge-influenced rock, **HOOBASTANK** had one the biggest hits in 2004 with "The Reason." After a succession of radio and MTV hits that included "Crawling in the Dark" and "Running Away," "The Reason" finally helped the band reach mainstream success. The Southern California-based quartet formed when singer Doug Robb met guitarist Dan Estrin at a battle-of-the-bands competition in high school. Soon after, they added bassist Markku Lappalainen and drummer Chris Hesse, and Hoobastank remains one of the best young bands in rock today.

THE REASON

Words and Music by
DANIEL ESTRIN and
DOUGLAS ROBB

The Reason - 4 - 1

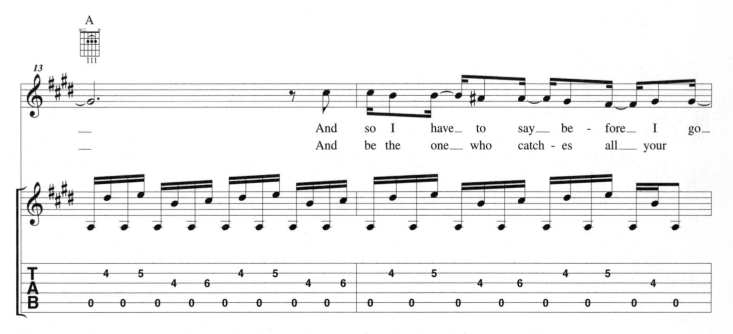

The Reason - 4 - 2

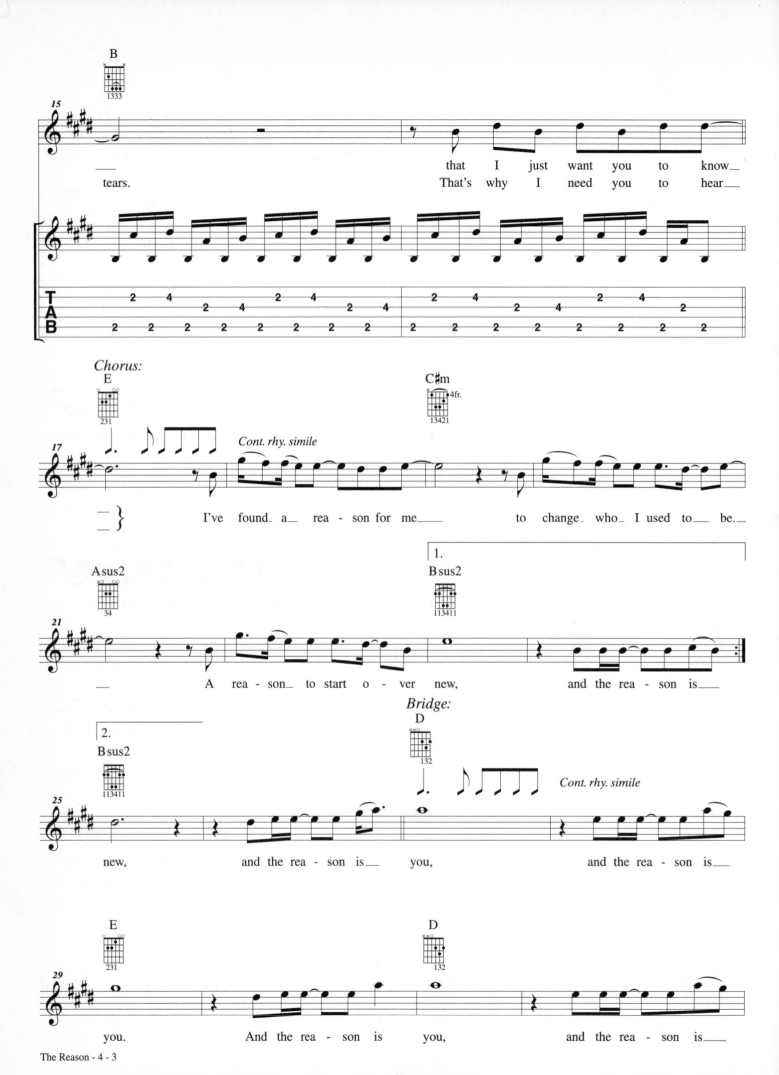

Sunshine of Your Love

Cream is widely recognized as the first true rock supergroup—a band formed by musicians already recognized as superstars in their own right. The band had a knack for finding the perfect riff, and the riff to "Sunshine of Your Love" may be their most famous.

"Sunshine of Your Love" begins with a stripped-down version of the riff. When you listen to the recording, you'll notice that the notes have a low, thick sound, even though they are in a relatively high range for a riff of this type. The fullness of the sound comes from playing these notes on low strings up around the tenth fret. If you were to play the same notes in first position, you'd get a much weaker, thinner tone. To really nail Clapton's sound, you need to add a wide vibrato to the F note by rapidly bending the string (toward the floor) and returning. The opening two bars are shown below, with a wavy symbol over the F to indicate the vibrato.

After the initial single-line statement of the riff, Clapton fattens it up by playing the first four notes as power chords and the last three notes an octave higher. The riff has gone from a one-dimensional linear melody to suddenly having a low bottom end (from the power chords) and a striking high end (the high octave ending).

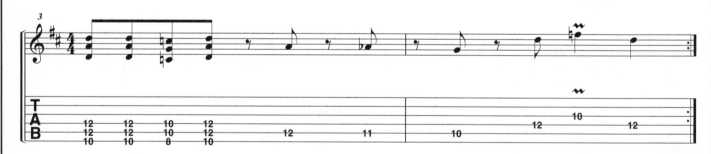

☆ Fun Fact ☆

After deciding "Sweet 'n' Sour Rock 'n' Roll" just wasn't quite the right name for them, the band went with "Cream" instead. It was a much more appropriate name for the trio, who were considered to be the "cream of the crop" amongst blues and jazz musicians in the British music scene.

SUNSHINE OF YOUR LOVE

Words and Music by
JACK BRUCE, PETE BROWN
and ERIC CLAPTON

To Coda ⊕ Chorus:

I've__ been wait - ing so__ long

to__ be where__ I'm go - ing in__ the sun - shine of__ your

love.____

1.

Sweet Child O' Mine

Key Thoughts

The opening guitar riff of "Sweet Child O' Mine" was originally intended as a technical exercise. Played completely unaccompanied on the recording, the riff propelled the band to national prominence and the song to No. 1, becoming one of the critical must-know licks for an entire generation of rock guitarists.

Take Note

To match the recording, you'll have to tune all your strings down one half step. This is very common in hard rock guitar because it makes the strings a little "softer" for easier bends and vibrato, and it also give the notes a thicker tone.

The beauty of the signature riff is its simplicity. It is played entirely in the twelfth position, so lock your 1st finger at the twelfth fret. The riff is a basic pattern that repeats over three chords: D, C, and G. The genius of its construction is that only the first note of the pattern must change in order for it to conform to each new chord—D for the D chord, E for the C chord, and G for the G chord. Everything else remains the same. The pattern is shown below with some fingering to help you out. Be sure to use lots of overdrive on your amplifier.

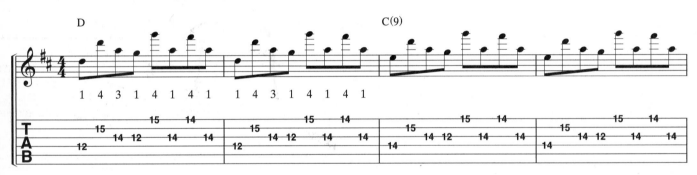

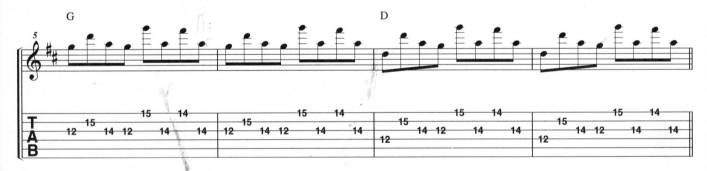

Guitar Gods

In 1987, the arrival of **GUNS N' ROSES'** explosive debut, *Appetite for Destruction*, marked the return of rock and roll. Coming out at a time when dance music and hair metal were dominating, Guns N' Roses proved that pure old-school hard rock was still viable. *Appetite for Destruction* included some of the greatest hard-rock hits of all time. The track "Welcome to the Jungle" has reached near iconic status, while songs like "Paradise City" and "Mr. Brownstone" are modern-day classics. The album's centerpiece may very well be the power ballad "Sweet Child O' Mine," showcasing Axl Rose's sensitive side. (Who knew he had one!)

SWEET CHILD O' MINE

Words and Music by W. AXL ROSE, SLASH, IZZY STRADLIN,
DUFF McKAGAN and STEVEN ADLER

To match recorded key, tune guitar down one half step.

Where do we go?___ Where do we go___ now?

Where do we go?___ Where do we go___ now?

No, no, no, no, no, no, no, sweet child,___ sweet

child___ of mine.___

Truckin'

Key Thoughts

"Truckin'" pretty much sums up the "hang it up and see what tomorrow brings" life-style associated with Grateful Dead. The main guitar riff is an infectious boogie riff that's easy and fun to play.

Take Note

"Truckin'" is in $\frac{12}{8}$ time. Like most songs in this meter, you should feel it as four strong beats per measure, with three equal eighth notes per beat. You can really see this subdivision in bar 2 of the opening blues lick. A typical E blues guitar rhythm pattern begins in bar 3.

Starting at the chorus, you'll see rhythm slashes for the acoustic rhythm guitar, which basically just plays a strong shuffle rhythm strum. For the muted chords with "x" note-heads on beats 2 and 4, strike the strings with a short stab of the pick to create a percussive *back beat*, which accents beats 2 and 4.

The most memorable riff from the song begins around bar 16 with Rhythm Figure 1. Jerry inserts this lick towards the end of each chorus and verse, wherever there are four bars of an E chord. The lick is played on electric guitar. To get the right sound, use your lead pickup near the bridge, and bring your pick down toward the bridge as well to create a bright "twangy" sound.

☆ Fun Fact ☆

Despite their studio successes, Grateful Dead kept their focus primarily on being a live act. Tours were lengthened, shows added, and the mass of loyal fans who followed the band in their tie-dyed clothes and VW Microbuses soon became known as "Deadheads."

TRUCKIN'

Moderately fast ♩. = 114

Intro:

Words by ROBERT HUNTER
Music by JERRY GARCIA,
BOB WEIR and PHIL LESH

Chorus 1:

Truck - in',___ got_my chips cashed_in,___ keep truck-in',___ like the doo-dah___ man._____ To-

geth - er,___ more or less in___ line.___ Just keep truck - in' on._____

Welcome to the Jungle

"Welcome to the Jungle" was Guns N' Roses' first single from their first album, and it quickly catapulted the band to the top of the hard rock heap in the late '80s. Axl Rose's lyrics were inspired by an encounter with a homeless man in New York City, who asked the young man, "Do you know where you are? You're in the jungle, baby. You're gonna die!"

Like "Sweet Child O' Mine," "Welcome to the Jungle" is played with the guitar tuned down. To match the recording, tune all your strings a half step low.

On the original recording of "Welcome to the Jungle," the intro riff is heavily processed with delay. The delay echoes the notes in the spaces between where they're played, so they overlap and create a cascading torrent of sound. The notes themselves are from a relatively simple descending B minor pentatonic scale. Follow the alternating pick directions shown below, and the rhythm should come easily.

The verse riff is a classic rock riff based on an open-position A5 chord. Again, follow the alternating pick directions shown here to help with the rhythm.

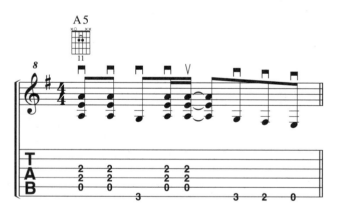

Fun Fact

Not many bands can boast the distinction of having their music used as a tool for psychological torture, but "Welcome to the Jungle" was indeed employed for such a purpose in 1989. When U.S. troops could not extricate deposed Panamanian dictator Manuel Noriega from his compound, they set up loudspeakers and blasted hard rock music to "irritate and intimidate" him into surrendering. The kickoff song in this new form of warfare? "Welcome to the Jungle."

The E5 riff at the end of each verse adds a slight rhythmic variation. Instead of two sixteenth notes in the second half of beat two, there is only one.

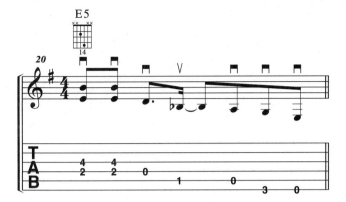

Here's a further variation on the fourth repetition of the E5 riff, immediately preceding the return to the beginning of the verse.

If the written part in Guitar Solo 1 proves too difficult, you can play the rhythm figure below in its place.

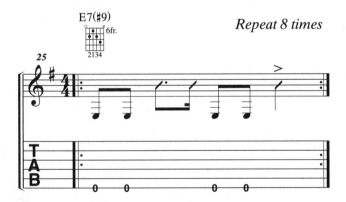

Now drop your axe down around your knees, don your top hat, and prepare to feel your serpentine.

WELCOME TO THE JUNGLE

To match recorded key, tune guitar down one half step.

Words and Music by
W. AXL ROSE, SLASH, IZZY STRADLIN,
DUFF McKAGAN and STEVEN ADLER

Welcome to the Jungle - 6 - 1

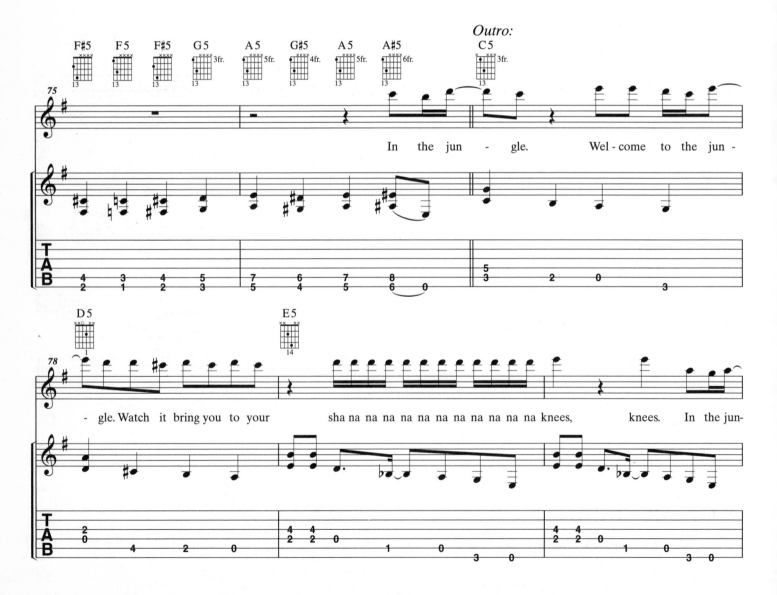

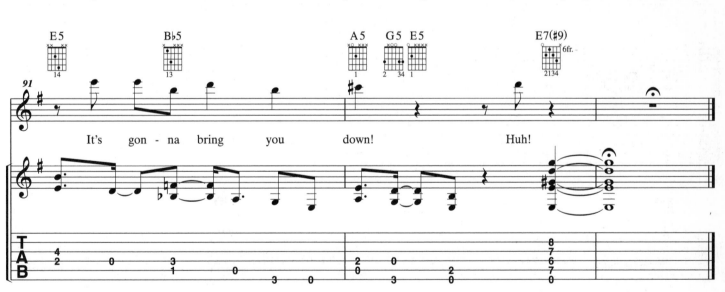

Verse 2:
Welcome to the jungle,
We take it day by day.
If you want it, you're gonna bleed,
But it's the price you pay.
And you're a very sexy girl
Who's very hard to please.
You can taste the bright lights,
But you won't get them for free.
In the jungle.
Welcome to the jungle.
Feel my, my, my, my serpentine.
Uh ah. I wanna hear you scream!
(To Interlude:)

Verse 3:
Welcome to the jungle,
It gets worse every day.
You learn to live like an animal
In the jungle where we play.
If you got a hunger for what you see,
You'll take it eventually.
You can have anything you want,
But you better not take it from me.
In the jungle.
Welcome to the jungle.
Watch it bring you to your
Sha na na na na na na na na na na na na
Knees, knees.
Uh. I'm gonna watch you bleed.
(To Bridge:)

When I Come Around

Green Day's mud-splattered performance of "When I Come Around" at Woodstock '94 helped elevate the band from punky cult status to mainstream pop-rock stardom. The basic riff is a prime example of how a simple chord progression can be combined with a poppy bass part to create a catchy hook.

The chords in the opening riff are pretty simple. With the exception of a quick down-up stroke on the sixteenth notes that come before each chord change, hammer out the rhythm with all down-strokes as shown below.

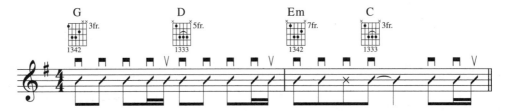

The all-down-stroke picking is even more important on the chorus, where the sixteenth-note embellishments are done away with in favor of a straight, driving eighth-note pattern.

Guitar Gods

GREEN DAY hit it big in 1994 with their major-label debut, *Dookie*. The album almost single-handedly reestablished punk rock music in the mainstream and helped the genre reach levels it had never seen before. *Dookie* featured the MTV-approved singles "Longview," "Basket Case," and "When I Come Around," and has sold over 20 million copies worldwide, making it the best-selling punk album of all time. By the time Green Day released the critically acclaimed album *American Idiot* in 2004, they had already become established as a mainstay on rock radio, and their successes have paved the way for many pop-punk, punk metal, and ska bands.

The guitar solo is a prime example of minimalist proto-punk guitar playing. Except for an occasional A note, even when the chords change to Em and C, Billie Joe never veers away from the notes G–D–G until the end.

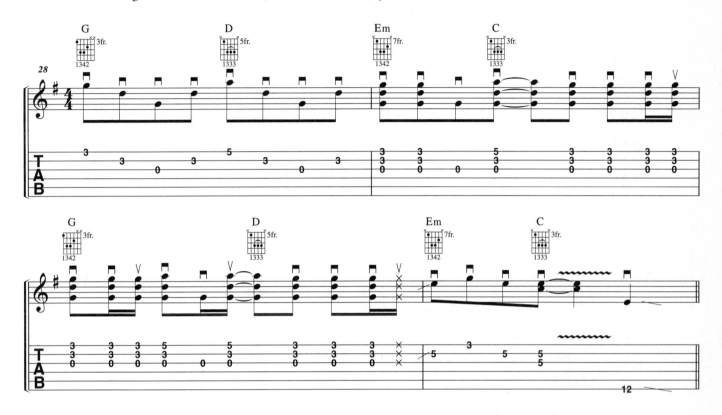

WHEN I COME AROUND

Lyrics by BILLIE JOE
Music by GREEN DAY

To match recorded key, tune guitar down one half step.

Moderately ♩ = 100

Intro:

Play 3 times

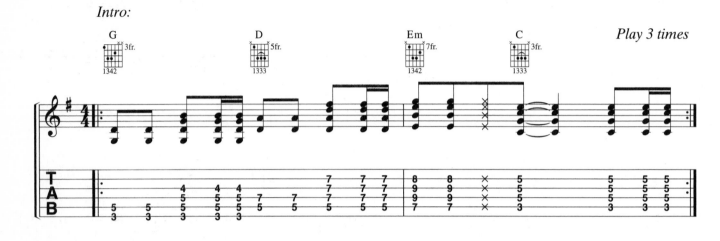

Verse:

Cont. rhy. simile

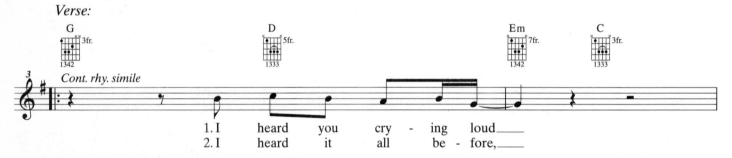

1. I heard you cry - ing loud___
2. I heard it all be - fore,___

all the way___ a - cross town.___ You've been search-
so don't___ knock down my door.___ I'm a los-

- ing for that some - one, and it's me,___ out on the prowl.___ As
- er and a us - er so I don't___ need no ac - cus - er to

When I Come Around - 4 - 1

'cause you know___ where I'll be found   when I come a-round.___

Ooh.

Guitar Solo:

Elec. Gtr. 2

Cont. in slashes

Chorus:

No   time   to   search   the   world   a - round

Wild Night

Key Thoughts

From the rollicking strummed intro of "Wild Night" to its infectious opening guitar and bass riff, Van and the band really nailed the groove. At any Van Morrison show, as soon as the guitar strikes that opening Em chord, the entire audience is on its feet and dancing in the aisles. It's that joyous groove that you should be striving for as you play this song.

Take Note

The intro rhythm guitar part looks a lot more complicated than it really is. Measures 1 and 2 are just a strummed Em chord in first position, then seventh position. Measures 3 and 4 are a classic rock and roll rhythm pattern.

To play bars 1 and 2, begin with a first-position Em chord and imitate the accents and rhythm you hear on the original recording. Strum with a constant down-up motion and use your ear to imitate the accent pattern. The strums in between the accented chords will then fall into place on their own. These two measures are shown below. Note that the last G chord is really an anticipation (meaning the chord is played before the first beat of the bar), so don't think of it as the last chord of the measure—it's really the first chord of the next measure.

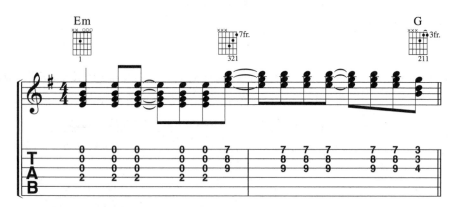

Guitar Gods

Born George Ivan Morrison in Belfast, Northern Ireland, the sometimes-rock, sometimes-blues, sometimes-another-genre-altogether artist **VAN MORRISON** got his start at age 15 while touring military bases throughout Europe with the R&B group the Monarchs. Several years later, Morrison's next gig with his own band, Them, yielded several U.K. hits, including the rock staple "Gloria." After leaving Them in 1966, he ventured out and began recording as a solo artist with lasting hits like "Brown-Eyed Girl," and his 1968 release *Astral Weeks* became regarded as one of the greatest LPs ever produced. Morrison recorded several albums after relocating to California with his new wife, Janet Planet, and capped off 1971's *Tupelo Honey* with an introspective, thoughtfully melodic expression of blissful marriage in the song "Wild Night."

Now let's look at the second half of the intro rhythm figure, which starts at bar 3. The whole pattern is basically two beats of G chord with an inside bluesy pattern on the 3rd string: B–B–C–B♭. Then those two beats repeat over and over. For practice, it's a great idea to play just the 3rd-string notes as a constant eighth-note pattern to get the sound in your head before trying it as part of the chord strum.

Once you have the sound of that inside pattern in your head, try the full pattern. Follow these steps:

◆ Hold a full G barre chord and strum down-up.

◆ Quickly flatten your 4th finger across the middle strings at the fifth fret, and quickly stand it back up to create the move from C to B♭ on beat 2. Note that as you flatten your 4th finger, you have to release your 2nd finger from the 3rd string to get the B♭—but that action happens fairly automatically as you flatten the 4th finger.

◆ Even though all six strings are indicated in the music, focus the up-down strumming of your pick mostly on the middle strings, with larger accents hitting more strings.

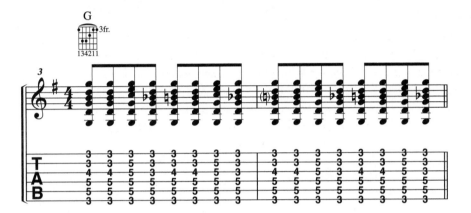

After the first four bars, the second guitar enters and doubles the signature bass line riff. That riff is shown below.

163

WILD NIGHT

Moderately fast ♩ = 152

Words and Music by
VAN MORRISON

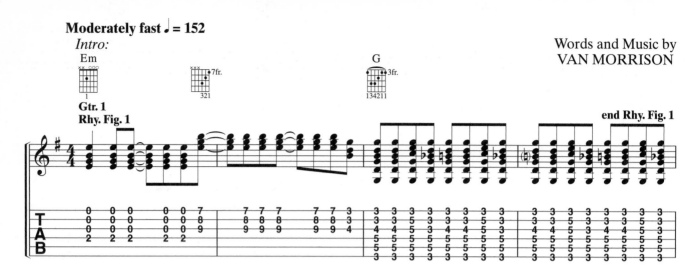

Intro:

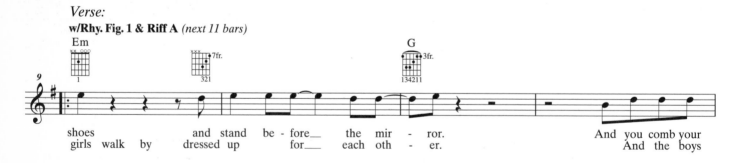

Verse:

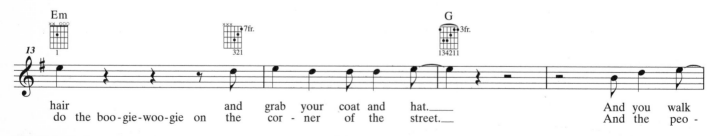

Wild Night - 4 - 1

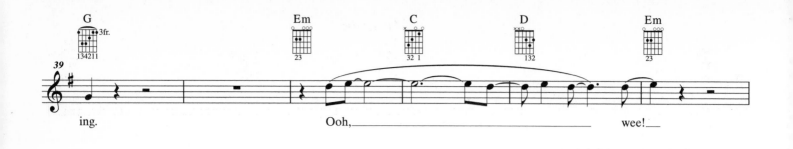

ing.   Ooh,_____ wee!__

The wild_____ night   is call - ing.   2. All the

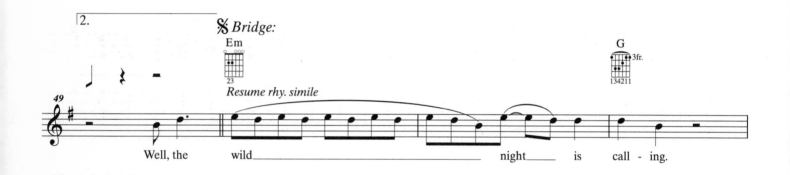

Well, the wild_____ night____ is call - ing.

The___ wild_____ night____ is call - ing.

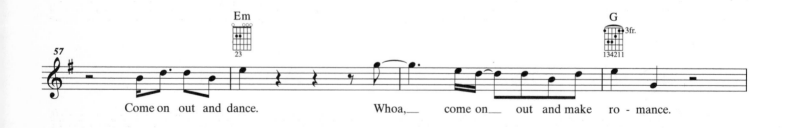

Come on out and dance.   Whoa,___ come on___ out and make ro - mance.

Come on out and dance.   Come on____ out,   make ro - mance.__

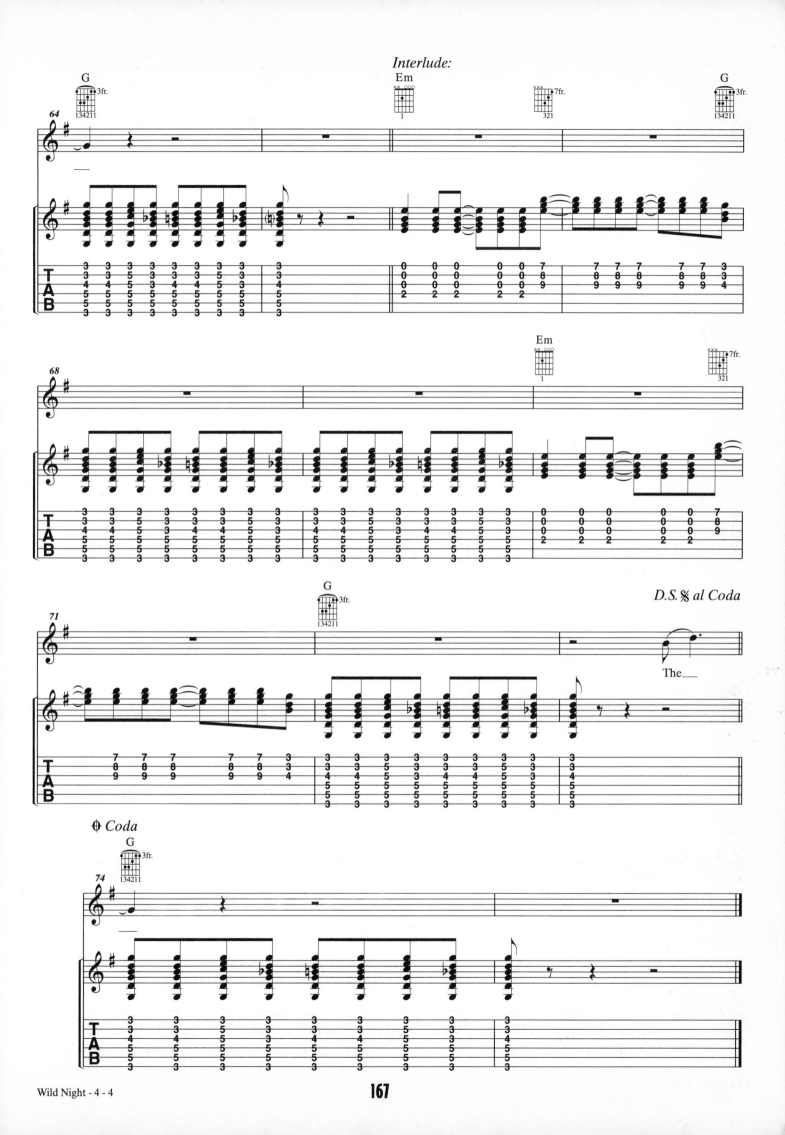

Appendix

Chord Theory

You don't have to understand the music theory of chord construction to play the songs in this book. The notation, TAB, and chord diagrams tell you everything you need to know to play the music correctly. Someday, though, you're bound to find music that doesn't give you as much information as we have, and you'll need to know at least a little bit about chords to get it right. This section should help you out in those situations, and also add some basic chops to your knowledge of music.

Intervals

Play any note on the guitar, then play a note one fret above it. The distance between these two notes is a *half step*. Play another note followed by a note two frets above it. The distance between these two notes is a *whole step* (two half steps). The distance between any two notes is referred to as an *interval*.

In the example of the C major scale on the following page, the letter names are shown above the notes and the *scale degrees* (numbers) of the notes are written below. Notice that C is the first degree of the scale, D is the second, and so on.

The name of an interval is determined by counting the number of scale degrees from one note to the next. For example, an interval of a 3rd, starting on C, would be determined by counting up three scale degrees, or C–D–E (1–2–3). C to E is a 3rd. An interval of a 4th, starting on C, would be determined by counting up four scale degrees, or C–D–E–F (1–2–3–4). C to F is a 4th.

Intervals are not only labeled by the distance between scale degrees, but by the *quality* of the interval. An interval's quality is determined by counting the number of whole steps and half steps between the two notes of that interval. For example, C to E is a 3rd. C to E is also a *major* third because there are 2 whole steps between C and E. Likewise, C to E♭ is a 3rd. C to E♭ is a *minor* third because there are 1½ steps between C and E♭.

There are five qualities used to describe intervals: *major, minor, perfect, diminished,* and *augmented.*

Interval Qualities

Quality	Abbreviation
major	M
minor	m
perfect	P
diminished	dim or °
augmented	aug or +

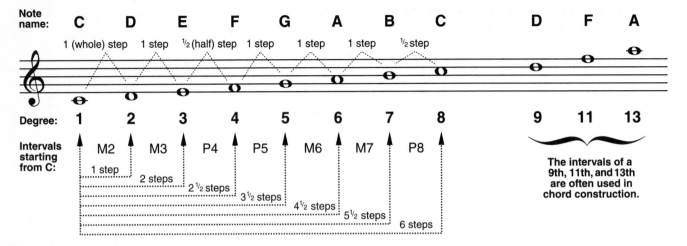

Particular intervals are associated with certain qualities. Not all qualities pertain to every type of interval, as seen in the following table.

Interval Type	Possible Qualities
2nd, 9th	major, minor, augmented
3rd, 6th, 13th	major, minor, diminished, augmented
4th, 5th, 11th	perfect, diminished, augmented
7th	major, minor, diminished

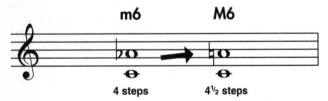

When a major interval is made smaller by a half step, it becomes a minor interval.

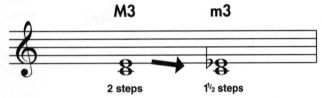

When a minor interval is made larger by a half step, it becomes a major interval.

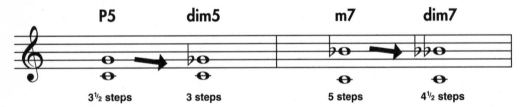

When a perfect or minor interval is made smaller by a half step, it becomes a diminished interval.

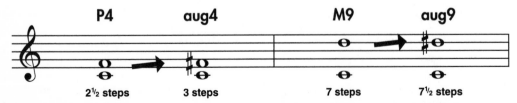

When a perfect or major interval is made larger by a half step, it becomes an augmented interval.

170

Following is a table of intervals starting on the note C. Notice that some intervals are labeled *enharmonic*, which means that they are written differently but sound the same (see aug2 and m3).

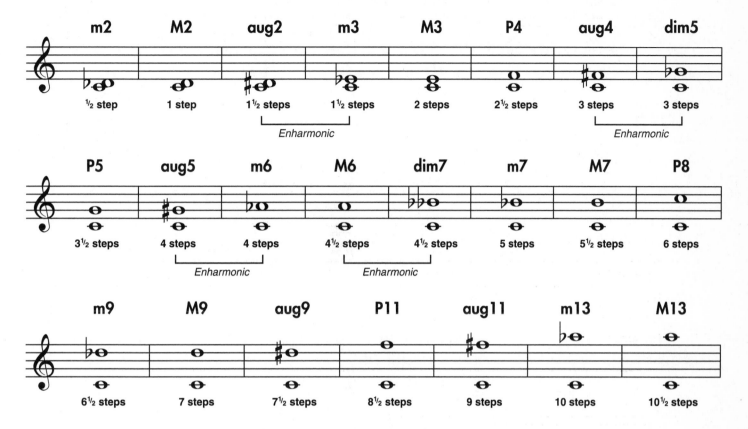

Basic Triads

Two or more notes played together are called a *chord*. Most commonly, a chord will consist of three or more notes. A three-note chord is called a *triad*. The *root* of a triad (or any other chord) is the note from which a chord is constructed. The relationship of the intervals from the root to the other notes of a chord determines the chord *type*. Triads are most frequently identified as one of four chord types: *major*, *minor*, *diminished*, and *augmented*.

Chord Types

All chord types can be identified by the intervals used to create the chord. For example, the C major triad is built beginning with C as the root, adding a major 3rd (E) and adding a perfect 5th (G). All major triads contain a root, M3, and P5.

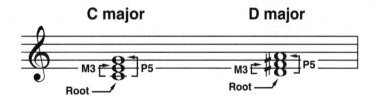

Minor triads contain a root, minor 3rd, and perfect 5th. (An easier way to build a minor triad is to simply lower the 3rd of a major triad.) All minor triads contain a root, m3, and P5.

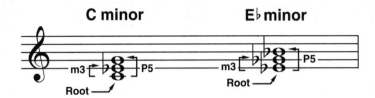

Diminished triads contain a root, minor 3rd, and diminished 5th. If the perfect 5th of a minor triad is made smaller by a half step (to become a diminished 5th), the result is a diminished triad. All diminished triads contain a root, m3, and dim5.

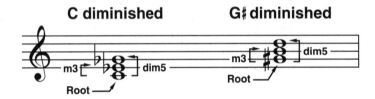

Augmented triads contain a root, major 3rd, and augmented 5th. If the perfect 5th of a major triad is made larger by a half step (to become an augmented 5th), the result is an augmented triad. All augmented triads contain a root, M3, and aug5.

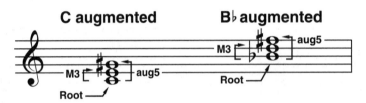

Chord Inversions

An important concept to remember about chords is that the bottom note of a chord will not always be the root. If the root of a triad, for instance, is moved above the 5th so that the 3rd is the bottom note of the chord, it is said to be in the *first inversion*. If the root and 3rd are moved above the 5th, the chord is in the *second inversion*. The number of inversions that a chord can have is related to the number of notes in the chord: a three-note chord can have two inversions, a four-note chord can have three inversions, etc.

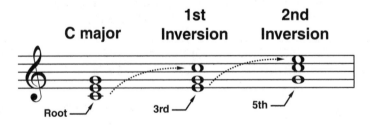

Building Chords

By using the four chord types as basic building blocks, it is possible to create a variety of chords by adding 6ths, 7ths, 9ths, 11ths, and so on. The following are examples of some of the many variations.

C Major Suspended Fourth
Csus

C Flat Fifth
C(♭5)

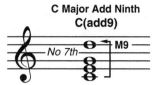

C Major Add Ninth
C(add9)

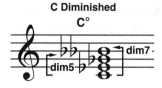

C Diminished
C°

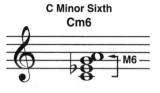

C Major Sixth
C6

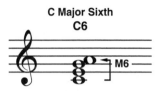

C Sixth Add Ninth
C6/9

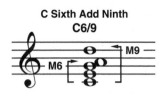

C Minor Sixth Add Ninth
Cm6/9

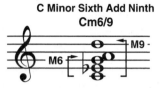

C Minor Sixth
Cm6

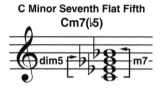

C Seventh
C7

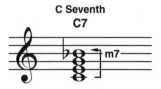

C Seventh Suspended Fourth
C7sus

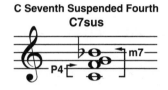

C Minor Seventh
Cm7

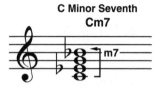

C Minor Seventh Flat Fifth
Cm7(♭5)

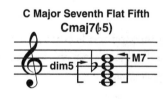

C Seventh Augmented Fifth
C7+

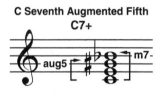

C Seventh Flat Fifth
C7(♭5)

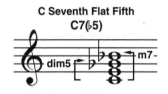

C Major Seventh
Cmaj7

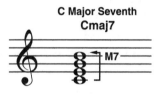

C Major Seventh Flat Fifth
Cmaj7(♭5)

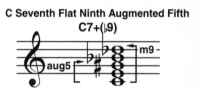

C Minor Major Seventh
Cm(maj7)

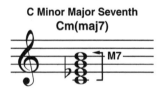

C Seventh Flat Ninth
C7(♭9)

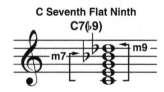

C Seventh Augmented Ninth
C7(♯9)

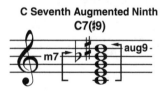

C Seventh Flat Ninth Augmented Fifth
C7+(♭9)

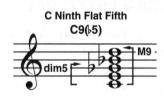

C Minor Ninth
Cm9

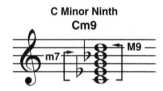

C Ninth
C9

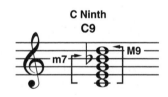

C Ninth Augmented Fifth
C9+

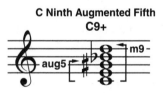

C Ninth Flat Fifth
C9(♭5)

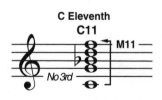

C Major Ninth
Cmaj9

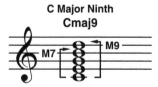

C Ninth Augmented Eleventh
C9(♯11)

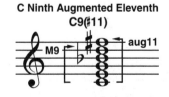

C Minor Ninth Major Seventh
Cm9(maj7)

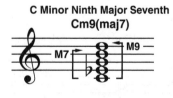

C Eleventh
C11

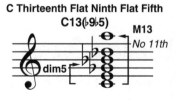

C Minor Eleventh
Cm11

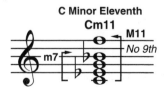

C Thirteenth
C13

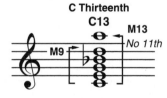

C Thirteenth Flat Ninth
C13(♭9)

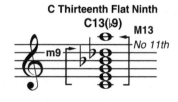

C Thirteenth Flat Ninth Flat Fifth
C13(♭9♭5)

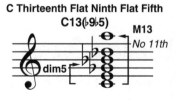

So far, the examples provided to illustrate intervals and chord construction have been based on C. Until you're familiar with chords, the C chord examples on the previous page can serve as a guide for building chords based on other notes. For example, to construct a G7(♭9) chord, you can first determine what intervals are contained in C7(♭9) and use the steps below to build the same chord starting on G.

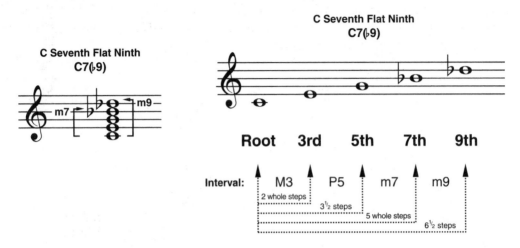

- ◆ First, determine the *root* of the chord. A chord is always named for its root, so G is the root of G7(♭9).
- ◆ Count *letter names* up from the *letter name of the root* (G) to determine the intervals of the chord. Counting three letter names up from G to B (G–A–B, 1–2–3) is a 3rd, G to D (G–A–B–C–D) is a 5th, G to F is a 7th, and G to A is a 9th.
- ◆ Determine the *quality* of the intervals by counting half steps and whole steps up from the root. G to B (2 whole steps) is a major 3rd, G to D (3½ steps) is a perfect 5th, G to F (5 whole steps) is a minor 7th, and G to A♭ (6½ steps) is a minor 9th.

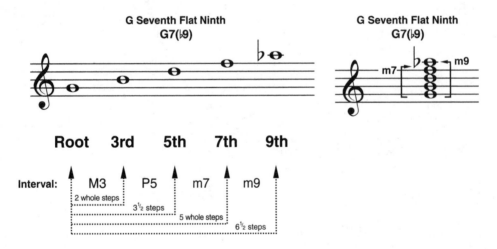

Follow this general guideline for determining the notes of any chord. As interval and chord construction become more familiar to you, you'll be able to create original fingerings on the guitar. Don't be afraid to experiment!

The Circle of Fifths

The *circle of fifths* will help to clarify which chords are enharmonic equivalents (yes, chords can be written enharmonically as well as notes). The circle of fifths also serves as a quick reference guide to the relationship of the keys and how key signatures can be figured out in a logical manner. Moving clockwise (up a P5) provides all of the sharp keys by progressively adding one sharp to the key signature. Moving counter-clockwise (down a P5) provides the flat keys by progressively adding one flat to the key signature.

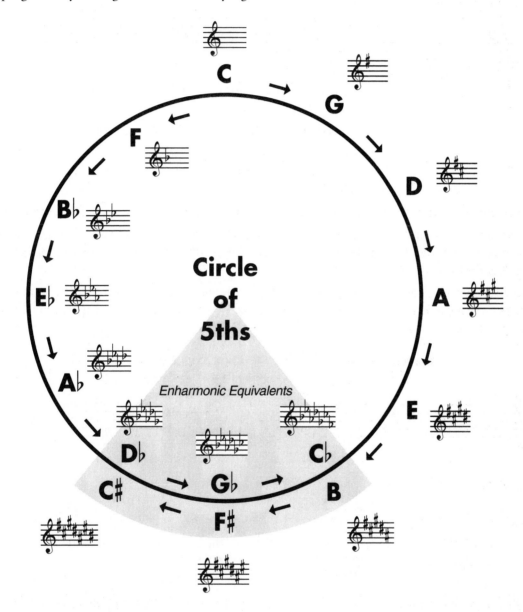

Chord Symbol Variations

Chord symbols are a form of musical shorthand that provide you with as much information about a chord as quickly as possible. The intent of using chord symbols is to convey enough information to recognize the chord, yet not so much as to confuse the meaning of the symbol. Chord symbols are not universally standardized and are written in many different ways—some are easy to understand, others are confusing. To illustrate this point, following is a list of some of the variations copyists, composers, and arrangers have created for the more common chord symbols.

C	Csus	C(♭5)	C(add9)	C5	Cm
C major	Csus4	C-5	C(9)	C(no3)	Cmin
Cmaj	C(addF)	C(5-)	C(add2)	C(omit3)	Cmi
CM	C4	C(♯4)	C(+9)		C-
			C(+D)		

C+	C°	C6	C6/9	Cm6/9	Cm6
C+5	Cdim	Cmaj6	C6(add9)	C-6/9	C-6
Caug	Cdim7	C(addA)	C6(addD)	Cm6(+9)	Cm(addA)
Caug5	C7dim	C(A)	C9(no7)	Cm6(add9)	Cm(+6)
C(♯5)			C9/6	Cm6(+D)	

C7	C7sus	Cm7	Cm7(♭5)	C7+	C7(♭5)
C(addB♭)	C7sus4	Cmi7	Cmi7-5	C7+5	C7-5
C7̶	Csus7	Cmin7	C-7(5-)	C7aug	C7(5-)
C(-7)	C7(+4)	C-7	Cø	C7aug5	C7̶-5
C(+7)		C7mi	C ½dim	C7(♯5)	C7(♯4)

Cmaj7	Cmaj7(♭5)	Cm(maj7)	C7(♭9)	C7(♯9)	C7+(♭9)
Cma7	Cmaj7(-5)	C-maj7	C7(-9)	C7(+9)	Caug7-9
C7	C7̶(-5)	C-7̶	C9♭	C9♯	C+7(♭9)
CΔ	CΔ(♭5)	Cmi7̶	C9-	C9+	C+9♭
CΔ7					C7+(-9)

Cm9	C9	C9+	C9(♭5)	Cmaj9	C9(♯11)
Cm7(9)	C7^9	C9(+5)	C9(-5)	C7̶(9)	C9(+11)
Cm7(+9)	C7add9	Caug9	C7$^9_{-5}$	C7̶(+9)	C(♯11)
C-9	C7(addD)	C(♯9♯5)	C9(5♭)	C9(maj7)	C11+
Cmi7(9+)	C7(+9)	C+9		C9̶	C11♯

Cm9(maj7)	C11	Cm11	C13	C13(♭9)	C13($^{♭9}_{♭5}$)
C-9(♯7)	C9(11)	C-11	C9addA	C13(-9)	C13(-9-5)
C(-9)7̶	C9addF	Cm(♭11)	C9(6)	C$^{13}_{♭9}$	C(♭9♭5)addA
Cmi9(♯7)	C9+11	Cmi7$^{11}_{9}$	C7addA	C(♭9)addA	
	C7$^9_{11}$	C-7($^9_{11}$)	C7+A		

Reading Chord Frames

Guitar chord frames are diagrams that show the fingering and position of a particular chord on the neck of the guitar. Vertical lines represent the strings, and horizontal lines represent the frets. Dots on the diagram show exactly where to place the fingers, and corresponding numbers at the bottom of the frame tell which fingers to use.

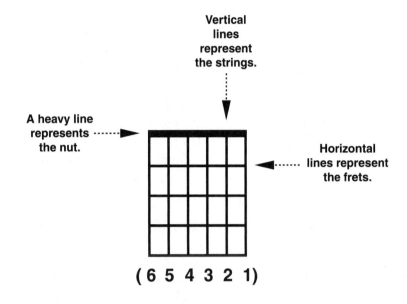

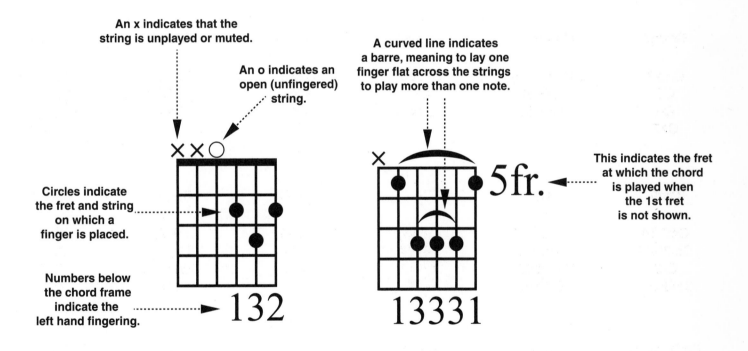

Appendix

B

Guitar Fingerboard Chart

Frets 1–12

FRETS	STRINGS					
	6th	5th	4th	3rd	2nd	1st
Open	E	A	D	G	B	E
1st Fret	F	A#/Bb	D#/Eb	G#/Ab	C	F
2nd Fret	F#/Gb	B	E	A	C#/Db	F#/Gb
3rd Fret	G	C	F	A#/Bb	D	G
4th Fret	G#/Ab	C#/Db	F#/Gb	B	D#/Eb	G#/Ab
5th Fret	A	D	G	C	E	A
6th Fret	A#/Bb	D#/Eb	G#/Ab	C#/Db	F	A#/Bb
7th Fret	B	E	A	D	F#/Gb	B
8th Fret	C	F	A#/Bb	D#/Eb	G	C
9th Fret	C#/Db	F#/Gb	B	E	G#/Ab	C#/Db
10th Fret	D	G	C	F	A	D
11th Fret	D#/Eb	G#/Ab	C#/Db	F#/Gb	A#/Bb	D#/Eb
12th Fret	E	A	D	G	B	E

Glossary

accent   Emphasis on a beat, note, or chord.

accidental   A sharp, flat, or natural sign that occurs in a measure.

altered tuning   Any tuning other than standard tuning on the guitar.

arpeggio   The notes of a chord played one after another instead of simultaneously.

bar   See *measure (or bar)*.

bar line   A vertical line that indicates where one measure ends and another begins.

barre   To fret multiple strings with one finger.

barre chord   A chord played by fretting several strings with one finger.

bend   A technique of pushing a guitar string up or down with the fretting finger to change the pitch.

bridge   The part of the guitar that anchors the strings to the body.

brush stroke   To lightly strum the guitar strings with the index finger of the right hand.

capo   A device placed around the neck of the guitar to raise the pitch of the strings.

chord   A group of three or more notes played simultaneously.

chord progression   A sequence of chords played in succession.

chromatic   Notes that move in half steps.

common time   The most common time signature in music; there are four beats to every measure and the quarter note gets one beat. Same as $\frac{4}{4}$.

countermelody   A melody played at the same time as the main melody.

cut time   A time signature that usually indicates a faster tempo where there are two beats to every measure and the half note gets one beat. Same as $\frac{2}{2}$.

distortion   An electronic effect that alters the sound of an amplified instrument by distorting the signal. Compared to *overdrive*, distortion produces a higher level of signal alteration or "fuzz."

dotted note   A note followed by a dot, indicating that the length of the note is longer by one half of the note's original length.

double bar line   A sign made of one thin line and one thick line, indicating the end of a piece of music.

double stop   A group of two notes played simultaneously.

downbeat   The first beat of a measure.

down-pick   To pick the string downward, toward the floor.

down-stroke   To strike the strings downward, toward the floor.

down-strum To strum the strings downward, toward the floor.

drop D tuning An altered tuning in which the 6th string of the guitar is lowered from E to D.

economy of motion A concept for efficient playing that involves moving as few fingers as little as possible when changing chords.

eighth note A note equal to half a quarter note, or one half beat in $\frac{4}{4}$ time.

eighth rest A rest equal to the duration of an eighth note.

fermata A symbol that indicates to hold a note for about twice as long as usual.

fifth The fifth note of a scale above the root note, the distance of seven half steps.

fingerboard See *fretboard*.

fingerpicking A style of playing that uses the right hand fingers to pluck the guitar strings rather than using a pick.

fingerstyle To play the strings with the fingers of the right hand rather than using a pick.

flat A symbol that indicates to lower a note one half step.

fret The metal strips across the fretboard of a guitar.

fretboard The part of the guitar neck where the frets lie.

fuzz An electronic effect that is one of the first guitar effects ever produced. The sound produced is an extremely high level of distortion.

G clef See *treble clef*.

groove The sense of rhythm in a piece of music.

half note A note equal to two quarter notes, or two beats in $\frac{4}{4}$ time.

half rest A rest equal to the duration of a half note.

half step The distance of one fret on the guitar.

hammer-on A technique by which a note is made to sound after playing the string with the right hand by tapping down on the string with another finger of the fretting hand.

harmonics The notes of the harmonic series that sound clear and bell-like when played, produced by lightly touching a string at various points on the fretboard and indicated in notation with diamond-shaped symbols.

harmony The result of two or more tones played simultaneously.

Hertz (Hz) The unit of measurement for the frequency of vibration.

interval The distance in pitch between notes.

key The tonal center of a piece of music.

key signature The group of sharps or flats that appears at the beginning of a piece of music to indicate what key the music is in.

ledger lines Short horizontal lines used to extend a staff either higher or lower.

major chord A chord consisting of a root, a major third, and a perfect fifth.

major scale The most common scale in music, consisting of a specific order of whole and half steps: W-W-H-W-W-W-H.

major third A note that is four half steps up from the root.

measure (or bar) Divisions of the staff that are separated by bar lines and contain equal numbers of beats.

minor chord A chord consisting of a root, a minor third, and a perfect fifth.

minor third A note that is three half steps up from the root.

mode A set of notes arranged into a specific scale.

mute To stop a note from ringing on the guitar by placing either the right or left hand over the strings.

natural A symbol that indicates a note is not sharp or flat.

note   A symbol used to represent a musical tone.

nut   The part of the guitar at the top of the neck that aligns the strings over the fretboard.

octave   The interval between two immediate notes of the same name, equivalent to 12 frets on the guitar, or eight scale steps.

open E tuning   An altered tuning for the guitar in which the strings are tuned from low to high E-B-E-G♯-B-E.

open G tuning. An altered tuning for the guitar in which the strings are tuned from low to high D–G–D–G–B–D.

open position   Fingering for chords that incorporates open strings and no barre.

overdrive   An electronic effect that alters the sound of an amplified instrument by slightly distorting the signal. Overdrive produces less signal alteration than distortion.

palm mute   A technique of muffling the guitar strings with the right hand palm at the bridge of the guitar.

palming the pick   A technique of holding the pick in the palm of the hand with the ring finger, while keeping the index and middle fingers free.

pentatonic scale   A five-note scale.

pick   A device used to pluck or strum the strings of a guitar.

pickup   A device on the body of an electric guitar that converts the vibrations of the strings into electronic signals, enabling them to be amplified.

pitch   The location of a note related to its lowness or highness.

position   The location of the hand on the fretboard at a particular fret.

power chord (or "5" chord)   A chord consisting of only the root and fifth, without a third or other additional notes.

pull-off   A technique in which two notes are fingered on the same string, and the lower note is then made to sound by pulling the fretting finger off the higher note.

quarter note   A note equal to one beat in $\frac{4}{4}$ time; the basic unit of musical time.

quarter rest   A rest equal to the duration of a quarter note.

repeat signs   A group of various symbols indicating sections of music to be played over again.

rest   A symbol representing measured silence in music.

rhythm   The musical organization of beats.

riff   A short, repeated melodic pattern.

root note   The fundamental note of a chord, and also the note that gives the chord its letter name. The root is the first note of the corresponding major scale.

scale   A set of notes arranged in a specific order of whole steps and half steps. The most common scale is the major scale.

sharp   A symbol that indicates to raise a note one half step.

shuffle rhythm   A rhythm in which eighth notes are played in an uneven, long-short manner.

sixteenth note   A note equal to half an eighth note, or one quarter beat in $\frac{4}{4}$ time.

sixteenth rest   A rest equal to the duration of a sixteenth note.

slide   1. A technique of moving smoothly from one note to another. A note is fingered by the left hand and played by the right hand, then the left hand finger maintains pressure while sliding quickly on the string to the next note without interrupting the sound or picking the note again. Indicated in notation with a diagonal line between notes. 2. A metal or glass tube that fits over a left hand finger, used to fret the strings and produce slide notes.

staccato   To play notes in a short, distinct manner. Indicated in notation by a dot directly over or under the note or chord.

staff   The horizontal lines and spaces upon which music notes are placed to designate their pitch.

standard tuning   The normal tuning for the guitar in which the strings are tuned from low to high E-A-D-G-B-E.

strum   To play several strings by brushing quickly across them with a pick or the fingers.

swing   To play eighth notes in an uneven, long-short rhythm.

syncopation   A shift of rhythmic emphasis to the weak beat, or to a weak part of a beat.

TAB   Abbreviation for *tablature*.

tablature   A system of guitar notation that uses a graphic representation of the six strings of the guitar with numbers indicating which fret to play.

tempo   The speed at which music is played.

tie   A curved line that joins two or more notes of the same pitch, indicating to play them as one continuous note.

time signature   A sign resembling a fraction that appears at the beginning of a piece of music. The top number indicates how many beats are in each measure and the bottom number indicates what kind of note gets one beat.

tone control   An adjustable knob on the body of an electric guitar that controls the amount of treble or high-frequency output.

treble clef   A symbol at the beginning of the staff that designates the second line as the note G. Also called the *G clef*.

tremolo bar   See *whammy bar*.

triplet   A group of three notes played in the time of two.

unison   The same pitch played at the same time on different strings of the guitar.

up-pick   To pick the string upward, toward the ceiling.

up-stroke.   To strike the strings upward, toward the ceiling.

up-strum   To strum the strings upward, toward the ceiling.

vibrato   A rapid alteration of pitch slightly higher or lower than the main pitch, usually achieved by rapidly bending the string.

volume control   An adjustable knob on the body of an electric guitar that controls the overall output of the instrument.

whammy bar.   A handle attached to the body of an electric guitar below the strings, used to alter the pitch of the strings by moving the bridge.

whole note   A note equal to four quarter notes, or four beats in $\frac{4}{4}$ time.

whole rest   A rest equal to the duration of a whole note, or the duration of any full measure.

whole step   The distance of two frets on the guitar.

The following blank chord frames and staff systems may be used to keep track of new chords, songs, and riffs. Write them here as you learn so you won't forget them.

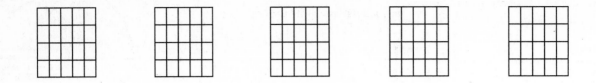

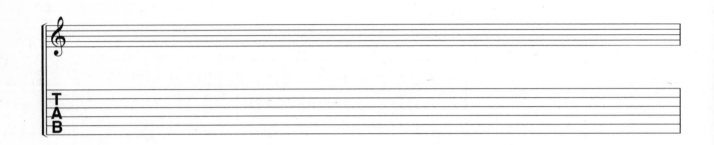

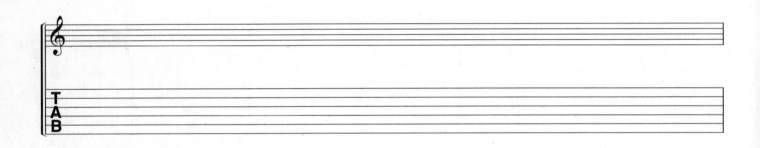

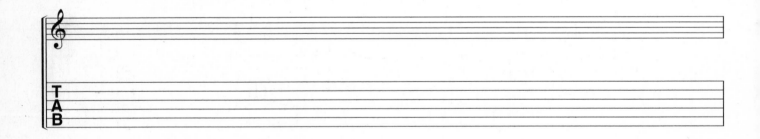